The Canada IFLA Adventure

85 Years of Canadian Participation in the International Federation of Library Associations and Institutions 1927 to 2012

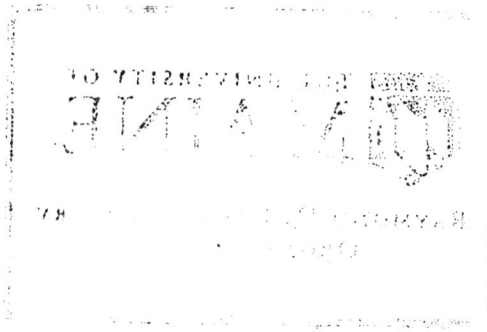

Judith Saltman, Dan Gillean, Jamie Kathleen McCarthy, Myron Groover, J Jack Unrau, and Rachel Balko

Library and Archives Canada Cataloguing-in-Publication

Saltman, Judith, author
    The Canada IFLA adventure : 85 years of Canadian participation in the
International Federation of Library Associations and Institutions, 1927 to 2012 /
Judith Saltman, Dan Gillean, Jamie Kathleen McCarthy, Myron Groover,
J Jack Unrau, and Rachel Balko.

Includes bibliographical references.
ISBN 978-0-88802-339-1 (pbk.)

    1. International librarianship--History--20th century. 2. Libraries--Canada--
International cooperation--History--20th century. 3. Library science--Canada--
History--20th century. 4. Librarians--Canada--History--20th century.
5. International Federation of Library Associations and Institutions--History--
20th century. I. Gillean, Dan, author II. McCarthy, Jamie Kathleen, 1987-, author
III. Groover, Myron, 1983-, author IV. Unrau, J. Jack, 1980-, author V. Balko,
Rachel, 1974-, author VI. Canadian Library Association VII. Title.

Z672.3.S24 2013   021.6'40971   C2013-904260-1

Cover design: Beverly Bard
Cover photo: Participants at the 1967 IFLA Conference in Toronto.
*Photograph from IFLA Headquarters Archives, sent to IFLA by l'Office du film
de la province de Québec, ca. 1967.*
Photographer unknown. Permission courtesy of IFLA Headquarters.
There are instances where we have been unable to trace or contact the copyright
holders. If notified the publisher will be pleased to rectify any errors or omissions
at the earliest opportunity.
Layout and design: Beverly Bard

Published by the Canadian Library Association/Association canadienne des
bibliothèques
1150 Morrison Drive, Suite 400
Ottawa, ON K2H 8S9

Printed and bound in Canada

Table of Contents

List of Photographs

Foreword: A Message from Ingrid Parent, IFLA President, 2011 to 2013

Eighty-five years ago, the group that was to become the International Federation of Library Associations and Institutions—otherwise known as IFLA—was established in Scotland.

Today, IFLA is the largest international library organization in the world, and Canadians have played a key role in the group's development since its beginnings.

As the first Canadian President of IFLA, it is a great honour to provide some opening remarks for *The Canada IFLA Adventure*—the first account of Canada's participation in the federation. This entertaining and informative book is a worthy tribute to those Canadians whose passion for libraries and literacy has greatly contributed to IFLA's emergence as a global force.

Books such as this one are labours of love—and I would like to thank the talented team of writers behind *The Canada IFLA Adventure*: Judith Saltman, Dan Gillean, Jamie McCarthy, Myron Groover, Justin Unrau, and Rachel Balko. I would also like to thank the IFLA staff at the Netherlands headquarters, including Communications Officer and Web Content Editor Louis Takács, for their invaluable assistance in scouring the IFLA archives to assist with this book's production.

Since 1927, Canadians have been instrumental to IFLA's progress. It is my sincere hope that future generations of librarians will be able to read about our efforts, reflect on our successes and continue to enhance IFLA's Canadian legacy for many decades to come.

Ingrid Parent

President of IFLA, 2011–2013,
President Elect, 2009–2011,
University Librarian, University of British Columbia

June 2013

Preface

The book you now hold in your hands is the culmination of nearly two years of research by students at the University of British Columbia's School of Library, Archival, and Information Studies. Initiated at the request of Ingrid Parent (UBC Librarian and IFLA President, 2011–2013) and carried out under the supervision of Professor Judith Saltman, this manuscript was originally intended as a brief overview of the historical relationship between Canada and the International Federation of Library Associations and Institutions (IFLA). As our research progressed, however, it became clear that our research project was much more complex than originally envisioned. No one had yet documented the history of Canadian involvement in IFLA; in fact, we could not find evidence of any other attempts to capture the contributions of a single nation to IFLA over the course of its entire history. Secondary sources were scarce; primary sources were scattered across the country and at IFLA Headquarters in The Hague. We decided that, if we were to pursue this project, it would require original research. A major part of this effort, it seemed to us, would involve interviewing Canadian IFLA members who had been actively involved over the course of the last three decades; this would furnish us an opportunity to capture not just the bare facts, but some of the personal stories that enrich our understanding of what it means to be involved with an international federation. And so began our own Canadian IFLA adventure: what follows in these pages has been assembled from a combination of archival research, interviews, e-mail exchanges, and secondary sources.

Carried out as a combination of course work, paid research, and seemingly endless volunteer hours, it stands as only the briefest summary of the many ways in which Canadians have contributed to IFLA throughout the Federation's history: a complete telling might take many years of research and a far larger manuscript! Many sources, both primary and secondary, were inaccessible to us due to time and financial restrictions; similarly, we were unable to pursue research with many wonderful individuals we would have liked to interview. There will be Canadians whose contributions deserve greater recognition for their efforts than this treatment, and the sources we were able to find to support it, has allowed. Geographical and linguistic constraints, in particular, have prevented us from speaking with many of the franco-phone IFLA members who have been significantly involved in the Federation. While we have done everything we could to eradicate errors and inaccuracies from the text, such lacunae will inevitably be present. It is therefore our hope that this will be viewed as an initial offering and that in the future, others might continue the work we have begun in documenting the Canadian IFLA adventure. Despite these challenges, it has been remarkable and inspiring to learn of the many influential ways in which Canadians have helped to shape the Federation over time; we hope that other countries might consider documenting their own roles in IFLA so the unique perspectives and contributions of each can be celebrated.

All of our interviewees and correspondents spoke warmly of the benefits that involvement in IFLA brings, both personally and nationally. Kelly Moore, Executive Director of the Canadian Library Association and former IFLA Manager of Membership and Corporate Relations, notes:

> [I]t is a unique experience to be at a conference with 3,000 other people from all around the world who are sharing their concerns, and the issues and the joys and trials and everything of librarianship all there, and just engaging in a whole different way from what we normally do on a day-to-day basis. Just being able to have that input from other people's experiences and what they go through to try to make things happen. It puts your own work in a really different light when you see what happens in different countries.[1]

Victoria Owen, Head Librarian at the University of Toronto Library and current Chair of IFLA's Copyright and other Legal Matters Committee, echoes this sentiment. She adds that IFLA makes an "opportunity for the world to share at an international level, the library world, community, to share . . . internationally. [M]oving around the world in the different venues for the conferences, I think, gives people a real opportunity to understand library services in many, many areas of the world. And appreciate our own all the more."[2] Frank Kirkwood, who retired from the Library of Parliament in 2011 and is past Chair of IFLA's Government Information and Official Publications Section, views IFLA as "a place of activism, a place to accomplish change in the world through libraries and information services, [and] make a difference in people's lives,"[3] calling himself an "IFLA activist for life."[4] Barbara Clubb, retired City Librarian for the Ottawa Public Library and a previous Chair of the Public Libraries section, recalls that "in the Ottawa Public Library, if you go to a conference, you've got to write a report, so I wrote a report and gave it to the board. And I remember one of our members said, 'If any one of us doubted whether or not going to an international conference like IFLA was of use, Barbara's report has proven that it is of extreme value.'"[5] Marianne Scott, former National Librarian of Canada and the first Chair of the IFLA Committee on Copyright and Other Legal Matters, wryly adds that "You don't go and hear intelligent people talk about . . . issues . . . without it rubbing off. It's hard to pick it out and say 'Well, it was that thing,' but it helps your formation, your development."[6]

When asked whether Canadians have, in fact, been very involved in IFLA, all respondents were emphatic in their responses. Clubb recalls that at one point she "did a . . . tally; it would have been in '89 or '90 because I remember writing it up in my report to the board and . . . there were 14 sections where Canadians were not only members, but they were chairs of those sections."[7] Parent concurs, adding that "out of 50 participants, not too long ago at IFLA, about 35 of them are on committees, and some of them chair and some of them are officers of committees because they feel that they can do things and help and make a difference and that to me is what is Canadian."[8] Kelly Moore relates that:

> When we had the conference last year during the Canadian caucus meeting we . . . asked people in the room to indicate what their IFLA affiliation was at the time if they had one. And out of maybe 70 people in the room, almost everyone in the room was there because they were working on a particular committee, or working in a particular group, or doing something specific for the Federation, and that was just great to see that everybody's . . . there to be engaged. They're not there just to attend a conference.[9]

This involvement was viewed by our interviewees as part of a Canadian ethos in international librarianship; as Parent aptly summarizes, "I think our character is [that] we step up. Not forcing ourselves out there, but when needed, we step up."[10] Clubb agrees, noting that Canadians "have a very good work ethic and we go, and we work."[11] Scott tempers this by reflecting on the importance of having fun through IFLA:

> I have that sense that the general thing that we brought was serious hard work. And fun. That was another thing, because the Canadians were always . . . able to have fun. We always enjoyed getting together and I think that . . . [we] were really generally well liked on the committees. I think [we] were open to diversity without being obvious about it.[12]

Others point to the multicultural makeup of Canada as informing the role of Canadians in an international context. Moore sums up how this informs Canadian participation within the Federation in particular:

> Part of it is the bilingual nature of the country, the multicultural nature of the country—the way that we approach different issues, the way we work in international crowds, because a lot of us do that on a daily basis. . . . We're working with people who come from different cultures and different countries, so going to an IFLA conference and doing that in another country is not odd for us, the way it might be for people who live in more homogeneous societies. It's not weird to sit down in a room of people who all come from different places. So that, I think, helps us. It's a bit of an advantage in our perspective and [in] how we approach that kind of work.[13]

Réjean Savard, Professor at the Université de Montréal's École de bibliothéconomie et des sciences de l'information and a former IFLA Governing Board member,[14] attributes this to Canada's perception as having "a very dynamic library community,"[15] while Ralph Manning, now retired from Library and Archives Canada and a former Chair of the IFLA Professional Board,[16] believes that Canadians have typically "been seen as the arbiters"[17] in international contexts. Parent aptly encapsulates these ideas, noting that:

> Canadians in general . . . are very valued within IFLA, very trusted, very fair. There are strong political views within IFLA between certain countries, and Canada is not one of them. Canada kind of plays a mediator role between some of the stronger, larger countries. I think it's appreciated that we're there to do that. I use the word "honest broker" sometimes; but you know, I think people trust us, other countries trust us and . . . have faith in what we propose. We're not just talking about silly things. We actually are seen to have results and to actually do the work.[18]

What follows, then, is an attempt to capture this Canadian ethos in deed, by documenting some of the ways in which Canadians have actively contributed to the growth, internationalization, and importance of IFLA in the last 85 years.

Bringing together such a manuscript naturally could not have occurred without the support and assistance of many wonderful institutions, associations, and individuals. This book has been published with support from the University of British Columbia's Faculty of Arts' Humanities and Social Sciences Research Grant; the University of British Columbia's School of Library, Archival, and Information Studies (SLAIS); and Ingrid Parent. These sources of funding have enabled us to travel to archives and libraries across Canada, complete a series of interviews, and recruit student assistants to aid in our research and editing. Additional funds provided by the University of British Columbia (UBC) Library have supported research and editing costs at critical junctures.

Ingrid Parent deserves special recognition for being the impetus behind this project—and for providing us with a list of initial contacts and considerations, networking on our behalf at every opportunity, and acting as an inexhaustible well of moral support. Without her proposal, and her continued efforts to help us realize it, this manuscript would never have come into being.

Transforming the dry facts of this history into a rich narrative, and connecting the dots where our secondary-source research fell short of revealing the whole picture, could not have occurred without the participation of our thirteen interviewees: Hope Clement, Barbara Clubb, Tom Delsey, Frank Kirkwood, Ralph Manning, Kelly Moore, Victoria Owen, Ingrid Parent, Réjean Savard, Marianne Scott, Erik Spicer, Paul Whitney, and Nancy Williamson. Terry Kuny provided invaluable correspondence via e-mail, particularly about Canada's role in the establishment of IFLANET. These Canadian IFLA members have generously shared their time, knowledge, perspectives, and passion with us through audio interviews, correspondence by post and e-mail, and further discussion via telephone—many of them more than once! Without them, we simply could not have completed this book. Not every individual we have interviewed has been quoted in the book, but all provided substantive information, background, and context for our research. In many ways, they constitute a living history of Canada's engagement with IFLA, and their experiences, memories, and reflections have immeasurably enriched our understanding of the events we describe. The audio recordings of our interviews will be housed in the University of British Columbia Archives for future researchers to access.

Marianne Scott, Ingrid Parent, and Réjean Savard have also taken an active role in the creation of this manuscript by contributing their words directly to the final publication. Parent has provided the Foreword and Afterword; Scott has written the Introduction; and Savard has contributed the profile on ASTED, l'Association pour l'avancement des sciences et des techniques de la documentation. Our manuscript is stronger for their involvement, and we thank them for taking an active interest in seeing this book realized. Scott has also been a tireless advocate on our behalf, reaching out to Canadian IFLA members and encouraging them to speak with us, and providing valuable sources to support her recollections—even now, she continues to network on behalf of IFLA, and without her support, we might never have made the connections we needed.

Learning about Canadian involvement in IFLA's formative years has required primary-source research in various archival institutions and in the records of several associations. We would like to thank the individuals who have facilitated this access, beginning with the staff at IFLA headquarters in The Hague—particularly Louis Takács, IFLA Communications Officer and Web Content Editor, who enthusiastically scanned a remarkable number of documents for us from the IFLA Geneva Fonds following a great deal of correspondence and a research visit graciously carried out on our behalf by Ingrid Parent and Paul Whitney. Without Louis's support, we would not have been able to report on Canadians' involvement during IFLA's "early years." Kelly Moore—an active IFLA member and former IFLA employee herself—has also gone to great lengths to support our research, including the coordination of arrangements for our researchers to visit the Canadian Library Association Headquarters to examine its records. Robin Dumais (President) and Suzanne Morin (General Manager) of ASTED extended their gracious assistance in allowing us access to ASTED's records, in spite of our most unfortunate timing in the midst of their moving offices! At Library and Archives Canada (LAC), Mélanie Brunet provided invaluable reference assistance and research support, one component of which may actually have been history in and of itself; we participated in LAC's first-ever Skype reference interview! Bill Hamade, Senior Department Head of the Special Collections Department at the Toronto Public Library, also assisted us greatly by providing remote access to documents from the Harry Campbell Fonds. Lynne Howarth, Chair of the Ph.D. program at the University of Toronto's iSchool and an active IFLA member in her own right, kindly put us in touch with Bill Hamade when our research on Campbell came to a temporary dead-end. Caroline Haythornthwaite, Director of SLAIS, provided steady encouragement throughout the research, and helped locate the means by which to finish it. Last but by no means least, Harry Young, Executive Coordinator of the University Librarian's Office at UBC, patiently coordinated with us to gain access to IFLA materials held in Ingrid Parent's office, and generally acted as our point person at the UBC Library—coordinating travel, disbursing funds, and smoothing out rough edges here, there, and everywhere. Without these dedicated individuals, we could not have completed this work.

The manuscript has been enriched by the inclusion of the wonderful photographs kindly provided to us by their copyright holders. Julie Grahame, representing the estate of Yousuf Karsh; Yves Tessier of Les Productions Tessier; Ross Becker; UBC Library; IFLA Headquarters; the Canadian Library Association; and ASTED have all contributed in making the inclusion of these images possible.

Behind the scenes at UBC, other students from SLAIS have contributed their time and energy in support of this endeavour—in particular, the tireless research and consistently positive attitude of Stephanie Dror enabled the inclusion of our appendices, while Victoria Killington's eagle eye has ensured that our citations have been checked and double-checked for accuracy.

Of course, this book would not exist were it not for the support of the Canadian Library Association, which agreed to bring our manuscript into print. In particular, we would like to thank Kelly Moore and Judy Green for their assistance in helping us realize this goal and Beverly Bard for her fine design skills.

And what would a book be without a reader? Thank you for your interest in our work. Now, prepare yourself for an adventure!

The Canadian IFLA Research Team

June 2013

Introduction: A Message from Marianne Scott, former National Librarian of Canada, 1984 to 1999

It is a pleasure to have the opportunity to write a few words to welcome readers and to thank Ingrid Parent, the person who initiated this research study to document Canadian involvement in the first 85 years of IFLA.

For the novice, IFLA can be a confusing organization at first sight. However, some of its complexity is its strength. Over the years, it has developed systems and structures to deal with over 1,500 members from approximately 150 countries, increased the number of official languages to seven, and more importantly, continued to expand its capability to deal with members' ever-changing information needs.

The following pages tell the story of how Canadian librarians, with the support of their libraries, contributed to IFLA in numerous ways. They have given of their expertise by way of workshops and presentations, in writing for IFLA publications, as members of the various structural units that covered a myriad of professional interests, and by serving on the governing board.

In the world of librarianship, it appeared for a long time that Canada was not very prominent internationally. In fact, we relied very much on the development and expertise happening in the United States and, as documented in this study, our American colleagues often represented us at IFLA in the early years. However, Canadian librarians truly appreciated the benefits of collective activity and, after the Second World War, library associations flourished in Canada and interest in international happenings increased.

Reading these pages has been a wonderful walk down memory lane for me. It has brought back memories of friendships made with colleagues that you perhaps only saw once a year, meetings with great discussions, opportunities to learn so much about what was happening outside Canada, and of course, some of the memorable social activities at IFLA.

Canadians can sometimes be a little diffident and perhaps some of our IFLA participants do not realize the value and importance of their particular contribution to the whole. I hope that this study will bring some of the many pieces together. I, for one, am so very proud of the Canadian contribution recognizing the many volunteer hours spent at home base to develop the programs, write the papers, and provide the necessary administrative support for the various committees, sections and divisions to assist IFLA in reaching our collective goals.

However, while looking back over IFLA's many wonderful accomplishments during the past 85 years is time well spent, we must not relax our participation in this important organization. I can only hope that the active role of the Canadian library and information community within IFLA will continue to grow. As always, we have much to share and to learn.

Marianne Scott

Former National Librarian of Canada,
Former President, Canadian Library Association,
Former Chair, Conference of Directors of National Libraries,
Former Chair, IFLA Committee on Copyright and Other Legal Matters

May 2013

Chapter 1

IFLA: A General History, 1927 to 2012

O n 30 September 1927, at the annual meeting of the British Library Association in Edinburgh, representatives from 15 member countries came together to found an organization that was to become the International Federation of Library Associations and Institutions (IFLA).[19] Over 85 years later, now with over 1,500 members from 151 countries,[20] IFLA has become the world's largest international library association. Committed to expressing "the aspirations and international outlook of librarians,"[21] IFLA has provided the world's librarians with an open and diverse forum for communication, collaboration, and professional development. The organization has continued to grow throughout the tumultuous events of the past century, enduring and thriving in the face of the Second World War, the Cold War, economic depressions, technological advancements, and innumerable changes and challenges to the profession. In the words of IFLA historian Jeffrey M. Wilhite, the organization has "no limit to its future progress."[22]

The decade that followed the First World War saw a growing interest in internationalism, perhaps best symbolized by the founding of the League of Nations in 1919.[23] Embodying a prevailing sentiment of the era, the League "inspired great hopes and strengthened to an extraordinary extent the awareness among individual States of their obligation to promote cooperation and understanding across their national frontiers."[24] By this time, national library associations were already firmly established in various countries, including the American Library Association (founded in 1876), the British Library Association (1877),[25] and the French Library Association (l'Association des Bibliothécaires de France; 1906).[26] These efforts were furthered in the 1925 establishment of the League of Nations' International Institute for Intellectual Cooperation, which included the League of Nations' Library Conference.[27] As remembered by Joachim Wieder, who served as IFLA's Vice President from 1967 to 1973,[28] "Librarians now sought to join in the general movement towards worldwide cooperation by means of a permanent international professional organization in an effort to ensure maximum effectiveness of their manifold activities and their weight in cultural policy."[29]

The idea of an international library association moved one step closer to reality in July 1926, when a proposal for such an organization was tabled by Gabriel Henriot at the International Congress of Librarians and Booklovers in Prague. Henriot, then head of the French Library Association, would later be referred to as the "spiritual father of IFLA."[30] In October of the same year, the proposal was formally discussed by international delegates from 13 countries at the American Library Association's (ALA) General Conference in Atlantic City, New Jersey, and Philadelphia, Pennsylvania.[31] The results of these deliberations, which took place under the auspices of the ALA Committee on International Relations, were then presented by ALA delegates to the 1927 Annual Meeting of the British Library Association (BLA) in Edinburgh.[32]

Intrigued by the proposal, the BLA's International Library Cooperation Section formed a working group to consider the idea on 27 September 1927.[33] Chaired by Isak G. A. Collijn of Sweden, the committee also counted among its members Vincenzo Fago of Italy, Henry Guppy of the United Kingdom, Hugo Kruss of Germany, Henri Lemaitre of France, Carl H. Milam of the United States, and Zdenek Vaclav Tobolka of Czechoslovakia.[34] In the Mahogany Room of the North British Hotel, this committee officially declared the foundation of the International Library and Bibliographical Committee—subsequently renamed the International Federation of Library Associations—on 30 September 1927.[35] The resulting document, a seven-point resolution widely considered to be IFLA's "Magna Carta,"[36] was signed by 21 delegates from Austria, Belgium, Canada, China, Czechoslovakia, Denmark, France, Germany, Great Britain, Holland, Italy, Norway, Sweden, Switzerland, and the United States.[37] Collijn, who chaired the BLA working group, was elected IFLA's first Chairman—a title that would later be changed to President.[38]

The following year, Rome played host to the 15 delegates who comprised the first session of the International Library and Bibliographical Committee.[39] Later in the year, the second session was held in conjunction with the first International Congress of Libraries and Bibliography, also in Rome.[40] According to Carol Henry and Donald G. Davis, Jr.:

> The new organization was predominantly an association of library associations, aiming at the promotion of regular world conferences. Originally, IFLA was a meeting point for leading librarians from Europe and America and continued as such for a long time. In the early years, notable personalities—true representatives of their profession—defined IFLA's profile. It became a kind of "conference family," where personal friend-ships led to close cooperation in such areas as international loan and exchange, bibliographical standardization, and library education.[41]

Although in 1930 IFLA was still very young, and perhaps not yet truly international (in the sense that librarians from the United States and Europe almost entirely dominated the organization), the foundation of the organization marked the 1920s as an important watershed moment for international librarianship.

The 1930s saw sessions move outside of Rome—over the course of the decade, meetings were held in Stockholm (1930), Cheltenham (1931), Berne (1932), Chicago/Avignon (1933), Madrid/Barcelona (1934), Warsaw (1936), Paris (1937), Brussels (1938), and The Hague (1938).[42] This was a time of growth for IFLA which saw the organization become better established. While session attendance grew steadily, Wilhite maintains that during the 1930s, "IFLA suffered from the perception that it was a gentleman's club, a reference to its smallness and informality in conducting business. And in reality in the pre-World War II years, IFLA did not produce very many tangible results."[43] Never-theless, by the end of the decade, IFLA did boast a handful of members from outside Europe and North America, including China, Egypt, India, Japan, Mexico, Palestine, and the Philippines.[44] The organization was not yet wholly international in membership or outlook, however; when China and India proposed that the 1936 session be held in Asia, IFLA declined because of "financial strictures."[45]

The harsh realities of the Second World War caused numerous setbacks for IFLA; no annual sessions were held between 1940 and 1946. Despite operations being suspended for the duration of the conflict, there was still "behind the scenes work done to keep the organization alive, and help with the war effort"[46]—most of it coordinated from IFLA's temporary headquarters in Switzerland.[47] The country's neutral stance during the war was beneficial to IFLA, insofar as it "allowed for the circulation of information by correspondence and the maintenance of certain contacts which made possible various interventions and relief actions."[48] IFLA's President during this time was Marcel Godet, Director of the Swiss National Library in Berne, who had taken the helm at IFLA in 1936 and remained President until 1947, despite the fact that in 1939, "IFLA's German delegation (obligated to officially represent Hitler's National Socialist regime) was laying claim on the leadership of IFLA."[49] IFLA's then–Assistant Secretary A. C. Breycha-Vauthier used his position at the League of Nations Library and his membership on the Advisory Committee on Literature for Prisoners of War and Internees (directed by the Red Cross[50]) to facilitate IFLA's involvement "in the distribution of large numbers of books to various camps,"[51] presumably prisoner-of-war and internee camps.[52]

In 1945, the United Nations formed the United Nations Educational, Scientific, and Cultural Organization (UNESCO) as a successor to the League of Nations' International Commission for Intellectual Cooperation, which provided librarians with "hope that it would give libraries international direction after so many years of war."[53] After the 1946 reinstatement of IFLA, sessions were held in Oslo (1947), London (1948), and Basel (1949).[54] The 1947 session in Oslo, where representatives from both UNESCO and the International Federation for Documentation (FID) were in attendance,[55] was made possible, in part, due to a grant of $9,000 (USD) from the Rockefeller Foundation.[56]

The 1950s saw IFLA redevelop and rebuild itself slowly (largely due to a lack of funds); again, the organization held no sessions outside of Europe. Conferences were held in London (1950), Rome (1951), Copenhagen (1952), Vienna (1953), Zagreb (1954), Brussels (1955), Munich (1956), Paris (1957), Madrid (1958), and Warsaw (1959).[57] Although locations were all European, two of these conferences (i.e., Zagreb and Warsaw) took place in the Eastern Bloc, reflecting political inclusivity during a time of Cold War tensions. The Warsaw conference was held three years after the official formation of the Warsaw Pact. During this time, the Cold War was taking its toll on IFLA. As summarized by Henry and Davis: "The Cold War also brought tensions between some members from Eastern-bloc countries and those from Western nations, especially when conferences were held in Eastern Europe."[58] In the same vein, Wilhite recollects that "the IFLA of the 1950s closely resembled the tight-knit IFLA of the 1930s."[59] Concerns regarding IFLA's insularity were given voice in 1954, when respected Indian library theorist and leader S. R. Ranganathan wrote the ground-breaking article "IFLA—What It Should Be and Do." In this article, Ranganathan confirmed what many suspected; IFLA, being dominated by the viewpoints of Western European and North American institu-tions, was far from being truly international. This was not, perhaps, deliberate—Ranganathan commented that it may have been "uncon-scious and even unmeant"—but it was glaringly obvious and "clear as daylight in the tropics."[60] In recognition of this, IFLA began to take small steps towards a more outward-looking attitude in the 1950s, prompted by both philosophical and budgetary concerns—conferences, for example, were held in conjunction with those of the International Federation for Information and Documentation, an organization with which IFLA attempted to work more closely in general.[61]

After the slow growth of the 1950s, IFLA saw huge expansion throughout the boom years of the 1960s. Membership nearly tripled, increasing from 81 members in 1960 to 231 members in 1969,[62] thanks in part to a 1964 change in the IFLA *Statutes* that created an "Associate" membership category,[63] which meant that libraries, bibliographical institutes, schools of librarianship, and other groups could be considered members.[64] Conferences were held in Lund and Malmö (1960), Edinburgh (1961), Berne (1962), Sofia (1963), Rome (1964), Helsinki (1965), The Hague (1966), Toronto (1967), Frankfurt (1968), and Copenhagen (1969).[65] Only one conference (i.e., Sofia) was held in an Eastern Bloc country during the 1960s, in comparison to the two that were held in the 1950s—a possible reflection of the increasing Cold War tensions of the era. Although the Sofia conference was viewed as "a further important step in strengthening the library ties and collaboration between East and West," the Head of the Library Section of the Committee of Culture and Arts in Bulgaria criticized the Executive Board of the time for being "without any representative from the USSR, a state with more than 300,000 libraries."[66]

As IFLA developed more sections catering to different portfolios and different types of librarians, the organization's responsiveness and productivity also increased, "enabling IFLA to react adequately to urgent library problems."[67] Cataloguing also became a more important topic for IFLA with the 1961 Parisian International Conference on Cataloging Principles, which, for the first time, urged international standardization in cataloguing.[68] The organization was also self-conscious in looking to its own future, culminating with the 1963 publication of *Libraries in the World*. This landmark document, in which the future development of IFLA was outlined by Leendert Brummel with contributions from Sir Frank Francis, F. G. B. Hutchings, and Herman Liebaers, was the product of a long-running project to envision a viable future for the organization.[69]

IFLA celebrated its 50th anniversary in 1977—a highlight of a very successful decade for the Federation, which saw among other things, the appointment of its first female Permanent Secretary General (Margreet Wijnstroom, 1971–1987)[70] and President (Else Granheim, 1979–1985).[71, 72] IFLA conferences also started to include exhibitions on technology, and membership grew vastly—from 257 in 1970 to 906 in 1979.[73] More international members joined, including "the Democratic Republic of Korea (1970), Singapore (1972), [and] Indonesia and Malaysia (1973)."[74] By 1974, IFLA could finally claim "virtually universal international membership with 600 members in 100 countries."[75] During this time of unprecedented growth, IFLA's *Statutes* and *Constitution* were revised to accommodate the needs of the larger organization, and the beginnings of the IFLA publishing program were developed; the *IFLA Directory* was first published in 1971 and the *IFLA Journal* in 1975.[76] In 1971, "[IFLA President] Herman Liebaers advanced the idea of Universal Bibliographic Control (UBC), an idea so successful that in 1974 the organization's London office became the IFLA International Office for UBC."[77] Wilhite notes, however, that "all was not clear sailing for IFLA during the 1970s, as rocky waters were hit when UNESCO briefly dropped its consultative status with IFLA over issues concerning South African Apartheid," [78] which included IFLA taking no action against members who supported racial segregation. Conferences were held in Moscow (1970), Liverpool (1971), Budapest (1972), Grenoble (1973), Washington, DC (1974), Oslo (1975), Lausanne (1976), Brussels (1977), Strbske Pleso (1978), and Copenhagen (1979).[79] The Moscow conference, in particular, suggests a waning of Cold War tensions during this period, with a then-record number of conference attendees and the inclusion of a special plenary session on "Lenin and Libraries" to coincide with Lenin's centenary that year.[80]

The geographic focus of IFLA shifted dramatically in the 1980s, with the Federation hosting its first conferences in Asia, Africa, and Australia. Sessions were held in Manila (1980), Leipzig (1981), Montreal (1982), Munich (1983), Nairobi (1984), Chicago (1985), Tokyo (1986), Brighton (1987), Sydney (1988), and Paris (1989).[81] Throughout the decade, IFLA undertook a series of initiatives aimed at universalizing the sharing of information, including the Universal Availability of Publications Program and the Advancement of Librarianship Program.[82] As Harry Campbell states, these were evidence of a new direction for the organization:

> During the 1980s the theme of information services and their place in libraries was highlighted at various annual IFLA conferences. The theme of Universal Access to Publications and access to world-wide information had been chosen for the 1978 meeting in Strbske Pleso, in the Czech Republic and in 1985 in Chicago, and it was to be featured again in succeeding years.[83]

The decade was not without controversy, however; during the 1980s, IFLA was forced to adjust to worries over apartheid, the liberalization of the Soviet economy, and a particularly contentious incident whereby China, as a condition of its accession to the organization in 1981, demanded that IFLA "[drop] . . . the membership of the Taiwanese associations."[84] The outcome and rationale behind IFLA's cooperation in this matter is unclear, but Wilhite notes the following in his summation of the 1981 conference:

A significant change occurred in the work of IFLA once The People's Republic of China joined the Federation. The People's Republic of China had only agreed to join IFLA on the condition that the memberships of the library associations of the Republic of China (Taiwan) were suspended. IFLA agreed to this in 1974 and suspended the memberships of the Taiwanese associations, but did not suspend the memberships of individual Taiwanese libraries.[85]

The 1990s saw IFLA place a renewed focus on technological advancements and their potential for advancing connectedness between people and information, mirroring the history of a tumultuous decade which "appeared at first divergent but eventually brought people all over the world together."[86] The organization's official website, IFLANET, was launched in 1993, a testament to IFLA's early understanding of the Internet's transformative potential, and from that point on, the Federation increasingly used information technology to communicate through e-mail and online publishing.[87] This increased technological investment, in turn, did much to promote international discussions outside of session gatherings. The 1990s also saw the creation of six new discussion groups and the foundation of the Freedom of Access to Information and Freedom of Expression (FAIFE) Committee and the Committee on Copyright and Other Legal Matters (CLM).[88] The creation of FAIFE and CLM were both seminal moments for the organization, and promoted the role of libraries in the distribution of knowledge on a global scale. The decade also saw a growing emphasis on collaboration with organizations outside traditional librarianship. Campbell elaborates:

> IFLA established working relations with a variety of other bodies with similar interests, providing an opportunity for a regular exchange of information and views on issues of mutual concern. It has Formal Associate Relations with UNESCO, observer status with the United Nations, associate status with the International Council of Scientific Unions (ICSU) and observer status with the World Intellectual Property Organization (WIPO) and the International Organization for Standardization (ISO). IFLA offered consultative status to a number of non-governmental organizations operating in related fields, including the International

Federation for Information and Documentation (FID) and the International Publishers Association (IPA). It became a member, along with the International Council of Archives (ICA), International Council of Museums (ICOM) and the International Council on Monuments and Sites (ICOMOS), of the International Committee of the Blue Shield (ICBS).[89]

The conferences of the 1990s were held in Stockholm (1990), Moscow (1991), New Delhi (1992), Barcelona (1993), Havana (1994), Istanbul (1995), Beijing (1996), Copenhagen (1997), Amsterdam (1998), and Bangkok (1999).[90] The Moscow conference was significant for taking place during the August Putsch (the attempted Soviet coup d'état)—a pivotal moment in world history.

IFLA has remained an important force in the world of librarianship in the opening years of the new millennium. Conferences have been held in: Jerusalem (2000), Boston (2001), Glasgow (2002), Berlin (2003), Buenos Aires (2004), Oslo (2005), Seoul (2006), Durban (2007), Quebec (2008), Milan (2009), Gothenburg (2010), San Juan (2011), and Helsinki (2012).[91] The decade opened with controversy for IFLA, however, when, in the face of the increasing violence in the Palestinian territories that would lead to the Second Intifada, there was "an almost total boycott" of the 2000 conference in Israel by the Federation's Islamic members, and the Arab Federation for Libraries and Information hosted its own rival conference in protest in August, in Cairo.[92] Wilhite remarks that in President Deschamps' closing speech, "she stated that the decision to hold the conference in Israel was made years ago, and was not decided to make a political statement about the present Middle East situation."[93]

In 2000, conscious of the need to remain relevant and fresh, IFLA undertook a major revision of its *Statutes* and *Rules of Procedure*; this effort to adapt was continued in 2001 when the first postal ballot was conducted to choose the organization's President-Elect.[94] In 2006, IFLA reached its highest membership to date—1,784 members—and in 2008, partially in recognition of this increasing membership, the *Statutes* received another revision.[95] As IFLA nears its 100th birthday, the organization continues to grow, and to support both international librarianship and global access to information.

Profile: Elizabeth Morton

E lizabeth Homer Morton (b. 13 February 1903, Tunapuna, Trinidad; d. 6 July 1977) served as Executive Director of the Canadian Library Association from 1944 to 1968; in partial recognition of this service, she was awarded the Order of Canada in 1968.[96] An article on Library and Archives Canada's website celebrating women's achievements in Canada named Morton "truly a national figure in the history of Canadian librarianship."[97] Born to Canadian missionaries in Trinidad,[98] Morton attended secondary school in Saint John, New Brunswick[99] before pursuing a Bachelor of Arts from Dalhousie University (1926), a teacher's licence from the Normal School in Truro, Nova Scotia (1926), and finally a qualification from the Ontario Library School (1926).[100, 101] This early education was followed some decades later by a Master of Arts from the University of Chicago's Graduate Library School in 1969, an LL.D. from the University of Alberta (1969), and a D.Litt. from Sir George Williams (now Concordia) University (1970).[102]

Figure 1: Elizabeth Morton, Canadian Library Association Executive Director (1946–1968).

Permission courtesy of the Canadian Library Association.

After her initial sojourn at the Ontario Library School in the 1920s, Morton worked in the cataloguing department of the Toronto Public Library and later accepted a position to organize a library at the Saint John Vocational School, New Brunswick, in 1928.[103] This accomplished, she worked from 1931 to 1944 in the reference department of the Toronto Public Library.[104] This vocational experience was complemented by her enthusiastic participation in professional organizations; Morton served as Secretary for the New Brunswick

Library Commission from 1930 to 1931 and then, as Secretary-Treasurer of the Ontario Library Association from 1936 to 1943.[105] She also had active memberships in the American Librarian Association, the Special Library Association, and the Canadian Association for Adult Education.[106]

In 1944, Morton became the Executive Secretary of the newly incorporated Canadian Library Council, where she played a pivotal role in the foundation and establishment of the Canadian Library Association (CLA). She served as the fledgling organization's first Executive Director from its inception in 1946 until 1968, where she worked "with a small staff and often inadequate budget to bring the goals of the CLA into being."[107] During her time as Executive Director, the CLA lobbied successfully for the establishment of the National Library. Morton also served as Editor to the *Canadian Library Journal* and *Feliciter*, while the *Canadian Periodical Index* flourished during her time as Director.[108] In her role as CLA Executive Director, Morton corresponded with IFLA, and attended the 1961 IFLA conference in Edinburgh and the 1963 conference in Sofia. Later, she served as Secretary for the IFLA Organizing Committee of the 1967 IFLA meeting in Toronto.[109]

After her retirement from the CLA, Morton began a library consulting group, Elizabeth Morton and Associates, which conducted a comprehensive survey of the National Library's resources.[110] In 1972, she worked with the United Nations Educational, Scientific, and Cultural Organization (UNESCO) to create a report entitled *Trinidad and Tobago: Development of Library Services* (1974).[111] A frequent public speaker, she also delivered many lectures and penned numerous articles and reviews in professional publications. Two years after Morton's retirement from the CLA, Helen Howard, Director of McGill University's Graduate School of Library and Information Studies, recognized the importance of her work:

> Since 1946 many new libraries have been built in Canada, and Canadians have better access to books and instructional materials than ever before. This impetus for change has come largely from the Canadian Library Association, working with governments and interested groups. Perhaps more than anyone else, Miss Morton has been the powerhouse within it.[112]

In commemoration of this outstanding legacy, CLA, with support from the Ex Libris Association, established a trust called the Elizabeth Morton Memorial Fund in 1988.[113] In 1995, the funds raised from the trust resulted in a publication celebrating the CLA's accomplishments under Morton's leadership, entitled *The Morton Years: The Canadian Library Association, 1946–1971.*[114]

Spotlight: Canadian Library Association (CLA)

The Canadian Library Association/l'Association canadienne des bibliothèques is "a national, not-for-profit, voluntary organization, governed by an elected Council and Board of Directors."[115] First proposed in 1900 while the American Library Association (ALA) held its annual conference in Montreal (which led instead to the creation of the Ontario Library Association),[116] and again in 1934 (which led to the formation of the CLA's predecessor, the Canadian Library Council, a regional branch of the ALA),[117] the CLA was created to represent the interests of Canadian libraries and librarians nationally[118] and internationally. Officially founded in Hamilton, Ontario, in 1946,[119] the CLA was incorporated under the Companies Act on 26 November 1947.[120] George Locke, Head of the Toronto Public Library and Canadian signatory to the IFLA founding charter, played an instrumental role in the early days leading up to the official formation of the Association, as did its principal proponent, University of British Columbia Librarian John Ridington,[i] as well as many others, including Fred Landon, Mary Black, Carl Milam,[121] and Margaret S. Gill.[122]

Currently, the Association "includes five constituents that represent the interests of academic libraries, public libraries, school libraries, special libraries, and library trustees,"[123] and its Executive Council is advised by a series of "Networks, Advisory Committees and Standing Committees."[124] To complement the activities of these committees, the Association hosts an annual conference which is held in a different Canadian city each year. The CLA has been instrumental in Canada's participation in IFLA; it joined the international organization in 1946 and has encouraged the participation of other Canadian library associations and individuals in IFLA ever since. Elizabeth Homer Morton, the CLA's first Executive Director, was a driving force in encouraging Canadian associations to participate in IFLA; she acted as the Secretary of the 1967 IFLA Conference Organizing Committee shortly before

---

[i] Ridington was nominated as the first CLA President in 1927, although the Association existed in name only, its official incorporation happening 20 years later. See: Stuart-Stubbs, "1927–30: The Muddle Years," 148-149.

her retirement.[125] Many other CLA Presidents have also been major participants in IFLA, including Erik Spicer,[126] Marianne Scott,[127] Harry Campbell[128], Barbara Clubb,[129] and Paul Whitney.[130]

Today, the CLA continues to participate in IFLA and to advocate on behalf of libraries and librarians throughout Canada. In the Association's own words: "We champion library values and the value of libraries. We influence public policy impacting libraries. We inspire and support learning. We collaborate to strengthen the library community."[131]

Chapter 2

1927 to 1959

T he Canadian library community's involvement with what was to become IFLA dates back to the organization's inception. In the aftermath of the First World War and the establishment of the League of Nations, an increasing sense of internationalism contributed to a growing consensus among librarians that they should form an international organization for their mutual benefit. This movement began to take formal shape at the 1927 conference of the British Library Association, held in Edinburgh, where a resolution was passed to create an organization called the International Library and Bibliographical Committee.[132]

This "Edinburgh Resolution" was unanimously signed by all delegates of the 15 countries present:[133] Austria, Belgium, Canada, China, Czechoslovakia, Denmark, France, Germany, Great Britain, Holland, Italy, Norway, Sweden, Switzerland, and the United States.[134] George H. Locke, Chief Librarian of the Toronto Public Library from 1908 to 1937,[135] was Canada's signatory.[136] Canada and the United States were represented jointly at the committee's 1928 inaugural meeting in Rome by William W. Bishop, Director of the University of Michigan Library.[137] Bishop represented Canada again at the historic 1929 meeting,[138] also held in Rome,[139] where the Committee unanimously took on a new name and so officially became the International Federation of Library Associations.[140]

IFLA's 1930 meeting in Stockholm featured a report on "The Library Year in the United States and Canada" by Sarah C. N. Bogle,[141] the Assistant Secretary of the American Library Association (ALA).[142] A similar report, "Libraries of the United States and Canada, 1931–1932," was presented by Carl H. Milam, the Secretary of the ALA, at the 1932 IFLA meeting in Berne.[143] As these reports were prepared by US librarians, it is perhaps not surprising that they focused overwhelmingly on the status and issues of libraries in the United States. The 1932 report does, however, mention a study by a commission of Canadian librarians on "library needs and conditions throughout the Dominion."[144]

The extent of Canadians' involvement in IFLA before the Second World War is not well documented, although one Helene Grenier, a librarian from the Catholic School Commission of Montreal, is known to have attended IFLA's early meetings.[145] In IFLA's 1938 *Répertoire des Associations de Bibliothécaires Membres de la Fédération Internationale*, C. R. Sanderson of Canada (presumably Charles R. Sanderson, the Chief Librarian of the Toronto Public Library from 1937 to 1956)[146] is listed as a member of the Sub-Committee on Popular Libraries.[147] Amid the chaos of the war and its aftermath, IFLA was inactive from late 1940 until May 1946, when the Executive Board was finally able to meet again in Geneva.[148]

Early in its own history, the Canadian Library Association (CLA) joined IFLA, although there is contradictory evidence about precisely when that took place. Most of IFLA's records indicate that the CLA joined in 1946,[149] the year of CLA's founding.[150] In a 1947 letter from CLA Executive Secretary Elizabeth H. Morton to IFLA Secretary General Tietse Pieter (T. P.) Sevensma, Morton remarked that the CLA would not be able to send an official representative to the 1947 IFLA conference in Oslo,[151] adding:

> Miss Margaret Gill [the Chief Librarian of Canada's National Research Council Institute for Scientific and Technical Information from 1928 to 1957[152]], who attended the UNESCO [United Nations Educational, Scientific, and Cultural Organization] Conference and the informal Committee Meeting at Geneva, has suggested the advisability of our Association joining the International Federation of Library Associations. Such a move will be discussed at the C.L.A. Executive Meeting on June 21. Unofficially, I doubt if our budget can bear the tax suggested in your Constitution, and it is more than probable that we shall regretfully have to refuse this opportunity.[153]

It appears that the CLA Executive Meeting to which Morton refers, did, indeed, result in the decision to join IFLA. As Kelly Moore, in her role as the Executive Director of the CLA, wrote in 2010: "One of our Association's first resolutions in 1947 was to apply for membership in the International Federation of Library Associations and Institutions (IFLA), and we have maintained this membership ever since."[154]

In an undated letter from Morton to Sevensma, she indicates that the CLA chose Leon Carnovsky of the University of Chicago "to represent Canada and to present the Canadian report at the Oslo conference" (presumably the 1947 IFLA conference).[155] The letter enclosed a six-page report by Morton on the state of "Libraries in Canada."[156]

In IFLA's 1948 *Repertoire of the Associations of Librarians Members of the International Federation*, the Sub-Committee on Special Libraries and Documentation Centres listed Margaret Gill, representing the National Research Council Library in Ottawa, as a member.[157]

In a June 1950 letter to Sevensma, Morton confirmed that William Kaye Lamb, the Chief Dominion Archivist and the Chairman of the National Library Advisory Committee of Canada, and Peter Grossman, the Director of Regional Libraries for the province of Nova Scotia, would be the CLA's representatives to the 1950 conference in London.[158]

At the conference, a report on the subject of "Canadian Library Affairs, 1949–1950" was presented to the delegates. Authored by Morton, the report mentioned, among other points, changes to Canadian legislation regarding public libraries, new buildings for both public and university libraries across Canada, and newly introduced Master's courses in librarianship at the University of Toronto and the University of Ottawa.[159] In Morton's words, the "outstanding event of the past two years" for Canadian libraries was the appointment of a National Library Advisory Committee by the Canadian government.[160]

Morton wrote to Sevensma again in August 1950, asking for IFLA's assistance in verifying the qualifications of "European librarians who have immigrated to Canada and are without professional papers."[161] Morton requested that IFLA "compile a study regarding training received in the different countries of Europe, [as] it would be of great assistance to those countries in the new world which are taking in European librarians."[162]

This "taking in" of librarians appears to have been a result of the many upheavals in Europe resulting from the Second World War; Morton describes the particular case of a Latvian librarian who "was placed in a displaced persons camp in Germany and is now in Canada" with "no papers substantiating his claim" to have graduated from university and received training in librarianship.[163] A subsequent letter from Morton to Sevensma, written in December 1950, thanks Sevensma for supplying "[p]hotostats of library training in Esthonia [*sic*] and Latvia, which I have found most helpful."[164]

In 1951, Harry C. Campbell (later the Chief Librarian of the Toronto Public Library) attended the IFLA conference in Rome; he went on to work with both IFLA and the International Federation for Information and Documentation in organizing the 1955 World Congress of Libraries in Brussels.[165] The early 1950s also saw two francophone Canadian library organizations join IFLA: the Association of French Canadian Librarians (Association canadienne des bibliothécaires de langue française) in 1951, and the Canadian Association of Librarians of the French Language in 1953.[166]

The lack of funds impeding official CLA representation at IFLA conferences, mentioned by Morton in her 1947 correspondence, appears to have continued into the 1950s. In a letter to Sevensma written in April 1952 regarding that year's conference in Copenhagen, Morton wrote that she would "advertise the dates of your meeting and discover if one of our members is in the locality and would be prepared to attend at their own expense."[167] This letter also discussed how CLA was behind in its dues to IFLA:

> I shall take up the matter of our dues with the Council of this Association when it meets in June. In 1950 Canadian Library Association accounts showed a deficit and in 1951 there was a balance of $1.24. Our finances appear to be better this year and it might be possible for us to again pay a fee to IFLA and we shall hope, if our finances improve, to be able to make some payment on our past fees.
>
> This organization is not one which can bear any but its national expenses and I have wondered if perhaps our fees could be accepted in publications of which we appear to have a considerable unsold quantity. We could provide copies of the Canadian Index for which a subscription is %50.00 [*sic*] per year in Canadian funds.[168]

It appears that Canadian representatives did attend the 1952 Copenhagen conference, as the passage of the Canadian National Library Bill was discussed there.[169] It is likely that there were also Canadians in attendance at the 1955 conference in Brussels, where the building projects of the CLA were discussed.[170]

In October 1958, Morton wrote to Sevensma that no official representative of the CLA would attend that year's IFLA conference in Madrid, but that she would ask John Mackenzie Cory, "who has frequently attended CLA meetings" to represent Canada there.[171] Cory was, at that time, the Chief of the New York Public Library's Circulation Department.[172]

It appears that the CLA continued the practice of asking Canadian librarians who were abroad for their own reasons to attend IFLA conferences if they could. In 1959, Amy M. Hutcheson, the Chief Librarian of the New Westminster Public Library from 1954 to 1973,[173] wrote to IFLA Secretary General Joachim Wieder[174]—on stationery from the Grand Hotel Terminus Saint Lazare in Paris —that "I regret to say that I have already made arrangements to return to England from the continent to-morrow [*sic*] so it will not be possible for me to attend your Congress."[175]

Feliciter (the official newsletter of the CLA, which describes itself as "the only national magazine dedicated to serving the Canadian library and information services community"[176]) was an important source of information for Canadian librarians regarding IFLA's activities in the late 1950s. The January 1959 edition of *Feliciter* featured a six-page report by Sevensma on the proceedings of the 1958 conference in Madrid.[177] An unattributed report on the 1959 conference in Warsaw appeared in *Feliciter* in December 1959, and included the names of three of the Canadian delegates to the conference: Robert H. Blackburn (the Chief Librarian of the University of Toronto Library), Jack E. Brown (the Chief Librarian of the National Research Council of Canada Library), and William A. Roedde (the Assistant Director of the Provincial Library Service of the Ontario Department of Education).[178]

At the 1957 conference in Paris, the Executive Board discussed the possibility of holding a future IFLA session in Canada at a time when the Canadian and US library associations would be holding their conferences together.[179] In an October 1958 letter to Sevensma, Morton wrote:

> Plans for the proposed 1960 meeting of IFLA in Canada are progressing. Mr. Jack Brown has offered the facilities of the National Research Council building for general meetings and for committees. This building is close to the Archives where committee meetings could also be held. There should be no expense with regard to arranging for the conference as this can be undertaken by the Canadian Library Association. . . . Canadian librarians look forward to welcoming the 24th session of the Council of IFLA to Ottawa in 1960 if you decide to cross the Atlantic. Miss Alberta Letts, past-president of our Association, is now in Asia and reports that several Asian librarians would be interested in attending.[180]

The letter also discussed arrangements that were being made regarding transportation and accommodation for IFLA Council members in order to spare them expense wherever possible during the proposed conference.[181]

There is evidence that serious consideration was given to the proposal that Canada host the 1960 IFLA conference, as Sevensma refers to it in his 1958 conference report:

> From the Canadain [*sic*] Library Association a letter has been received confirming the invitation to I.F.L.A. for 1960 and giving more details about the ways and means this session may be effectuated with the cordial collegial assistance of the Canadian Association and its members individually.[182]

Joachim Wieder, Sevensma's successor as the Secretary General of IFLA,[183] wrote to Morton in April 1959:

> We are very glad indeed to know that the plans for the proposed 1960 meeting of IFLA in Canada are progressing. With particular joy we have learnt that you are all greatly interested in the

international activities of our Federation, and this is one more reason why we should extremely like to organize our 26th session in Ottawa. To hold the 1960 Council meeting in Canada, in a country with such important library efficacy, would be of utmost importance for strengthening our ideas and IFLA work outside Europe. We vividly [*sic*] welcome your proposals and also the project of organizing a round table on comparative library education.

The friendly invitation of the Canadian Library Association will be submitted again to the members of our Executive Board, which will hold a meeting at Geneva on the 25th and 26th of April. There we shall especially discuss the possibilities of national and international assistance in order to find some satisfactory solution to the rather difficult problem of trans-portation.[184]

It appears that IFLA found "the problem of transportation" insurmountable, as IFLA President Gustav Hofman[185] informed Morton in May 1959 that IFLA would not hold the 1960 conference in Canada:

I was asked to thank you most kindly for your invitation and for the friendly hospitality offered to us. The Board has once more very carefully examined all your arguments and balanced the pros against the cons. As to the comparatively short time in which the great difficulties of the transportation problem should have to be overcome—and this not only for European, but also for Asian librarians—,[*sic*] The Board thought it wiser to abstain from the 1960 plan. We are all very sorry not to be able to realize [*sic*] the promising conference together with the Canadian colleagues, but we hope that in the some years [*sic*] to come it will be possible to organize an IFLA meeting in Canada, a plan which is considered very important in view of our federal projects.[186]

This decision was described in *Feliciter*'s 1959 conference report in this way: "As for the next Council sessions, the President informed the assembly that the acceptance of the Canadian invitation was postponed in accordance with a wish expressed by the Canadian colleagues themselves."[187]

This was not the first time IFLA had declined requests to hold the annual conference outside of Europe. China and India had invited IFLA "with insistence" to hold its 1936 conference in Asia and were denied due to financial considerations.[188] By 1960, only one IFLA annual conference had been held in a non-European location: the 1933 conference in Chicago.[189]

The 1960 annual conference took place in Lund and Malmö, but IFLA representatives did participate in the joint conference of the CLA and the ALA held in Montreal in June 1960.[190]

Profile: Erik Spicer

Erik Spicer, Parliamentary Librarian of Canada from 1960 to 1994, holds the distinction of being Canada's "longest continually serving official with the rank of Deputy Minister, serving under eight Prime Ministers and reporting to twelve Speakers of the Senate and ten Speakers of the House of Commons."[191]

Born in Ottawa on 9 April 1926, Spicer received a Bachelor of Arts from Victoria University (College) at the University of Toronto (1948), a Bachelor of Library Science from the University of Toronto Library School (1949), and a Master of Arts in Library

Figure 2: Erik Spicer, Parliamentary Librarian of Canada (1960–1994).

Permission courtesy of the Canadian Library Association.

Science from the University of Michigan (1959).[192] Before his training in library science (and a stint as Deputy Chief Librarian of the Ottawa Public Library from 1954 to 1960), Spicer served Canada in several regiments during the Second World War, attaining the rank of Major in the Governor-General's Foot Guards by the end of his military career.[193] He credits his military background with developing his work ethic, stating "there, you learned to concentrate."[194]

A longstanding participant in professional library organizations, Spicer has been named a Life Member of the Canadian Library Association (President, 1979–1980), the Ontario Library Association (President, 1962–1963), and the Ottawa Historical Society.[195] He was also actively involved in the Association of Parliamentary Librarians in Canada, of which he is a past President.[196] He first became involved with IFLA after the longstanding Executive Director of the Canadian Library Association, Elizabeth Morton, invited him to deliver a keynote address to the 1965 IFLA session in Helsinki.[197] Although he did not actually present at this conference due to budgetary restrictions,[198] he did go on to serve as a Canadian delegate to IFLA in 1966[199] and afterwards spoke to librarians in Ottawa about his experience.[200] He later wrote a paper for IFLA on better communication amongst parliamentary librarians.[201]

In 1973, Spicer campaigned to become IFLA President, gaining the Ontario Library Association's endorsement and running against fellow Canadian Harry Campbell[202] (both were unsuccessful).[203] During his many active years with IFLA, Spicer served as Director (1967–1973)[204] and Standing Advisory Committee Member (1973–1976)[205] of the Special Libraries Section; Chairman[ii] (1972–1980),[206] Standing Advisory Committee Member (1972–1975),[207] and Standing Committee Member (1981–1989[208]; 1993–1997)[209] of the Parliamentary Libraries Section; Standing Advisory Committee Member of the Section of Administrative Libraries (1973–1977);[210] and Member of the Committee on Official Publications (1972–1978).[211] He was also Vice-Chairman of the IFLA 50 Year Anniversary Program Planning Committee (1975–1977).[212] Spicer was an official Canadian delegate to dozens of IFLA annual meetings (1966–1997 and 2001)[213] and received a Tabula Gratulatoria from IFLA in 1977. [214]

In addition to his work with IFLA, Spicer was also engaged in international librarianship through his involvement with the European Conference on International Exchange of Publications (Vienna, 1972), the Intergovernmental Conference on the Planning of National Documentation for Library and Archives Infrastructures at the United Nations Educational, Scientific, and Cultural Organization (UNESCO; Paris, 1974), UNESCO's workshop on Development of Parliamentary Libraries (Nigeria, 1982), and the Commonwealth Library Association Council Meeting and Seminar (Nairobi, Kenya, 1983).[215]

[ii] Contrary to the information contained in the IFLA Directories from the 1970s, Spicer has also been reported as being first called President of the Parliamentary Libraries Section from 1972 to 1976 and then Chairman from 1976 to 1980. Source: Browne, Lynn N., and Gwen Peroni. "Mr. Erik John Spicer." *Canadian Who's Who: 2011*. Orillia: Third Sector Publishing, 2011. Accessed 22 December 2012. http://canadian-whoswho.ca/.

In recognition of his remarkable achievements, Spicer was named Parliamentary Librarian Emeritus and Honourable Officer of both Houses by resolution of both the Senate and the House of Commons in 1994.[216] He has been granted numerous awards, medals, and fellowships, including the Library Service Fellowship from the University of Michigan (1974), the Queen's Silver Jubilee Medal (1977), the Distinguished Graduate Medal from the Faculty of Library and Information Sciences at the University of Toronto (1989), the Henrik Schauman Medal, Finland (1991), the Canada 125 Medal (1992), the Outstanding Service to Librarianship Award from the Canadian Library Association (1994), and the Queen's Golden Jubilee Medal (2002).[217]

Spotlight: Library of Parliament

Responsible for over 17 linear kilometers of textual, graphical, and digital material, the Library of Parliament is the primary institution dedicated to serving Canadian parliamentarians' research needs. As designated by the Parliament of Canada Act, it is also the repository for "all books, paintings, maps and other articles that are in the joint possession of the Senate and the House of Commons."[218] Under the direction of the Parliamentary Librarian and counting among its officers the Poet Laureate of Canada,[219] the Library undertakes a wide range of advisory and support capacities in the realms of public policy, legislation, and administration.

The history of the Library of Parliament has its beginnings in the mid–18th century, when legislative libraries for the provinces of Upper and Lower Canada were established.[220] When the provinces were united in 1841 as the single Province of Canada, the collections of these libraries were merged; the books and manuscripts spent the better part of the next two decades following Parliament itself from city to city.[221] During that time, the collection was subject to various adventures and mishaps; the most severe of these came in 1849, when an angry mob protesting the Rebellion Losses Bill set fire to the Legislature in Montreal, destroying all but 200 of the 12,000 books in the collection at that time.[222]

When Ottawa was selected as the capital in 1857, preparations began to be made to transfer the collections to that city, and a facility to house them was designed in 1859.[223] In 1865, the Library of Parliament's collection "took its last journey when 55,000 volumes were moved from Quebec to Ottawa by barge."[224] Building the Library took nearly 20 years in the face of various political scandals and setbacks, during which time Confederation came to pass and the Dominion of Canada was established. After Confederation, the collections—and a building to house them—were officially recognized and given a statutory role as the Library of Parliament in 1871, and the new building was completed and formally opened in 1876.[225]

Taking its architectural cues from the Victorian Gothic Revival, the building incorporated a number of forward-thinking design features. The Library's massive iron doors are arguably the only thing that protected it from burning with the rest of the Centre Block when a fire broke out in 1916.[226] The Library was not so fortunate in 1952, when yet another fire caused significant damage to the facility;[227] renovation was extensive but piecemeal, culminating in a major renovation between 2002 and 2006 that brought the building up to modern standards, with extensive work on internal climate control and electrical infrastructure.[228] Erik Spicer, the library's first professionally trained librarian, was appointed in 1960,[229] and served under eight Prime Ministers before his retirement in 1994.[230] Spicer was incredibly active in IFLA for more than 30 years, and encouraged other parliamentary librarians to become involved as well, including Parliamentary Librarian Richard Paré, who chaired the Section on Library and Research Services for Parliament (1999–2001).[231] In addition, the Association of Parliamentary Libraries in Canada is a member of IFLA and provides leadership in the Library and Research Services for Parliaments Section.[232]

Chapter 3

1960 to 1979

T he 1960s saw greatly increased Canadian participation in IFLA. Over the course of the next two decades, Canada would host two IFLA conferences, field several candidates for the IFLA Executive Board, and double the number of Canadian member associations and affiliates participating. The profile of Canadian involvement began to shift, as well; during this period, two of Canada's National Librarians and its Parliamentary Librarian, among others, became actively engaged with IFLA. This was instrumental in encouraging others to take an active role in the Federation, which in turn raised the visibility of IFLA within the Canadian library landscape, as Canadian organizations and associations began paying more attention to the activities of IFLA and to international librarianship in general—despite an ongoing lack of funds to support such endeavours.

Late in 1960, le Service des bibliothèques publiques du Québec decided to join IFLA.[233] The following year, l'Association canadienne bibliothécaires de langue française (ACBLF)'s President, Auguste Morrisset, noted in a letter to the IFLA Treasurer that his association would send one official delegate, accompanied by at least five other librarians, to represent French Canada at the October 1961 International Conference on Cataloging Principles in Paris.[234] Although the Canadian Library Association (CLA) lacked funds to send an official delegate to the 1963 IFLA Council meeting in Sofia, Elizabeth Morton observed that "[s]everal Canadians expect to be in Southeastern Europe this coming summer and if the dates were known fairly soon it is quite likely that arrange-ments could be made for a representative from Canada to be present at the Sophia [sic] meeting."[235] These types of informal arrangements characterized Canada's increasing awareness of the importance of international participation, which still often depended on the willingness of Canadian librarians to incorporate their professional activities with their personal travels for the benefit of their profession. Even when financial challenges prevented large-scale participation, interest and correspondence with IFLA Executive Board members remained constant.

In May 1963, Harry Campbell wrote to IFLA Secretary General Anthony Thompson to congratulate him on his recent appointment to the IFLA secretariat, and to express interest in attending the Sofia conference.[236] Campbell, then Chief Librarian of the Toronto Public Library[237] and a longstanding participant in IFLA and the United Nations Educational, Scientific, and Cultural Organization (UNESCO),[238] went on to mention that he was "particularly interested in arranging a joint UNESCO-IFLA seminar on young peoples [*sic*]/boys & girls library work to be held in Canada (Toronto) in the future if possible."[239] IFLA responded with enthusiasm, but was unable to provide funds to support the conference.[240] Undeterred, Thompson (with the support of IFLA President Sir Frank Francis) continued to write letters in search of funding.[241] In spite of ongoing concerns about finances, the IFLA International Seminar on Children's Library Services (entitled "Highroads to Pleasure through Books") was scheduled for June 1965 in Toronto, with sponsorship from the IFLA Section on Library Work with Children.[242] Campbell's involvement in IFLA would continue over the course of the next two decades, mirroring an increased interest in IFLA by Canadians more generally.

Erik Spicer, Canada's Parliamentary Librarian from 1960 to 1994,[243] in many ways exemplified this increasing participation in IFLA.[244] In 1965, Spicer was encouraged by Elizabeth Morton to accept an invitation to deliver a keynote address at the 1965 IFLA conference in Finland, but last-minute budgetary restrictions prevented him from accepting.[245] Spicer recounts how this redoubled his intention to attend the next IFLA conference in The Hague: "I thought, 'Okay, I'll get to it next time. I couldn't get to it this time, but I'll get to it next time.'"[246] The following year, Spicer's investment in the Federation was immediate and, sent as a voting delegate to a conference in which Canada's own National Library was not represented, he attempted to "cover as many meetings as possible," picking up papers in both French and English for the National Library, the CLA, and the Library of Parliament.[247] Spicer remarks that his first impression of IFLA's conference was "extraordinarily ill-planned and amateur,"[248] but this only encouraged him to take a more active role.

During his first IFLA Section on Parliamentary and Administrative Libraries meeting in 1966, Spicer introduced a motion to split the section in two—one to represent parliamentary libraries and one to represent the libraries of government departments, in an effort to increase the efficiency of each.[249] The motion was not without controversy, eventually passing after an unorthodox double round of voting,[250] but was ultimately defeated after a third vote was called by the session's chair.[251] This incident served as Spicer's introduction to an extremely active involvement in IFLA that he was to sustain for many years. According to Spicer, "I was trying to build a team that could be a basis of a proper organization. . . . I saw a great opportunity to improve library services."[252] Spicer spoke of his IFLA experiences to local librarians upon his return to Canada, encouraging them to become involved in the organization.[253] He continued to attend conferences as a vocal participant, which propelled him to several leadership positions within IFLA. During his peak years of IFLA participation, Spicer served in various capacities including Director (1967–1973)[254] and Standing Advisory Committee Member (1973–1976)[255] of the Special Libraries Section; Chairman (1972–1980) of the Parliamentary Libraries Section;[256] Standing Advisory Committee Member of the Section of Administrative Libraries (1973–1977),[257] and Member of the Committee on Official Publications (1972–1978).[258] He was also Vice-Chairman of the IFLA 50 Year Anniversary Program Planning Committee (1975–1977).[259] In 1977, Spicer received a Tabula Gratulatoria from IFLA,[260] in "recognition for services rendered."[261]

Toronto, 1967

Figure 3: Participants at the 1967 IFLA Conference in Toronto.

Photograph from IFLA Headquarters Archives, sent to IFLA by l'Office du film de la province de Québec, ca. 1967. Photographer unknown. Permission courtesy of IFLA Headquarters.

Although Canada's bid to host the 1960 IFLA conference had been unsuccessful, Elizabeth Homer Morton and the CLA continued to campaign for Canada to play host to IFLA throughout the 1960s. Campbell recalls that Morton:

> had been at IFLA in Edinburgh in 1961 and Sofia in 1963. She had established good relations with Sir Frank Frances [*sic*], the President, Anthony Thomson and Margaret Wijnstrom [*sic*], members of the IFLA Secretariat. Mrs. Margaret Rudamino of the USSR, First Vice President of IFLA, as well as Sir Frank, both wanted IFLA to break away from past practice and meet outside of Western Europe. There were also other IFLA interests in Canada, particularly our financial aid to developing countries [*sic*] libraries. [262]

Hilda Gifford, a longstanding CLA delegate to IFLA throughout the 1970s and the University Librarian at Carleton University, adds that the "CLA invited IFLA to meet in Canada in 1964, and at the Helsinki conference of 1965 the invitation was renewed and accepted for 1967."[263] When Toronto was finally selected as the location for the 1967 IFLA Conference, Morton was (perhaps unsurprisingly) named secretary of the Organizing Committee.[264] She retired as the Executive Director of the CLA the following year, after 22 years of dedicated service, but continued to attend IFLA conferences whenever possible for years afterwards.[265]

The 1967 conference in Toronto was a first for IFLA in several ways. Not only was this the first large general meeting convened by IFLA in North America, it was in fact the first IFLA session "held entirely outside of Europe."[266] The conference theme was, appropriately enough, "Library Service for a Nation Covering a Large Geographical Area,"[267] and Klaus Plötz suggests that this was only the second time "a general theme had been chosen for the occasion"—a theme "not only for the plenary sessions but also for the open meetings of the Sections and committees."[268] Held at the University of Toronto, the conference was attended by approximately 312 participants representing 26 countries, with 64 Canadian participants registered.[269] Dr. W. Kaye Lamb, Canada's National Librarian and Dominion Archivist, addressed the session, as did CLA president John H. Archer.[270] Erik Spicer gave a presentation on the growth and challenges of special libraries in Canada, noting that from 1961 to 1967, their number had increased from 580 to about 1,200.[271] Mr. R. Boza, the Acting Director of the School of Librarianship at the Université de Montréal, presented on the state of librarian education in Canada at the Education Section meeting[272], while Harry Campbell and Virginia F. Ludlow, the Head of the Travelling Branch of the Toronto Public Library, made a joint submission on "the provision of library services to hospitals and the handicapped in Canada."[273] A paper on Canadian folklore by Professor Sheila Egoff of the University of British Columbia's School of Librarianship (later reprinted in a Festschrift in honour of Morton's retirement), was one of many Canadian presentations to the conference.[274]

One other notable outcome of the 1967 conference was the initial formation of the International Association of Metropolitan City Libraries (INTAMEL).[275] Initially, this organization maintained its independence from IFLA as a separate association with its own Executive Board and conferences, only to seek official IFLA membership in 1968.[276] Within IFLA, INTAMEL allied itself closely with the Public Libraries Section[277] as a Round Table[278] shortly after its first international conference and inaugural meeting at the Liverpool Public Library.[279] Campbell was closely involved in INTAMEL's formation, and would become its President from 1971 to 1974.[280] (INTAMEL has held its own annual conferences ever since, and became the Metropolitan Libraries Section of IFLA in January 2004.[281])

During the conference, day trips and library tours were organized in Montreal, Quebec City, Boston, Niagara Falls, and Ottawa,[282] where Spicer organized a luncheon on Parliament Hill for visiting delegates.[283] Post-conference trips were also organized to Washington, DC, and New York City.[284] In the final reckoning, 1967 had been something of a boom year for showcasing Canada's accomplishments to the world: the new National Library building had recently been completed in Ottawa[285] and Montreal played host to the World's Fair (Expo '67) the same year.[286]

The 1967 IFLA conference also provided the needed incentive for more Canadians to become involved with IFLA. Both the Ontario Library Association and the Quebec Librarian Association joined IFLA that year,[287] bringing the number of North American member associations in IFLA to 10; seven more members followed in 1968.[288] Echoing this trend, Guy Sylvestre, National Librarian from 1968 to 1983,[289] became a fixture at IFLA conferences and an active proponent of Canadian involvement in the Federation.

While Canadian participation in IFLA conferences overseas had previously been limited due to the distance and costs associated with attendance, the 1968 session in Frankfurt was attended by 22 Canadians, including Campbell, Spicer, Sylvestre, Hilda Gifford, and the new Acting Director of the CLA, Marion C. Wilson.[290] In a dramatic departure from tradition, this made Canada the fourth most-represented country at the session.[291] The 1969 Session/General Council in

Copenhagen was similarly well attended, with 23 Canadians participating.[292] Canada was instrumental in organizing IFLA's 1969 conference in Copenhagen; Georges Chartrand, who in 1978 would become the president of l'Association pour l'avancement des sciences et des techniques de la documentation (ASTED), later remarked that he had played a very active role in conference planning that year.[293] On all levels, Canadians were becoming more engaged participants with IFLA. As L. M. Harrod noted in 1967:

> Attendance at only two or three days of IFLA's five-day conference held at Toronto in August is enough to convince one of the great—and potentially much greater—value of this organization to the improvement of libraries throughout the world. As libraries and library schools join IFLA as Associate Members (which they are now able to do), so will their staffs become better informed of IFLA's work, and be able to take part in the annual conferences and contribute, both directly and indirectly, to the development of its work.[294]

Into the 1970s

The 1970s were a period of tremendous growth for IFLA as an organization. Wilhite writes that:

> Not only did IFLA have its first female Secretary General, but also its first female President. At Session, the first pre-session was held as well as its first technology exhibit. But the overall expression of the 1970's for IFLA was a time of stupendous growth. IFLA began the decade in 1970 with 257 members and ended it in 1979 with 906![295]

To accommodate such growth, IFLA's *Statutes* and *Constitution* were significantly revised; the *IFLA Journal* and *Directory* were also launched during the decade.[296] Canadian participation continued the steady growth seen since the end of the 1960s, with ever-increasing Canadian contribution to international projects sponsored by IFLA.

Throughout the 1970s, Canadian associate members continued to join IFLA as more and more Canadians reported back to their communities about the work taking place through the Federation. In1970, the Canadian Association of Library Schools joined IFLA,[297] while the Manitoba School Library Audio Visual Association joined in 1972.[298] This was followed by the Association of Parliamentary Libraries in Canada in 1976.[299] By 1974, Canada had six national members and 33 associate members in IFLA;[300] five further Canadian associate members joined after the 1974 IFLA conference in Washington, DC.[301] By the end of the decade, these numbers had risen to seven Canadian national members and 49 associate members.[302]

Conference attendance continued to fluctuate somewhat depending on the distance and costs involved in attendance, but remained relatively steady. There were at least 36 Canadian participants on record for the 1970 conference in Moscow,[303] and approximately 20 at the Liverpool[304] and Budapest[305] conferences of 1971 and 1972 respectively. General conference attendance increased during this period; each of the conferences since Toronto had set a record number for total attendees for IFLA.[306] Canadian delegate Madeleine Adorian remarked of the 1972 conference in Budapest that "a second room was provided with closed-circuit television for those unable to be placed in the great reception hall."[307] The 1973 IFLA conference in Grenoble saw at least 44 Canadian attendees including Erik Spicer, Guy Sylvestre, and Basil Stuart-Stubbs.[308] During this conference, the CLA had participants in at least 26 different committees, sections, and subsections, who could report back on their activities to other Canadian members.[309]

In preparation for the 1974 conference in Washington, DC, Dr. Laurent-G. Denis was nominated by the CLA/ACBLF Joint Committee to act on behalf of Canadian library organizations in organizing the conference, which was being handled largely by the American Library Association (ALA).[310] The 1974 conference naturally saw a sharp spike in Canadian attendance, with approximately 88 Canadian participants registered;[311] at least four Canadian papers were presented at the 40th General Council meeting[312] and several other Canadian presentations were made throughout the conference.[313]

As Canada's second National Librarian, Sylvestre began to play a more active role in the IFLA over time. Prior to the 1974 conference, Sylvestre organized and chaired a meeting of the Directors of National Libraries in Ottawa,[314] in part to foster better networking between national librarians who "have few colleagues within their own country."[315] These meetings were also held with an eye to forming a new organization for national librarians separate from the IFLA umbrella, as recent changes in IFLA's structure had made recognition as a delegate more difficult for national librarians. The outcome of these efforts was the founding of the independent Conference of Directors of National Libraries (CDNL), which tried to maintain a "good working relationship with IFLA as an organization, and in particular with the Section of National Libraries within IFLA."[316] The CDNL continues to this day.[317] Around this time, in 1974, future National Librarian of Canada Marianne Scott attended her first IFLA conference in Washington, DC,[318] although she would not become actively involved with IFLA until the 1980s.

The 1970s also saw an increasing number of Canadians take on active leadership roles within IFLA, culminating in Harry Campbell's seat on the IFLA Executive Board from 1973 to 1979. In April 1971, the New York-based Special Libraries Association took the extraordinary step of writing to the CLA to announce that its members intended to nominate Erik Spicer for the IFLA Executive Board.[319] The ALA received word of this and wrote in May to the CLA about its preferred alternate choice of candidate, Robert Vosper. Additionally, the CLA and ACBLF were unable to agree on an appropriate candidate, and ultimately, Spicer's run for one of the Vice President positions on the IFLA Executive Board was unsuccessful.[320]

In 1971, Campbell also became the President of INTAMEL, the organization he had helped to found at the 1967 Toronto conference.[321] The following year, in September, Campbell was elected to the IFLA Executive Board as a Vice President.[322] In April 1973, the CLA put forward the nomination of Campbell for First Vice President in the upcoming IFLA elections at the Grenoble conference, and began reaching out to other associations for support. This support did not manifest, however, with the Ontario Library Association's President writing to inform the CLA that they had "a commitment dating back to 1972 to support

Mr. Erik Spicer, Parliamentary Librarian. It is unfortunate that two Canadian nominations are going forward for different candidates in the same year and I can only hope that this will not prevent one of them being elected."[323] In the end, Campbell was successful, and was elected First Vice President of IFLA in 1973[324]—the same year he was elected President of the CLA.[325] In 1974, when IFLA President Herman Liebaers "resigned owing to his appointment to Grand Marshall of the Belgian Court,"[326] the CLA and ASTED quickly put forward a joint nomination for Campbell to take the President's seat, and began soliciting others for support.[327] Although Campbell received 20 votes in his favour, the presidency went to Preben Kirkegaard of Denmark's Royal School of Librarianship.[328] Campbell continued to serve as First Vice President until 1979, when he was made an Honorary Fellow upon his retirement from the Executive Board.[329]

In 1979, at what may have been Campbell's recommendation,[330] Hilda Gifford brought forward a motion to the CLA to nominate Sylvestre, Canada's National Librarian, for IFLA President. This followed on from Kirkegaard's 1978 announcement that he would be retiring before the next General Council in Copenhagen.[331] The CLA endorsed Gifford's recommendation in February 1979,[332] which quickly gained the support of all of Canada's national IFLA members.[333] Unfortunately, Sylvestre's campaign was not successful, and in 1979, Else Granheim, Director of the Norwegian Directorate for Public and School Libraries in Oslo, was elected, the first woman to hold the post in the Federation's 52-year history.[334] After his defeat, Spicer (by then the President of the CLA) wrote to Sylvestre thanking him for the attempt, noting, "though you were unsuccessful, the margin of your defeat supports the wisdom of our decision to nominate you and it is clear that a substantial number of your colleagues wished to have you as President. . . . This in itself will stand as proof to IFLA of Canadian interest in the International Federation of Library Associations."[335]

Canadian involvement in IFLA's international projects also grew significantly throughout the 1970s, particularly in the areas of international standards development, bibliographic control, and data exchange formats. For years, IFLA had been working to create a system of Universal Bibliographic Control (UBC), which led to efforts to compile an International Standard for Bibliographic Description (ISBD). These efforts arose first out of the UNESCO/IFLA International Conference on Cataloging Principles in Paris (1961)[336] and from a subsequent resolution passed at the International Meeting of Cataloguing Experts held in 1969, which was organized by the IFLA Committee on Cataloguing.[337]

In 1971, the ISBD(M) for monographs was published,[338] and shortly thereafter, an international working group was formed to begin work on a similar standard for serials designated ISBD(S).[339] The working group drew its membership from IFLA's Committee on Cataloguing and its Committee on Periodicals.[340] Dr. Jean Lunn, then the Director of the National Library of Canada Cataloguing Division, was involved in the creation of both standards[341] through her position on the Standing Advisory Committee (SAC) of IFLA's Committee on Cataloguing,[342] but is most associated with the creation of the ISBD(S). Lunn had previously worked on the first edition of the Anglo-American Cataloguing Rules (AACR) and the establishment of an International Organization for Standardization (ISO) Technical Committee 46 (Documentation).[343] A serious proponent of international exchange formats and standards, Lunn worked hard to ensure that Canada, through the National Library, would be actively involved in these standards' creation and maintenance. She believed that international exchange could not occur without first achieving national bibliographic control, and is chiefly remembered in Canada for her monumental contributions as the first editor of *Canadiana: The National Bibliography of Canada* in the 1950s.[344]

Speaking at a National Conference on Cataloguing Standards held at the National Library of Canada in May 1970, Lunn remarked on the challenges of coordinating services in a diverse, multilingual, large nation such as Canada: "Canada is a microcosm of the world. IFLA believes that there is some hope for world uniformity. Perhaps we can be at least equally optimistic."[345] By 1974, Lunn was on the Standing Committees of the Cataloguing, Serial Publications, and Bibliography Committees of IFLA.[346] Even after her retirement from the National Library in 1975, Dr. Lunn continued working to support a vision of internationally exchangeable formats and universal bibliographic control. She contributed to the AACR2 (1978) and helped to produce best-practice works such as UNESCO's 1981 *Guidelines for Legal Deposit Legislation*, which was intended as a "...model legislation for legal deposit, which would serve as a basis for Member States in attaining national bibliographic control."[347]

The 1970s also saw more Canadians getting involved with IFLA sections and committees than ever before. In July 1973, Jack Cain, Chair of the CLA's Committee on Cataloguing and Classification and the Head of the Cataloguing Department at the University of Toronto Library, was invited to participated in the ISBD(M) Revision meeting taking place at the Grenoble conference,[348] while J. McRee Elrod of the University of British Columbia Library and Francoise Lamy-Rousseau of the Ministry of Education in Quebec became formative members of a new IFLA working group to establish an ISBD for non-book library materials in 1975.[349] Hope Clement, then the Director of the Research and Planning Branch of the National Library, sat on IFLA's Committee on Mechanization, which by 1975, had set up a working group on content designators intended to "prepare an international format for the communication of bibliographic data in machine readable form."[350] Similarly, Hugo L. P. Stibbe of the Public National Archives of Canada acted as Chair of both IFLA's Section of Geography and Map Libraries, as well as chairing the initial Working Group on the International Standard for the Bibliographic Description of Cartographic Materials,[351] formed jointly with the IFLA Committee on Cataloguing, "whose task is to develop an ISBD for maps."[352] The resulting standard, ISBD(CM), was completed in 1977.[353] In Stibbe's own words:

> The publication of the ISBD(CM) and *Cartographic Materials* may surely be considered the most significant development for the cataloguing of cartographic materials. *Cartographic Materials* is now used and accepted in all of the English-speaking world and has been influential in other parts of the world. It also has been the basis for many of the enhancements and improvements to the Machine Readable Cataloguing (MARC) formats, used extensively in libraries and institutions adhering to library standards.[354]

During this period, Stibbe also became the General Editor of *Cartographic Materials: A Manual of Interpretation for AACR2*, which was published in 1982.[355] As a map archivist working in a field that overlapped significantly with the work of many special collections librarians, Stibbe was one of the few information professionals who moved freely between the library and archival spheres, making significant and lasting contributions internationally in each field over the next 25 years.[iii]

By 1975, Canadians were also represented on the SACs of several of IFLA's committees and sections, including R. Gerald Prodrick (School of Library and Information Science, Western), who sat on the SAC of the Section of Social Science Libraries;[356] Katherine Packer (Assistant Professor, Faculty of Library Science, University of Toronto) on the Committee on Statistics and Standards,[357] and Jacques Prémont (Director, Assemblée nationale du Québec)[358] on the SAC of the Section of Parliamentary and Administrative Libraries,[359] in addition to the many committees and sections in which Campbell, Spicer, and Lunn participated or chaired.[360] As the decade progressed, Canadians became

---

[iii] In addition to the contributions listed above, Stibbe represented the National Library on the Bureau of Canadian Archivists' Planning Committee on Descriptive Standards (1986–1996), the committee responsible for the first version of the Canadian Rules for Archival Description (RAD), and participating in the Choice of Access Points Working Group, 1988–1989 (BCA, *Rules for Archival Description*, vi-x). He also represented the National Library on the Canadian Committee on MARC (CCM) in 1987 (Stibbe, "Archival Descriptive Standards," 266). In 1991, Stibbe received an Honour Award from the Association of Canadian Map Libraries and Archives (ACMLA, "Awards"). He was active in the International Council on Archives (ICA), and became Project Director and Secretary of the ICA Ad Hoc Commission on Descriptive Standards (later the Committee on Descriptive Standards, or ICA/CDS), acting as Project Director and Secretary from 1990 to 2000, during which the first (1994) and second (1999) versions of ISAD(G) were developed, as well as the first version of ISAAR(CPF) (1996). Louis Cardinal, in remembering Stibbe's achievements upon his passing in 2003, adds that Stibbe also contributed to "the compilation of a bibliography of the two standards [ISAD(G) and ISAAR(CPF)] and of citation of articles which mention the standards; co-operation with IFLA for the design and eventual implementation of an international standard archival authority code similar to the ISBN and ISSN numbers; the planning with the Society of American Archivists regarding the development of an EAD (Encoded Archival Description) for contextual information associated with archival creators and the revision of EAD to conform with ISAD(G); and finally the development of guidelines for an archival finding aid typology and for standardization of finding aids" (Cabral, "In Memoriam").

increasingly invested in IFLA's core activities. In 1977, Basil Stuart-Stubbs (University Librarian, University of British Columbia) was on the SAC of the Section of University Libraries and Other General Research Libraries;[361] Edwin Buchinski (Chief, Office of Library Standards, National Library of Canada) and J. McRee Elrod (Head, Catalogue Division, UBC Library) sat on the SAC of the Section on Cataloguing;[362] Cynthia Durance (Director, Cataloguing Branch, National Library of Canada) sat on the SAC of the Section on Serial Publications;[363] Bruce Peel (Chief Librarian, University of Alberta Library) sat on the SAC of the Section on Rare and Precious Books and Documents;[364] J. Y. Gendreau (Directeur général, Services des bibliothèques, Université du Québec à Montréal) sat on the SAC of the Section on Official Publications;[365] and Katherine Packer joined the Section on Library Theory and Research as a non-voting member[366] in addition to her continuing role on the SAC of the Section on Statistics.[367] By 1978, Canada had 17 different members on 15 Standing Committees in IFLA, with Sylvestre chairing both the National Libraries Standing Committee and the Division of General Research Libraries, and Spicer continuing to chair the Parliamentary Libraries SAC.[368] During this period, Campbell, still First Vice President, continued to be actively involved in guiding IFLA through its growing pains as an organization, as it changed its name to include institutions, changed its voting and membership structure, and sought to address the needs of its members in developing countries. For his contributions during this period, he was made an Honorary IFLA Fellow upon his retirement from the Executive Board in 1979.[369] Throughout the 1970s, Canada's National Library also continued to subsidize IFLA's Universal Bibliographic Control Programme, another key Canadian contribution to IFLA-led international collaboration.[370]

In the 1970s, Canada also increased its financial support for developing countries that wished to become involved with IFLA but were impeded by cost and logistical concerns. By 1975, IFLA had member associations and institutions from 98 different countries, of which 59 were considered to be developing nations.[371] This was a testament to IFLA's efforts at reaching out to librarians in developing countries. As Wilhite notes of the 1971 IFLA conference in Liverpool, "a major first for this Session was the pre-session seminar for colleagues from developing countries on the topic *Latest Achievements in Advanced Librarianship.*"[372] Shortly thereafter, the CLA began efforts to secure Canadian funds in support of these activities, as attested by a July 1973 announcement to the Canadian library community:

> Gratifying progress has been made with regard to the IFLA Working Group on Developing Countries. On initiative of the Canadian Library Association a grant of $27,000 has been obtained from the Canadian International Development Agency in order to further the program of the Working Group. The grant will be used for:
>
> a) Travel costs to enable members of the Working Group to hold seminars, meetings and workshops as they require, and participate in such meetings organized by IFLA and other organizations in the field of library development;
>
> b) Research grants for projects to be undertaken by library associations in developing countries as part of their participation in the work of IFLA;
>
> c) Secretarial assistance.
>
> The Working Group Headquarters will be in Kuala Lumpur, where the chairman of the Working Group, Joseph S. Soosai, lives. The scope of the Working Group will be enlarged in the near future with an extension in the non-English speaking parts of the Third World.[373]

This funding continued throughout the 1970s and 1980s, provided both by the Canadian International Development Agency (CIDA) and Canada's International Development Research Centre (IDRC). Hilda Gifford's report to the CLA in 1976 provides further details: "Regional conferences are held such as the 1975 conference on universal bibliographical control in Southeast Asia. IDRC has assisted in paying the expenses of consultants and resource persons. CIDA has given a further grant of $50,000 towards an estimated $120,000 required for IFLA regional projects in 1976/7."[374] Parker describes IFLA's efforts in 1976 and 1977 to proactively address the growth of "Third World membership" in IFLA, noting that "in an attempt to give developing countries a more effective voice in IFLA, its new Constitution provides for the establishment of a new Division for Regional Activities (DRA) 'to promote and coordinate professional work of particular regional relevance, and more specifically to promote the objectives of the Federation in particular regions.'"[375] Somewhat critical of IFLA's efforts, Parker goes on to say that "despite the claim that the programme has been given 'very high priority', it is to receive no financial support from the Federation's regular budget, but is instead made entirely dependent on external aid." He adds:

> For 1976 and 1977, the work of the DRA will be financed by grants totalling some Can. $56,400 (about £ 34 thousand) from the Canadian International Development Agency and the Australian National Library. These funds are to be used to finance research and development projects in the regions and "to set up certain regional offices, and to enable colleagues from the various regions to participate in the seminars and workshops organized by IFLA and Unesco [*sic*] and in other meetings."[376]

According to Campbell, "the IFLA Division for Regional Activities was set up in 1976. The Canadian International Development Agency (CIDA) in Ottawa provided funds for these regional activities. I had been fortunate enough to be involved in these meetings and negotiations."[377] In 1974, the Harry Campbell IFLA Conference Attendance Grant was established to assist librarians from developing countries wishing to attend IFLA conferences.[378] Wieder's 1977 outline of IFLA's history adds the National Library of Canada to the list of IFLA's major sustainers offering "valuable financial support" to the Federation.[379] Through projects such as these, Canadians sought to make IFLA more inclusive and accessible as the organization grew throughout the 1970s.

Overall, the 1960s and 1970s represent a period of massive growth for IFLA itself and for Canadian involvement in the Federation. In celebration of the Federation's fiftieth anniversary in 1977, Spicer told colleagues the story of his first experiences with IFLA, noting that his first impression of the organization had been so poor that he couldn't get through a report to the CLA Council in 1966 without laughing:

"[T]he more I thought of the meetings and the more I tried to tell about their apparent disorganization, the more I laughed. The more I laughed, the more my audience laughed. . . . I sat down. There was wild applause. My IFLA report was over."[380] Despite this, Spicer's first impressions were soon transformed, and he would become deeply involved with the Federation for the next 30 years, contributing to its growth into a mature and influential international organization. This lifelong involvement and IFLA's increasing relevance and maturity were foreshadowed in Spicer's conclusion to his 1977 recollections, where he notes:

> In the last ten years I have enjoyed seeing the professional expertise of IFLA better organized, the devoted staff better supported, and the membership greatly increased. If we improve similarly over the next ten years, we may achieve fifty years progress in only ten! My message then is this: to the newcomer, IFLA will appear both confusing and ill-disciplined. For the persistent and perceptive, IFLA will soon appear useful, friendly, and addictive.[381]

Profile: Harry Campbell

Henry "Harry" Cummings Campbell (b. 22 April 1919, Vancouver, British Columbia; d. 31 July 2009, Toronto, Ontario) is recognized for his tenure with the Toronto Public Library as Chief Librarian from 1958 to 1978 and then as a Consultant until 1981.[382] Campbell received his Bachelor of Arts from the University of British Columbia in 1940, his Bachelor of Library Science from the University of Toronto in 1941, and a Master of Arts degree in Adult Education from Columbia University in 1948.[383] He co-founded the Books for the Developing World project in 1959, which eventually evolved into the Canadian Organization for Development through Education (CODE).[384] He was awarded the International Kalia Gold Medal for his achievements in 1984.[385]

Figure 4: Harry Campbell, Chief Librarian of the Toronto Public Library (1958–1978).

Permission courtesy of the Canadian Library Association.

Shortly after completing his degree in library science, Campbell started his career as a librarian for the National Film Board of Canada (1941–1943), where he became the Head of Foreign Collections (1943–1946).[386] While pursuing his Master's degree, he became a research associate for the Institute of Adult Education at Teachers College in New York City (1946–1948), subsequently working as a librarian and archivist for the United Nations (1948–1949), Head of Bibliographical and Research Library Development for the United Nations Educational, Scientific, and Cultural Organization (UNESCO; 1951–1956), and Head of the UNESCO Clearinghouse for Libraries (1951–1956).[387] From 1978 to 1981, Campbell worked as a library and information consultant for Espial Productions Ltd.[388] In 1990, Campbell became the General

Manager of Cinfolink Services, an organization focused on Internet and information services in China.[389] He was active in the Canadian Library Association (President, 1973–1974), the Canadian–China Friendship Association (President, 1985–1988), the Ex Libris Association (President, 2002), and the American Library Association.[390]

In a tribute to Campbell's life and work, the Canadian Library Association published in *Feliciter*:

> Throughout his life, Harry Campbell believed in the access of people in all countries to the knowledge and information that would help them in their social development. He was a strong supporter of IFLA's work, as he felt the Federation had an important role to play as an international non-governmental body in supporting library development in post-colonial and emerging nations.[391]

Campbell first became involved in IFLA in 1950 though his work with UNESCO.[392] In 1972, at the IFLA Council in Budapest, Campbell was appointed to the IFLA Executive Board; at the following IFLA Council in Grenoble, he was elected to the IFLA Executive Board as First Vice President.[393] In 1973 and 1974, Campbell campaigned unsuccessfully to become IFLA President.[394] In 1974, he established the Harry Campbell IFLA Conference Attendance Grant, which was intended "to assist librarians from developing countries to attend IFLA."[395] Campbell was also President of the International Association of Metropolitan Public Libraries (INTAMEL) at IFLA.[396] He continued to serve on IFLA's Executive Board until 1979, when he was named an Honorary Fellow of IFLA at the Copenhagen conference.[397] Campbell stated that the Honorary Fellowship was "a designation that [he] value[d] more than any other [he had] received."[398]

Spotlight: L'Association pour l'avancement des sciences et des techniques de la documentation (ASTED) by Réjean Savard, Professor, École de bibliothéconomie et des sciences de l'information, Université de Montréal

A STED is an acronym for l'Association pour l'avancement des sciences et des techniques de la documentation (Association for the Advancement of Documentation Sciences and Techniques). It was founded in 1943 as the ACBI, the Association of Catholic Institutions Libraries. Between 1948 and 1973, it was recognized as the Canadian Association of French-Speaking Librarians. It took its current name in 1973[399] in order to reflect the many changes that started to transform the profession at that time.

The objectives of ASTED have always been to promote excellence in libraries and documentation centres and also to play an important role in French-speaking library and information science in Canada. Its members may be individual or institutional. From the beginning, professional publications were an important activity at ASTED, and today its journal, *Documentation et bibliothèques*, which is now in its 59th year of existence, is recognized as one of the most important professional journal in the *francophonie*. ASTED is also an important publisher for French-speaking libraries: we can see in their catalogue many key publications for French-speaking professionals, among them the French version of the Dewey Decimal Classification and of the Anglo-American Cataloging Rules. Recently they published a new edition of standards to be used by public libraries.[400] ASTED offices are located in Montreal and have a staff of three persons.

Other activities of ASTED include the organization of an annual conference which is always well attended and which is now organized together with all the Quebec associations in library and information science (archivists, special librarians, library technicians, etc.). ASTED has also been involved for many years in continuing education. Over 20 committees are currently active within ASTED. We can really say that over the years, ASTED has been considered as an important leader among the francophone world of libraries.

Since 1966,[401] ASTED was always represented at IFLA conferences. Many influential members of ASTED served on IFLA sections and even on the Governing Board and Executive Committee. Moreover, ASTED was in charge of two IFLA conferences: the first in Montreal in 1982, and the second in Quebec City in 2008, both having been considered big successes and which have drawn the attention of librarians from all over the world to the successes of Canadian libraries.

Réjean Savard, Ph.D.

Former President of ASTED,
Former IFLA Governing Board and Executive Committee Member,
Professor, École de bibliothéconomie et des sciences de l'information
Université de Montréal

Chapter 4

1980 to 1999

Building upon the contributions of their colleagues in the 1960s and 1970s, the 1980s and 1990s saw increasing numbers of Canadians take on leadership positions within IFLA even as many of their colleagues approached retirement and scaled back their involvement within the Federation. One such was Hilda Gifford, the longstanding Canadian Library Association (CLA) delegate to IFLA and one of the few to actively attempt to chronicle Canadian participation within the Federation, who announced her retirement from the position in May 1979: "I have found my work and travelling as CLA Representative to IFLA very interesting and I hope I have been of use. There has been a considerable increase in the number of Canadians involved in IFLA so I hope that someone may be found to continue to provide at least a modicum of organization."[402] In contrast, other Canadians active in the 1970s continued to increase their involvement as they grew more comfortable in the Federation, and moving into the 1980s, a new wave of participants joined and began making significant contributions to IFLA and the international library community.

Much of this was made possible by the tireless efforts of Marianne Scott, Canada's third National Librarian, to encourage broad Canadian participation in the Federation—especially among the staff of the National Library. Although Scott had become aware of IFLA many years earlier (and had even attended the 1974 conference in Washington, DC), she points to the 48th IFLA General Conference as the real beginning of her involvement with IFLA: "It was going to be in Montreal, and as Director of McGill Libraries, I sort of naturally got swept into it. I think that's about the best way to describe it."[403] In March 1978, l'Association pour l'avancement des sciences et des techniques de la documentation (ASTED) had sent a formal invitation to IFLA's President, Preben Kirkegaard, with a proposal to host the 1981 General Council and Conference in Montreal.[404] Germany had also sent a 1981 invitation, however, and the Secretariat announced that the "possibility of dividing these invitations over 1981 und [*sic*] 1982 is being examined."[405] By the end of 1978, ASTED had agreed to host the 48th IFLA General Council in 1982.[406]

Scott, at the time still the Director of McGill Libraries, soon found herself on the Honour Committee for the Montreal conference. In this capacity, she came into regular professional contact with Erik Spicer, who had been invited by ASTED's Guy Cloutier to join the Honour Committee in 1979 during Spicer's term as President of the CLA.[407] As the association extending the invitation, ASTED had naturally taken the lead on conference organization with support from the CLA, and in 1979, Cloutier invited the CLA to appoint members to the Organization Committee and the Liaison Committee. The CLA chose Miriam Tees (Graduate School of Library Science, McGill University)[408] to stand on the Organizing Committee and Hans Möller (Redpath Library, McGill University) to represent the CLA on the Liaison Committee.[409] The Honour Committee also saw contributions from former National Librarian W. Kaye Lamb and Dr. Robert H. Blackburn, who had previously organized conference arrangements in Toronto in 1967,[410] among others. By 1980, Onil Dupuis (Research Officer, Conference of Rectors and Principals of Quebec Universities) was nominated the President of the Organizing Committee, as well as President of the Local Arrangements Sub-Committee; Lise Brousseau (Executive Director, ASTED) was the President of the Liaison Committee, and Gérard Lamarche (Director General, Régie de la Place des Arts) acted as President of the Honour Committee.[411]

Scott, wanting to connect further with the Federation, recalls that she "decided to go to the IFLA meeting in 1981 simply to find out what it was all about before these delegates landed on our doorstep."[412] It was likely a disorienting introduction to the world of international librarianship; held in Leipzig, the 47th session and General Council of IFLA saw 946 participants from 70 countries, with 229 professional meetings and 147 papers presented over the course of five days.[413] Guy Sylvestre was present, delivering a paper on "Training for Conservation in Canada,"[414] and Sieglinde Rooney (Head of Acquisitions Division, University Library of the University of Alberta) attended as the CLA's newest official delegate. Upon her return, Rooney gave a summary of her experiences in *Feliciter*, the CLA's official newsletter. Entitled "IFLA Congress Report: Papers Lack Originality," Rooney spoke to the *Feliciter* editorial staff of her "frustration with the lack of significant information and content in many of the papers delivered at the 1981 IFLA congress in Leipzig, East Germany," with the sense of spontaneity being suppressed in some sessions "by the presence of uniformed police" who, though ostensibly there for security, "conveyed a sense of the ubiquity of monitoring and control."[415] Rooney, herself a newly elected member to the Standing Committee on University Libraries, added on a somewhat more positive note that "whatever was lacking in the papers was more than made up for by the personal contacts made and through numerous discussions held over lunch or coffee."[416] Scott echoes this disorientation when recalling her experiences in Leipzig, noting that she "sort of wandered around, and felt very out of it because, while it was not cliquish, it was relatively small—but it was still not easy for somebody green to break into."[417] Nonetheless, she committed herself to organizing the Montreal conference, and after making many international connections, found herself agreeing to attend the following conference in Munich. There, she says she "began again to get a little bit better sense" of IFLA's organization, its role in the international community, and its importance.[418] Less than a year after that, in February 1984, Scott would be invited to become the next National Librarian of Canada.

Montreal 1982: IFLA Returns to Canada

Figure 5: Participants at the 1982 IFLA Conference in Montreal.

Photograph from IFLA Headquarters Archives, sent to IFLA by Georges Chartrand, Secrétaire générale of the ACBLF, ca. 1982. Photographer unknown. Permission courtesy of ASTED and IFLA Headquarters.

IFLA's 48th General Council and Conference—with the theme of "Networks"—was held in Montreal from 22 to 28 August 1982.[419] Wilhite remarks that "the Conference was attended by 1,915 participants, the largest IFLA Conference to date by more than 700 attendees."[420] According to the *IFLA Annual*, at least 245 of those registered were Canadians.[421] Two events were held leading up to the conference: a pre-conference themed "Education for Research, Research for Education,"[422] and the International Cataloguing-in-Publication (CIP) Meeting (Ottawa, 16–19 August 1982), organized by IFLA in cooperation with the United Nations Educational, Scientific, and Cultural Organization (UNESCO) at the National Library of Canada. Attended by approximately 45 people, the CIP meeting "was the first such international gathering for six years, the first with publishers participating and the largest ever."[423] Reporting on the event, Anne Adler of the American Library Association commented that "out of this meeting came the decision to set up a working group to study and implement a standardized format for the CIP record in the book. This would help advance UBC's [Universal Bibliographic Control] objectives—and underscore professional unanimity of purpose. This working group will come from the Cataloguing Standing Committee of IFLA."[424]

While the majority of the conference took place at the Queen Elizabeth Hotel, the opening session was held at the Salle Wilfrid Pelletier Place des Arts,[425] where delegates were welcomed by Onil Dupuis, Gérard LaMarche (President, Honour Committee), Roland Auger (President, ASTED),[426] a UNESCO representative, the Chairman of the Executive Committee of the City of Montreal, the Minister of Cultural Affairs for Quebec, the Minister of Communications Canada, and finally, IFLA President Else Granheim.[427] Céline Cartier, Director of Libraries at the Université Laval, delivered a keynote in the first Plenary Session which focused on the importance of networks (the conference's theme), touching upon both the promise and dangers of information technology's rising prominence in the library.[428] Basil Stuart-Stubbs (Director, School of Librarianship, University of British Columbia) spoke at the first session of the Second Plenary on the subject of "Networks of the '80s: Realizations," delivering a paper entitled, "Library Networks: The Canadian Experience."[429] In his address, Stuart-Stubbs stated: "With one network (UTLAS) and an integrated library system (GEAC) well established, successful national networking now depends on surmounting Canada's provincial differences—a challenge echoing IFLA's need to reduce international barriers."[430] On this challenge, Stubbs commented that "Librarians often fail to create or sustain the essential conditions for networking, beginning with the most basic: standardization."[431]

Meanwhile, at the Division of General Research Libraries meeting, Guy Sylvestre presented a paper entitled, "Canada: A Voluntary, Flexible Network."[432] He spoke of the importance of preservation in the age of networks and increasingly digital information, noting that "if we fail to move strongly in the direction of preservation, we shall eventually have huge banks of bibliographic data, part of which will describe publications that no longer exist, or, at least, are not where they are said to be."[433] He also emphasized the need for cooperative national and international acquisitions planning, stating that "every country ought to have a national acquisitions policy if it hopes to cope with the information explosion."[434] Cynthia J. Durance (Director, Office for Network Development, National Library of Canada) presented on a "Pilot Implementation of an Open Library Network Concept for Canada" in the Section on Information Technology,[435] observing that:

> The library network must be open in that it must provide a method by which large and small systems interact as peers, rather than maintain a master/servant relationship. A Canadian library network based on the concept of openness will therefore be decentralized and comprise the sum total of all systems which follow the standardized procedures for systems interface that are being developed in conformance with the OSI model. The concept of openness also has the advantage that each library system or network can be autonomous in its own development as long as it can translate its internal applications to interact with network standard data and control transactions.[436]

Dozens of other Canadians presented during the conference, including R. Brian Land (Ontario Legislative Library, Toronto),[437] Pierre Lepine (Département de cartes et plans, Bibliothèque nationale du Québec), Gilles Langelier (National Map Collection, Public Archives of Canada),[438] E. V. Smith (Canada Institute for Scientific and Technical Information), Leonard Wertheimer (retired, formerly Metropolitan Toronto Library Board), Marie Zielinska (National Library of Canada, Multilingual Biblioservice),[439] Michel Thériault (National Library of Canada), Louise Filion (Bibliothèque nationale du Québec),[440] Anne Alexander (University of Newfoundland), Michel Fournier (Université Laval), Sieglinde Rooney (University of Alberta Library), Andre Preibish (National Library of Canada), Jean Rémi Brault (Bibliothèque nationale du Québec),[441] Barrie A.F. Burns (National Library of Canada), Robert M. Bennett (Network Development Directorate, Communications Canada),[442] William Tetley (McGill University Law School),[443] and many others.

The conference was a resounding success—277 meetings were held and 170 papers were delivered over the course of the week.[444] Adler praised the translation services provided, noting that "one could get an immediate translation of the speeches in the four official languages of IFLA: English, French, German, or Russian. In addition, Spanish translations were provided for the first time, an important innovation for the Latin American and Caribbean members."[445] Outcomes of the conference included the formation of a new Working Group on the Education and Training of School Librarians and a new IFLA Round Table for the Management of Library Associations.[446] The Executive Board announced that funds donated by the Canadian International Development Agency (CIDA) had helped to establish home libraries in Zimbabwe, promote the development of reading in Senegal, provide library materials for blind children, assist library information systems in Botswana, and subsidize travel for new IFLA members from developing countries which had previously never attended an IFLA conference.[447] This magnanimity prompted President Granheim to thank CIDA for its support, saying that such efforts were "of great importance to users and potential users of libraries in the Third World," just before declaring the 48th General Conference open.[448] Following the conference, the IFLA Secretariat released a glowing statement in the *IFLA Journal*, stating:

> The 48th IFLA General Conference will be remembered in superlatives: there were more participants, more meetings, more papers than ever before. . . . The organizing committee availed itself of the services of over 200 persons to make sure that the Conference unfolded smoothly, that everyone received the papers they wanted (1,500,000 pages of text were reproduced), that—in short—everyone was as happy as they no doubt had expected to be when they decided to travel in the direction of Montreal. And the organizing committee, ably led by Onil Dupuis, succeeded. Never before was the ovation at the closing session so spontaneous and impressive.[449]

The review from the Secretariat went on to praise the quality and design of the daily output of printings during the conference—from the program to the daily *IFLA Express* newsletters to the Conference papers themselves—remarking that "it is doubtful whether in the coming decade there will be any Conference printing that can be compared with what the Canadians offered IFLA. Simply unsurpassable!"[450] To this the Executive Board added, "It was noted with appreciation and satisfaction that the Canadian organizing committee of the 48th IFLA General Conference had succeeded in publishing in advance a booklet with the abstracts of Conference papers. It was urged that this become a tradition."[451]

This is not to say that all aspects of the conference went flawlessly. The Division of General Research Libraries reported that "the concept of an Open Forum of the Professional Board (PB) at each IFLA General Conference is very welcome. However, it is disturbing to note the recent tendency of the PB to allow the time allocated to be used exclusively for formal presentation of aspects of work under its control to the detriment of open discussion and debate," submitting a resolution that the Professional Board review its practice "with a view to encouraging a greater sense of participation."[452] The Section of Art Libraries also protested the restrictions imposed by the Revised Professional Meeting Procedures, arguing that "if more meetings cannot be allowed during the week of the Conference, the Professional Board should authorize Sections to organize pre-session programs as part of the official Conference."[453] Despite the praise received elsewhere for the simultaneous translation services offered, the Coordinating Board of the Division of Libraries Serving the General Public expressed "its great concern for the lack of simultaneous interpretation at IFLA meetings. . . . For example in 1982 the Children's Libraries Section gave papers in French, an official IFLA language, and as no interpretation services were offered, the discussion became restricted because some participants did not understand or speak that language."[454] Despite these critiques, the majority of resolutions were outcomes of the work done by each section and division during the conference.

Perhaps the greatest point of tension for the Organizing Committee arose before the conference even began. Laurent-G. Denis (Professor, University of Toronto Faculty of Library Science) edited an in-depth overview of Canadian history, libraries, services, and associations, published in the *IFLA Journal* as "Libraries and Librarianship in Canada." Unfortunately, its significance was overshadowed by a careless generalization that inflamed many American IFLA members; the authors remarked early in the article that, "While we enjoy a standard of living comparable to that of the United States, we have managed to escape the backlash of violence and corruption, neurosis and insecurity, all too much a part of American life."[455] IFLA received numerous complaints, prompting the Federation and the Montreal Conference Organizing Committee to issue a statement in the following issue of the *IFLA Journal*:

> We have heard indirectly the reactions of some of our American colleagues to the article on Canadian librarianship entitled, "Libraries and Librarianship in Canada", published in *IFLA Journal*, Vol. 8, No. 1. We regret that certain passages in this article may give rise to an offensive interpretation. We reemphasize our friendship for our colleagues from the United States and assure them that we will make every effort to give them a pleasant and fruitful visit to Montreal for the 48th IFLA Conference next August. (Signed on behalf of the Organizing Committee by Hubert Perron, Vice-President of the Organizing Committee of the 48th IFLA General Conference, and University Librarian at the University of Quebec at Montreal).[456]

Despite these events, the conference was widely viewed as a success—and the biggest IFLA conference to date, not to be surpassed until the 1987 General Conference in Brighton.[457] During this time, Canadians continued to be incredibly active in IFLA, with approximately 18 Canadians acting as Standing Committee members in various Sections.[458] Sylvestre continued to sit as a Steering Committee member of the Conference of Directors of National Libraries and a member of the UBC Advisory Committee,[459] Francoise Hébert of the Canadian National Institute for the Blind (CNIB) was the Secretary of the Round Table of Libraries for the Blind, and Hope E. A. Clement of the National Library was Chair of the International Focal Point, MARC Programme.[460] The CLA, acting as IFLA's North American clearinghouse for publications, was selling at least 27 different IFLA titles in 1982.[461] Canada would manage to send at least 48 representatives to the 1983 conference in Munich,[462] presenting a strong presence as the 1980s unfolded.

New Levels of Engagement: IFLA and the National Library of Canada

As the 1980s progressed, there were shifts in the Canadian personnel active in IFLA, but the level of involvement itself never wavered; indeed, if anything, it only increased as more Canadians and Canadian associations became invested in IFLA's vision of global librarianship. Many Canadians who had become regular and active participants in the 1970s continued their involvement into the mid-1980s and beyond as Standing Committee members, including J. McRee Elrod (Section on Cataloguing),[463] Katherine Packer (Section on Statistics),[464] Erik Spicer (Section on Parliamentary Libraries),[465] R. Gerald Prodrick (Section of Social Science Libraries),[466] and Hugo L.P. Stibbe (Section of Geography and Map Libraries).[467] Others, who had been active IFLA participants for some time, saw their involvement deepen during the 1980s; these included many from the National Library of Canada. By the time Marianne Scott became the new National Librarian in 1984 and began considering how she might become more involved with IFLA, many of her colleagues were already deeply engaged with the Federation, leaving indelible changes and improvements through their participation and leadership.

Hope Clement, Associate National Librarian from 1977 until her retirement in 1992,[468] was one of those who increased her involvement in IFLA throughout the decade. Having first become involved with IFLA at the 1974 conference in Washington, DC, at the urging of Guy Sylvestre, Clement found that "a lot of the things that were going on at IFLA were very close to what was going on at the National Library," and once she became involved with the Federation, "I kept getting more and more involved."[469] By 1979, Clement was appointed Chair of the International MARC Network Study established by the Conference of Directors of National Libraries in 1975[470] which—thanks to Clement's advocacy and leadership—later evolved into the International MARC Network Advisory Committee, described as "a joint committee of the Conference of Directors of National Libraries and the IFLA Programme Management Committee" originally created to advise the IFLA International MARC Programme, and later established as an IFLA core program in 1983.[471] When Guy Sylvestre retired as National Librarian in 1984 and slowly began winding down his participation in IFLA, Clement also assumed his position on the UBC Advisory Committee, while further acting as a Standing Committee member of the Section on Interlending and Document Delivery.[472] She became Chair of the Section in 1985, and was subsequently elected Chair of its parent, the Division of Collections and Services—which made her a member of the Professional Board as well.[473] Clement continued to take on additional duties during her tenure on the Professional Board, acting as a member of the preparatory committee for the planning of a conference pre-session on "Access to Documents" in Paris, and joining a working group to develop a methodology to manage the finances and needs of IFLA's various divisions, sections, and round tables in 1988.[474] Clement was elected to chair the Professional Board in 1989[475]—the first Canadian ever to hold the position—and when the UBC and International MARC Advisory Committees merged, Clement became Chair of the UBCIM Advisory Committee from 1987 to 1991.[476] On her time as Chair of the Professional Board, Clement recalls that:

> It was a lot of work. You had two meetings a year in The Hague, and of course you always went to the annual conference. So you had a lot to do with planning the overall professional program of IFLA, and doing some of the planning for the annual conferences, too. It was quite interesting because you had about eight or ten people on the Board, and they were all from different countries, so they all had rather different agendas. It was sometimes quite difficult to get everyone to agree on things. But it was quite interesting. So twice a year, when I was Chair anyway, I would go to the Hague . . . and you'd go over all the planning for the next conference and the planning for all the Standing Committees and whatnot. I would also sit on the Executive Board Ex-Officio, so that was really . . . interesting. There was a lot of work to do in between, keeping everything going.[477]

When the Executive Board agreed to create a Publications Committee in 1989, Clement was appointed to it.[478] Despite her many commitments throughout IFLA, Clement excelled in her role as Chair, and when she declined to stand for a second term after deciding to retire at the National Library of Canada,[479] she was awarded an IFLA Medal "for her leadership of the professional board" at the closing of the 1991 IFLA Conference in Moscow.[480] At this point, Clement, looking forward to her upcoming retirement, "decided that I was through with IFLA. I mean it had been suggested that I should run for the Executive Board, but I didn't think I should."[481] Yet when the Chair of the Publications Committee also retired in 1991, he approached Clement to ask "whether I would take it on. So I did that . . . for two years, continuing to do that even after I had retired at the National Library."[482] Having helped to formulate IFLA's *Medium-Term Programme 1992–1997* and having significantly reformed how IFLA coordinated its activities during her tenure as Chair, Clement's contributions to IFLA continued to influence the Federation long after her active participation ended. Reflecting on the development of the 1992 to 1997 program in 1993, she noted:

> It is hoped that the new integrated structure for IFLA profes-sional programmes, long-term policy direction from the EB [Executive Board] and regular reporting on progress through the MTP period will result in stronger, more cooperative, but fewer projects, related to identified priorities and that the experience with these changes will simplify and improve the preparation and development of future Medium-Term Programmes.[483]

Another active member of the National Library who continued to deepen her IFLA involvement in the 1980s was Cynthia J. Durance. As the National Library of Canada's Cataloguing Branch Director since 1974,[484] Durance had been a member of the Standing Committee of the Section on Serial Publications since at least 1977,[485] and in 1978, she joined the Working Group on the International Standard Bibliographic Description for Analytic Entries.[486] In 1981, as her interests continued to shift toward exchange standards and data transmission, she joined the Standing Committee of the Section on Information Technology.[487] By 1983, "the Section's interest in networking led it to commission a study on transborder data flow, to investigate the potential and problems of networking across national boundaries . . . This focus of the Section led to the creation in 1985[iv] of a new core programme at the National Library of Canada, initially called Transborder Data Flow (but eventually changed to Universal Dataflow and Telecommunications (UDT)). The Section on Information Technology had an especially close relationship with this core program."[488] When the new IFLA core program was created at the National Library of Canada, Durance was named its Director.[489] In 1987, Durance became the Chair of the Section on Information Technology[490] and helped organize the first international seminar on Open Systems Interconnection (a networking exchange reference model) specifically for the library and information community, entitled "Open Systems Interconnection: The Communications Technology of the 1990's."[491] In 1988, Durance moved to the National Archives of Canada,[492] and Leigh Swain (Information Technology Services Branch, National Library of Canada) succeeded her as the Director of the International Office for UDT.[493] Consequently, while Durance's focus remained centred on international standards and data exchange, her work in the international arena shifted to collaborations with the International Council on Archives, and other international committees and standards bodies. Nonetheless, her library expertise helped to form one of IFLA's core programs and to situate its international office in Canada—which, in turn, would lead to Canada's pivotal role in the establishment of IFLA's website, IFLANET, in the early 1990s. Following her death in 2005, an obituary written by Ralph W. Manning in the *IFLA Journal* noted that:

> Cynthia was active in both IFLA and the ICA [International Council on Archives]. She chaired a number of national committees and working groups and was well known throughout the country for her work fostering systems, and the development of the Canadian library resource sharing network through the development of bibliographic and communications standards. She believed in the vision of universal access for Canadians and championed the development of key standards such as MARC, the ILL protocol and Z 39.50 for search and retrieval. She developed a reputation as a worldwide leader in bibliographic and communications standards and systems.[494]

[iv] Note that this date conflicts slightly with other IFLA sources. According to Kenneth Roberts, "In 1984 a special IFLA Task Force recommended, and the Executive Board approved—in addition to the three existing programmes which should be continued —the creation of three new core programmes: on Preservation and Conservation, Transborder Data Flow and related problems of data exchange, and on Advancement of Librarianship in the Third World." Source: Roberts, Kenneth H. "Special Issue on IFLA's Core Programmes." *IFLA Journal* 12, no. 4 (1986): 277-278. doi: 10.1177/034003528601200403 (p. 277).

Durance's work on the ISBD for Analytic Entries would be continued by a colleague at the National Library, Tom Delsey, whom she had encouraged to get involved with IFLA. As Delsey, who joined the National Library in 1977,[495] recalls:

> In 1979 IFLA was in Copenhagen and for some reason Cynthia either wasn't able to go at all or she wasn't able to go to the working group meeting which was a follow-on to IFLA. It was actually held in Lund, Sweden, just across the water there, so she asked me if I would go for her. That then got me involved in the work of that group, which continued on for another eight years . . . or more after that. Eventually, I became the chair or convenor of an ad-hoc group that finished up the work that group had started 10 years before.[496]

Renamed the International Standardized Bibliographic Description for Component Parts (ISBD[CP]), the standard was completed in 1988 by Delsey and others (in spite of its having nearly been abandoned in 1983).[497]

Once he was involved in IFLA, Delsey quickly became Chair of the IFLA Working Group on an International Authority System (1979–1983).[498] This later evolved into the Steering Group on a UNIMARC Format for Authorities, of which Delsey was a member from 1984 to 1989.[499] As the Chief of the Canadian MARC Office when he started with the National Library,[500] Delsey also joined the Section on Cataloguing's Standing Committee in 1981, and acted as its Chair for two consecutive terms, from 1985 to 1989.[501] He then joined the Standing Committee of the Section on Serial Publications, from 1989 to 1993,[502] but began phasing out his involvement with the conferences and committees, preferring the analytical work to the social and political aspects of the organization:[503] "[B]asically, I'm an analyst. I don't make any bones about it. Everybody knows that I have a very analytical mind. So for the past 30 years or more, I've applied that mostly in the area of bibliographic standards."[504] In fact, Delsey's contributions following his terms in IFLA's sections are arguably more enduring, as he became one of the primary authors of the FRBR Model, working as a consultant with the IFLA Study Group on Functional Requirements for Bibliographic Records:[505]

I guess my most heavy involvement was actually after I'd finished my responsibilities in the Section on Cataloguing and Division of Bibliographic Control. I got involved with the working group that was looking at the Functional Requirements—it was a study group actually—Functional Requirements for Bibliographic Records. So I stayed with them from '92 to the completion of that. We actually completed our work in '97 and got published in '98.[506]

Among the IFLA study group members with whom Delsey collaborated as a consultant was Nancy Williamson (Faculty of Information Studies, University of Toronto),[507] who had herself been a member of the Section on Cataloguing's Standing Advisory Committee since 1989.[508] Drawn from an application of the Entity Relationship Model traditionally associated with database design to the universe of bibliographic data, FRBR's impact since its approval by the Section on Cataloguing and subsequent publication by IFLA in 1998[509] has been significant. It led to immediate revisions to IFLA's ISBDs[510] and acted as the foundation for many future cataloguing standards and guides such as the International Cataloguing Principles of 2008[511] and six OCLC research projects, including giants such as WorldCat and FictionFinder.[512] When the *Anglo-American Cataloguing Rules* came under review for a third edition (which eventually became known as RDA, *Resource Description and Access*), the revisions were based on the FRBR model,[513] and Delsey was selected as the new edition's Editor.[514]

Another National Library of Canada staff member who had a significant impact on IFLA during this period was Marie Zielinska (Chief, Multilingual Biblioservices), who became a founding member of what would later become IFLA's Section on Library Services to Multicultural Populations. She recounts the history of the Section in a pamphlet prepared to celebrate the Standing Committee's 20th Anniversary in 2001:

In 1973, when Marie F. Zielinska was given the task of organizing at the National Library of Canada, a central library serving all Canadian ethnolinguistic communities through the network of public libraries, she gathered an informal circle of librarians interested in the exchange of information and ideas by correspondence. Some members from the group had the opportunity to meet in person at the IFLA conference in Brussels in 1977. Initial talks on the possibility of creating a suitable international forum for exchange of information bore fruit only three years later. In April 1980, at the request of Johannes Daugbjerg from Denmark, then chairman of the IFLA Division of Libraries Serving the General Public, as well as chair of its Public Libraries Section, IFLA's Professional Board agreed to create a Working Group for a three-year period.[515]

Following its formation, Zielinska acted as the working group's first Chair.[516] The group's first annual report and open meeting was presented at the 1981 conference in Leipzig,[517] and its second was presented at the Montreal conference in 1982 where, with some involvement from Zielinska, "the Multilingual Biblioservice of the National Library of Canada provided an exhibit of acquisition tools for books in various languages which attracted much attention."[518] Soon it "became apparent that within the three-year period of its mandate the Working Group was only able to break the ground . . . and a permanent body was needed to carry on the work."[519] Consequently, the Working Group's application to become an official Round Table of IFLA was approved in 1983.[520] However, as interest continued to grow over the next few years, "it was clear that the Round Table outgrew its definition both in size of would-be membership and the quantity and quality of work undertaken;"[521] at the 1986 conference in Tokyo, the Round Table became the Section on Library Services to Multicultural Populations.[522]

During this same period, Zielinska collaborated with Cynthia Durance to organize an IFLA pre-conference, themed "Automated Systems for Access to Multilingual and Multiscript Library Materials: Problems and Solutions," which was held from 21 to 22 August 1986 in Tokyo.[523] In 1989, Zielinksa became the Chair of the section[524] and began collaborating with Francis T. (Frank) Kirkwood on one of the section's major publications; *Multicultural Librarianship: An International Handbook* was eventually published in 1992.[525] Kirkwood, a colleague at Multilingual Biblioservices (1982–1989) who eventually moved to the Library of Parliament, speaks highly of Zielinksa, calling her an "extremely competent, famous librarian . . . to whom I owe a great deal."[526]

Kirkwood would accrue eight university degrees and learn 12 languages over the course of his career, and claims it was Zielinska who "got me working with languages big time, and was tolerant of my vices and generally helped me to get into the international arena,"[527] bringing him into contact with IFLA through the editing work on the manuscript. "So that was my introduction to IFLA and I actually attended the IFLA conference in Paris 1989 unofficially—I didn't register—just in order to meet a couple of Marie Zielinska's colleagues who I had struck up an acquaintance with when they came to Canada on visits. And to submit a draft report proposal on how the book is going to go, the structure, you know, the usual preliminary stuff."[528] In 1990, the two attended a pre-conference on multicultural libraries in Eskil Stunna, near Stockholm, where the general conference was being held.[529] The two attended another pre-conference seminar the following year in Riga, concerning "library services in a multicultural environment, east and west"—a session which Zielinksa, as Chair of the section, opened with "words of welcome."[530] The 1991 Riga pre-conference, where Kirkwood delivered his first IFLA paper[531] and Zielinksa finished her term as Chair of the section, "attracted a very large audience of librarians who were eager after many years of isolation by the Communist regime to meet colleagues from other parts of the world."[532] Zielinska kept up her relationship with the section even beyond her last term on its Standing Committee (1995–1999),[533] acting as a Special Advisor to the section[534] and compiling several articles on the section's history to celebrate its 20th anniversary. The Section on Library Services to Multicultural Populations continues to be a vital and active part of IFLA today.

Enter Marianne Scott: IFLA, 1984 to 1988

In 1984, Marianne Scott, then the Director of Libraries at McGill, was asked to be the next National Librarian of Canada following Guy Sylvestre's retirement.[535] Although she had already attended several IFLA conferences by that time, it was only after joining the National Library that Scott began actively engaging with the Federation. Much of this was inspired by the strong precedent for involvement that Sylvestre had set during his tenure. Scott recalls that "when the '84 Conference came around, I was by then the National Librarian, and I was told that it had been pretty well *de rigueur* for Guy Sylvestre to go to IFLA. So . . . I packed myself off to IFLA."[536] Scott found herself among a dedicated cadre of at least 22 Canadians already active within IFLA's Standing Committees.

In addition to the National Library of Canada staff already involved and the stalwarts of the 1970s (such as Spicer, Packer, Elrod, Prodrick, Stibbe, and Stuart-Stubbs) who continued to participate during this period, a number of other Canadians had joined the Standing Committees of IFLA's sections and round tables. These included Margaret Anderson (Faculty of Library Science, University of Toronto)[537] and Hans Georg Schult-Albert (Associate Professor, School of Library & Information Science, University of Western Ontario)[538] in the Section on Library Theory and Research; Donald Cook (Associate Professor, Faculty of Library Science, University of Toronto) in the Section on Cataloguing;[539] Melva Dwyer (Head Librarian, Fine Arts Division, University of British Columbia)[540] and Mary Frances Williamson (Fine Arts Bibliographer, Scott Library, York University)[541] in the Section on Art Libraries, with Williamson also serving on the Standing Committee of the Section on Classification and Indexing;[542] Anne Galler[543] in the Section of School Libraries; Jean-Yves Gendreau (Directeur, Collections spéciales, Université du Québec à Montréal) in the Section on Official Publications;[544] Miriam Tees (Associate Professor, Graduate School of Library Science, McGill University)[545] and Richard K. Gardner (EBSI, Université de Montréal)[546] in the Section on Library Schools and Other Training Aspects; Martha Stone (Associate Director, Information Sciences, International Development Research Centre) in the Section on Biological and Medical Sciences Libraries;[547] Judith and Paul Thiele (Charles Crane Memorial Library, University of British Columbia) in the Section of Libraries for the Blind;[548] and Jean Whiffin (Head Serials Division, University of Victoria Library) in the Section on Serial Publications.[549]

The 1984 IFLA conference was slated to take place in Nairobi, and Scott prepared herself to attend. Sixteen other Canadians made the journey, including regular attendees Durance, Spicer, Clement, Stibbe, and Prodrick.[550] The conference, attended by over 1,000 people representing 71 countries, was significant for being the first held in Africa since IFLA's founding.[551] It was also where "the establishment of the Universal Dataflow and Telecommunications Core Program at the National Library of Canada" was first publicly unveiled.[552] Scott had been introduced to a number of people at IFLA during previous conferences she had attended, largely through Miriam Tees, Françoise Hébert, and Erik Spicer, "so by the time I became NL [National Librarian] and went to Nairobi in 1984, I knew my way around in a basic way. Erik was definitely at the Nairobi meeting and as I said was sure [*sic*] that he introduced the new Canadian National Librarian to many of his friends. Cynthia Durance and I travelled together from London to Nairobi."[553]

Scott initially joined the Conference of Directors of National Libraries (CDNL), a smaller and more intimate meeting than the larger IFLA section meetings taking place during the conference. At the time, Scott says, "CDNL meant two things to me—first, it was a small focused group which I could relate to, and secondly, it was clearly a casual informal group which reminded me of other small specialized group meetings I had attended, also dominated by men. Very friendly, helpful . . . because I was very much the new person on the block."[554] It didn't take long for Scott to realize she wanted to be more actively involved, however: "I think it was in the next couple of years' meetings that I really came to the conclusion that just attending the Conference, going to meetings and talking to colleagues was not enough. You had to get involved in the Sections and Committees."[555]

In 1985, Scott also became a Standing Committee member of the Section on Conservation.[556] The conference that year, in Chicago, saw a higher attendance of Canadians than usual due to its proximity —at least 96 Canadians were registered by the end of July.[557] The following year, Scott and at least 28 other Canadians traveled to the IFLA conference in Tokyo.[558] By then, Donald Bidd (National Film Board of Canada) had become the Secretary of the Round Table on Audiovisual Materials;[559] Clement was Chair of the Division of Collections and Services and sitting on the Professional Board;[560] Delsey was Chair of the Section on Cataloguing;[561] Anne Galler had ascended to Chair of the Section of School Libraries;[562] Richard Landon (Thomas Fischer Rare Book Library, University of Toronto) was the Secretary of the Section on Rare and Precious Books and Documents;[563] Miriam Tees was the Secretary and Financial Officer of the Division of Education and Research;[564] and Mary F. Williamson was the Secretary of the Division of Special Libraries and the Secretary of the Section on Art Libraries.[565] Canadians were playing active roles in key positions within IFLA, and shaping its direction and structure through their contributions.

Tees and Galler: Canadian Contributors to School Libraries and Library Schools

Two Canadians in particular were noteworthy for their incredible engagement with IFLA during this period, which culminated in a term on the Federation's Professional Board for each. At the 1987 IFLA General Conference in Brighton, Miriam Tees was elected to chair the Section on Library Education and Training.[566] Already the Secretary and Financial Officer of the Division of Education and Research, Tees was simultaneously elected to become the Division's next Chair; this in turn, also made her Canada's very first member of the IFLA Professional Board.[567] At the Brighton conference, Tees reported on the section's pre-conference, an "International Colloquium on the Harmonization of Education and Training for Library, Information and Archival Personnel," which was attended by approximately 50 people from 38 different countries.[568] That same year, through the section, Tees also received IFLA funding to prepare "a course curriculum on teaching management to information professionals."[569]

In 1988, Tees retired from McGill, and "immediately took on assignments at the Asian Institute of Technology in Thailand, at the Curtin University in Perth, Australia, and at the University of British West Indies in Kingston, Jamaica, as well as travelling widely in Europe."[570] Even after her term as Chair ended, she retained a personal affiliate membership in IFLA and continued to be active. According to Galler, "an entire issue of the *IFLA Journal* (v. 17 (1991)) under the editorship of Miriam Tees is devoted to Education and Training."[571] In 1991, IFLA's Continuing Professional Education Round Table published its *Continuing Professional Education: An IFLA Guidebook*, in which Tees selected and edited a survey of continuing professional education activities from 14 countries worldwide.[572]

Anne Galler of Concordia University was also highly active in IFLA during this period. She chaired the Section of School Libraries for two consecutive terms (four years),[573] and in 1987, was elected as Secretary to the Coordinating Board of the Division of Libraries Serving the General Public.[574] Galler notes that "during my term as Chair, guidelines for school library service were updated and published and translated into several languages."[575] In 1989, Galler became the Chair of her division,[576] thereby joining the IFLA Professional Board that Tees had just left, and that fellow Canadian Hope Clement was currently chairing. Having reached the maximum number of consecutive terms as Chair of her section, Galler then became Chair and Financial Officer for the Section of Libraries Serving Disadvantaged Persons, serving two consecutive terms in the position; it was during this time that the "International Guidelines for Prison Service and for Services to the Deaf were published."[577] Also in 1989, *Managing School Libraries,* a manuscript she had prepared with Canadian Joan Coulter through an IFLA research grant, was published. Of these developments, Galler recollects that:

> I have always encouraged research in librarianship, thus it was most gratifying when I joined IFLA to be able to apply for grants for research at the international level. My very first research project, with the help of a small IFLA grant, became a manual for school librarianship, co-authored with a local practicing librarian. This manual, entitled *Managing School Libraries*, was originally intended for the third world, as it describes methods to run a library on a virtually non-existent or very minimal budget. It became a useful reference tool in Canada as well as in some European countries. It was also translated into French and Spanish.[578]

Galler's run chairing IFLA's various sections and divisions came to an end in 1991, but her contributions to IFLA would continue for the rest of the decade, culminating in the *School Library Manifesto* at the close of the century.

Scott, the Conference of Directors of National Libraries, and IFLA

As the decade closed, Scott had grown comfortable in IFLA and had committed herself to further participation: "After I'd had a couple of years, I had this sense of the only way to really go to IFLA was to be actively involved. That was my mantra. I felt this business of going and going to sessions and wandering around like an aimless duck didn't work."[579] Consequently, when William Welsh's term as CDNL Chair came to an end in 1988, Scott assumed his position chairing the Conference "and the secretariat returned to Canada (1988–1992)."[580] Since the Chair of the CDNL would regularly attend the meetings of the IFLA Programme Management Committee (PMC) to share activity reports,[581] Scott also replaced Welsh on the PMC.[582] While the organization had operated as an "informal association" since its inception in 1974,[583] it lacked a formal structure; similarly, while its members and Chairs had consistently emphasized the need to remain in close contact with IFLA to ensure cooperation without an overlap of mandates, it was "difficult for the two organizations to maintain a steady flow of information during the twelve-month gap between meetings."[584]

Scott, seeing the CDNL's utility and potential, set out with several CDNL colleagues to make it more effective; thus it was that, "during the chair of Marianne Scott, National Librarian of Canada, CDNL established its present statutes and rules of procedures, which g[a]ve the organization a much clearer and stronger foundation for its activities."[585] Scott also "sought to formalize the communication mechanism [with IFLA] when she took over the chair."[586] Ralph W. Manning, who would become involved in IFLA in 1993 at Scott's urging, adds that when Marianne was Chair of CDNL, "she was the one who actually gave it a kick in the pants and gave it a strong foundation for that organization. . . . Kudos to her."[587] Through all these changes, Scott notes, "we were suddenly beginning to add new members."[588] Today, CDNL persists, and its core structure still attests to the changes that Scott introduced during her tenure as Chair.

By 1990, Canada had at least 33 different representatives on section Standing Committees and the Executive Committees of round tables, with Adèle Fasick (Faculty of Library and Information Science,

University of Toronto) as Chair of the Section of Children's Libraries;[589] Donna Duncan (McLennen Library, McGill University) serving as Secretary for the Section on Classification and Indexing;[590] Lorraine McQueen (National Library of Canada) and Helen Perry (CNIB) both acting as Secretary for the Section of Libraries for the Blind;[591] Richard Landon now chairing the Section of Rare Books and Manuscripts;[592] and Beth Miller (University of Western Ontario) serving as Secretary to the Executive Committee of the Round Table on Continuing Professional Education.[593] This was all in addition to the continuing responsibilities of Clement, Galler, and Zielinska in their respective roles as Chairs, Leigh Swain's role as the UDT Programme Director,[594] and Nancy Williamson's role as a liaison with the International Federation for Information and Documentation (FID).[595] Canada had 43 institutional members registered in 1990 to 1991,[596] and at least 37 Canadians travelled to attend the 1990 IFLA conference in Stockholm.[597]

Into the 1990s

Along with her involvement with the CDNL, Scott continued to be a Standing Committee member of the Section on Conservation until 1993,[598] at which point she became a Standing Committee member of the Section of National Libraries—a position she would hold until 1997.[599] It was also during this period that, arguably, Scott's greatest contribution to IFLA began in earnest: recruitment. Scott recalls that, as the call for committee nominations was taking place:

> I thought to myself, "Well, let's see what we can do." I went down the list of Standing Committees and I identified the committees where I thought the National Library had to be. In fact for a number of years we had had someone from NLC on certain Committees. In my opinion NL had contributed quite a lot during Sylvestre's term and then mine to certain areas, such as Standards, ILL, and cataloguing. However in reviewing the membership in all the Sections, it was clear there was room for greater Canadian participation, so I started phoning.[600]

Ralph W. Manning was one of those encouraged by Scott to get involved with IFLA in 1993. Having worked for years in cataloguing before becoming the Director of the Office of Library Standards at the National Library of Canada, he recalls that as Scott's term on the Standing Committee of the Section on Conservation came to an end in 1993:

> [S]he was very keen to have somebody, a Canadian, on the committee and that was when I was actually working with her on the Canadian strategy for preservation, when such a thing was still in vogue. So she called me and asked if I would be willing to be a Canadian rep on the committee on conservation. So that was actually how it started. Not more complicated than that.[601]

Manning was already aware of IFLA through the activities of National Library of Canada colleagues such as Durance and Delsey: "I knew they'd been very involved in IFLA activities, so it wasn't new to me. It was a bit of a surprise, actually, that I was acclaimed to Section on Conservation rather than cataloguing but . . . [laughs]."[602] Manning took his new role seriously, immediately becoming the Secretary and Treasurer for the Standing Committee of the section as well as the Secretary for its parent, the Division of Management and Technology.[603] In addition to these responsibilities, he became the Chair of the division in 1995 (which came with a seat on the Professional Board).[604] Manning also agreed to act as the Professional Board's UDT Core Programme Liaison,[605] and as a Teller for the Executive Board.[606] He would continue to hold his position as Chair of the division until 1999, becoming the Editor of the Section on Preservation and Conservation's newsletter in 1997 while continuing to act as the section's Secretary and Treasurer.[607] In 1999, Manning became Chair of the Professional Board, the second Canadian since Clement to hold the title, thereby joining the Executive Board as an ex-officio member.[608] Throughout this period, Manning also compiled and edited *A Reader in Preservation and Conservation* with Virginie Kremp, drawing on contributions "from more than 20 countries" that "g[a]ve a broad overview of preservation and conservation activities."[609] The book, released as IFLA Publication No. 91, was announced in 2000.[610]

Reflecting on his accomplishments in IFLA, Manning emphasizes his attempts to move IFLA away from its heavy dependence on English as the lingua franca of all of its conferences and activities as one of the outcomes of his involvement. He points out that, despite IFLA's recognition of five official languages at that time,[611] "if you go to an IFLA conference, you don't hear any of those languages except English. And Canada's a bilingual country. A lot of Québecois and non-Québecois who speak French go to IFLA conferences—an awful lot of French-speaking people go to IFLA conferences. . . . And yet at every meeting, you spoke English."[612] Manning, who himself speaks four languages, says he "felt it rather keenly," and did what he could "in helping to ensure that IFLA actually was a cosmopolitan organization that could benefit from having five or six or seven official languages."[613] He points to the influence he had in changing the Section on Conservation's name to the "Section on Preservation and Conservation"—a change that was approved by the Professional Board in 1996.[614]

> Conservation and Preservation reverse meanings in the two languages [French and English]. So preservation, and the way that I always try to explain it, if you've heard of conserves and preserves? Well, conserves are where you have a cherry and it's still a cherry, whereas preserves are turning it into jam, so it's no longer in its original form. So in the brittle book days for example, or today if you made a digital copy of something, you're preserving it, whereas if you're de-acidifying it, you're conserving it. But in French, and I believe in some other languages, it's the reverse. Preservation and conservation are the reverse meanings. So finally we decided that the only way around it was to use both words. Finally, it became the Section on Preservation and Conservation, so whatever you were talking about is what we were talking about.[615]

Manning's fluency in French also gave him "the ability to run meetings in French, so I was able to do an awful lot within IFLA to promote francophonie."[616] His efforts to promote IFLA as a truly inter-national organization continued into his tenure on the Professional Board: "[O]ne thing that we worked on quite a bit was the intent to get much more involvement from countries that didn't participate as much."[617] Manning's involvement with IFLA committee work would end in 2001, but he has maintained a peripheral involvement with the Federation, participating in a gathering of all the former Professional Board Chairs in 2005[618] that would lead to the new *Statutes* and *Rules* accepted in 2008 when "the new professional structure for the organization was ushered in."[619]

Ingrid Parent (University of British Columbia Librarian; IFLA President, 2011–2013) attributes her involvement in IFLA to Scott as well. In 1993, when Parent was the Acting Director of the Acquisitions and Bibliographic Services Branch of the National Library,[620] Scott approached Parent to encourage her to consider becoming involved. Parent recounts that:

> [T]here was a vacancy on the cataloguing committee of IFLA because Nancy Williamson from the University of Toronto finished her mandate of eight years, I think. It was felt that Canada needed a representative on the cataloguing committee, and so Marianne talked to me about it and she said that this would be a good opportunity to begin to get involved with IFLA. I was quite surprised because I didn't know that much about IFLA and I really didn't know what they talked about there. But I said "Sure, I'll put my name forward."[621]

Like many new to IFLA, Parent was disoriented at first. She notes that "it took us a while to get, to understand what was happening. It felt like a Byzantine kind of institution/federation at the time; it was just hard to understand it."[622] Nonetheless, Parent involved herself, and ended up spending eight years affiliated with the section, four of them as Chair. "I think if you volunteer to help out in some way, you're tapped to be the Secretary or the Chair right away."[623] In 1995, Parent became Chair of the Section on Cataloguing;[624] by 1997, she was Chair of the Division of Bibliographic Control, serving on the Professional Board at the same time that Manning had become its Vice-Chair[625] while retaining her position as Chair/Treasurer of the Section on Cataloguing for a second term.[626]

In 1999, Parent decided to run for the Executive Board at the upcoming elections to be held during the IFLA conference in Bangkok. She describes the process as "a lot of lobbying:"

> I remember sitting outside in the summer at home in Aylmer, Quebec, writing letters. This was before . . . e-mail and the Internet got really, really important. We had to write letters and mail them. You'd write to every country and say "Would you support me?" And at that time, the elections took place during the annual conference, so you'd show up at the annual conference in August. Every candidate was there and the people wrote a ballot and put it in the box and the winners were announced.[627]

Following the elections, Parent joined the Executive Board[628] after receiving a stunning 626 votes in support of her nomination.[629] "The elections were very political and you had to be known. So my experience working up through the professional side made me known to many countries."[630] That December, at a meeting of the Executive Board, she was also made Chair of the Conference Planning Committee and appointed to the Publishers Liaison Committee.[631] Parent's involvement with IFLA would continue to grow over the course of the next decade, culminating in her 2011 to 2013 term as IFLA President.

Ralph Manning and Ingrid Parent were just two of many Canadian librarians that Scott would encourage to become involved with IFLA during her tenure as National Librarian, and both went on to have a profound impact on the direction of the Federation through their contributions and leadership. Canada's contributions to IFLA were not merely in the realm of personnel, however—Canadians also were helping to bring IFLA into the digital age with the advent of IFLANET.

Canada and the Rise of IFLANET

IFLANET arose out of the efforts of the Universal Data Flow and Telecommunications (UDT) Core Programme, and was based at the National Library of Canada (NLC) since its establishment. Leigh Swain had taken over from Cynthia Durance as the Programme Director in 1988.[632] The UDT Core Programme, under Swain's direction, began investigating the possibilities of establishing an Internet home for IFLA in late 1992:

> During the 1992 IFLA Conference in New Delhi, it was recognized by a number of groups including the Section on Information Technology, that IFLA should take steps to utilize the various resources available on the Internet to support IFLA's activities. As the UDT Core Programme has gained considerable expertise in this area, it was proposed that the UDT Programme assist IFLA HQ in their efforts to obtain an Internet connection for HQ offices and provide guidance on the use of the various resources available on the Internet. This activity began in the latter stages of the 1992 programme year and will continue as a central programme activity in 1993.[633]

Much of the initial project was established by Swain with the assistance of Gary Cleveland, another NLC staff member (Information Technology Services)[634] who had been working with the UDT Core Programme for some time and regularly collaborated with Swain.[635] In November 1993, Terry Kuny joined NLC, having been "hired to look at nascent Internet information retrieval, then using FTP archives and Gopher servers,"[636] and "was immediately assigned to work with the UDT Core Programme."[637] At the time, "Leigh Swain, Gary Cleveland and Fay Turner were all doing library and IT technologies and standards work for NLC. And NLC's sponsorship of the UDT programme allowed them to push some of their knowledge out more broadly."[638] Along with Louise Lantaigne, these five would become the core team that established and managed IFLANET until the end of the decade.

UDT quickly succeeded in establishing the IFLA-L list-serv, "possibly in late 1993,"[639] through a partnership with the US-based SilverPlatter (recalled as "a company that put databases on CDs"), which also had several early FTP servers used to host the list until the infrastructure for IFLANET was more robust:[640] "By 1993, IFLA headquarters was equipped for e-mail messaging, and the IFLA website, IFLANET, was created in 1994."[641] Kuny recalls that "IFLANET was the name I coined to reference *all* the electronic services of IFLA (mailing lists, web site)."[642] By the time the 1994 IFLA conference in Havana was underway, IFLA was ready to unveil its project. In fact, President Robert Wedgeworth's opening address, entitled "The Virtual IFLA: Moving Knowledge through Time and Space," was almost exclusively focused on this exciting new development:

> The establishment of IFLANET will create the means for member associations, institutions and individuals to participate in IFLA in far greater numbers than current limitations on time and expense will permit. It will allow developing library communities to communicate more readily with library communities with similar situations as well as with those with very different situations. . . . The tools and resources made available via IFLANET will create a "virtual IFLA" for those who, for example, are unable to attend the next General Conference. Imagine being able to access important IFLA documents and conference papers as they are produced. Imagine being able to comment on IFLA conference papers and have your opinions shared with those at the Conference site. Imagine being able to make access to IFLA less costly for all members. Admittedly, nothing could replace the experience of actually being in Cuba. But for those colleagues who are unable to attend conferences due to obligations at work or at home, IFLANET will be a welcome substitute.[643]

According to Frank Kirkwood's account in *Feliciter*, 1994 "was the year of the Internet at IFLA: telecommunications workshops for Internet novices, potential uses of the Internet in South America, and document delivery by Internet in North America," in addition to the announcement of IFLANET, "which will electronically link member libraries and IFLA officers throughout the world, and will be based in Canada."[644]

Throughout this period, Kuny, Cleveland, and Turner were doing all they could to push their research out to an international audience. Kuny describes it as doing:

double duty with much of our work. Within NLC, I started a series of Network Backgrounders that I and others put out. These were short (1–2) page articles about different new and emerging technologies. Many of these we distributed to IFLA as well. We took *boxes* of this stuff to the annual conference. It was quite the logistical chore and the admin assistant we had, Louise Lantaigne, was essential for keeping things going. Louise later was trained to help manage the IFLA site.[645]

As IFLANET took off, Kuny and Lantaigne acted as co-moderators of IFLA-L,[646] while Kuny managed the majority of IFLANET's construction and maintenance; IFLANET itself was administered by Swain, Kuny, Lantaigne, and Cleveland[647] (who would be Programme Officer for UDT by 1997).[648] Kuny would also curate web development resources to assist other information professionals interested in moving online, including a page of "Advanced HTML Resources" and "Notes on Background and Colours," one of IFLANET's most visited documents in its early days.[649]

By August 1995, IFLA-L had moved from SilverPlatter to IFLANET, and on 17 August 1995, Kuny announced that IFLANET would begin implementing "WWW Hypermail access" so that users would "be able to access list archives, read messages, and send commands to the listserv from your WWW browser."[650] Web access to IFLA-L (as well as DIGLIB and LIBJOBS, two other mailing lists Kuny helped to administer and moderate)[651] was announced the following day.[652] A few days later, at the 61st IFLA conference in Istanbul, Swain was elected as Chair of the Section on Information Technology[653] (he had been a member of its Standing Committee since 1989).[654] At the same conference, Swain and Cleveland delivered a half-day workshop with Steve Cisler of Apple Computers entitled "The Internet and the WWW," which drew over 100 participants and "gave an overview of the Internet and the World Wide Web, a tutorial on using Gopher and WWW navigation software, and practical information on constructing a Web site."[655]

IFLANET was a huge success. In the month of September 1995 alone, IFLANET delivered 26,438 documents to over 8,471 unique hosts.[656] Over the next year, IFLANET completed 691,408 requests, or an average of 1,889 requests per day, to 140,389 distinct hosts.[657] "In an average week, users in at least 50 different countries use the IFLANET

WWW service. Over 100 different countries have been identified as having accessed the WWW service alone. IFLANET delivers an average of over 10,000 documents per week through its WWW service."[658] By the end of 1996, IFLA-L had over 800 subscribers, with over 6,000 subscribers across all the lists that Kuny and the UDT staff moderated, for a total of over 5 million messages sent that year.[659]

UDT members would also coordinate with SilverPlatter each year to produce "the IFLANET Unplugged CD-ROM," a snapshot of all resources available on the site, which they distributed free of charge at the annual IFLA conferences; more than 3,000 were distributed at the 1996 conference alone.[660] In an effort to support the increasing demand, the first official mirror site of IFLANET was established in December 1996,[661] hosted by the Institut de l'Information Scientifique et Technique (INIST) in Vandoeuvre-les-Nancy, France.[662] Shortly afterwards, it was announced that "IFLA's Web Site in Canada was given a Gold Award by NetGuide (CMP Media Inc.) for being one of the best on the Web."[663] At the 1996 conference, Scott received the IFLA Medal, "in recognition for the development of IFLA's UDT Core Programme."[664] Throughout this period, IFLANET's administrators continued to be active in promoting information technology to library professionals whenever possible. At the 1997 IFLA conference in Copenhagen, Kuny presented two related papers and participated in a debate on "Copyright and Access in a Digital Era."[665] Swain and Kuny also gave a workshop on Internet metadata and Fay Turner presented a series of workshops on topics such as the Z39.50 standard and "ILL Protocol Standard: Interlibrary Loan in an Open Networked Environment."[666] According to Kuny, UDT members during this time "also did a lot of early policy development around how to provide electronic services. And a lot of training to the international community on standards, on web, on IFLANET. Gary and I did many workshops from 1995 to at least 2000 on various aspects of IFLANET services and new technologies."[667] The three would continue to be active conference participants past the close of the decade.

In June 1998, Cleveland announced the creation of the new IFLANET domain, www.ifla.org, which the Federation still holds today.[668] A full redesign of the IFLA website with the inclusion of full-text searching across the entire site was introduced in 1999; 14 new discussion lists had also been created that year, often for specific sections or committees as part of an effort to "integrate the use of IFLANET into regular IFLA activities, and to promote its use in all areas of IFLA."[669] At least 400 new documents were also added to IFLANET in 1999, not including the many edits and updates to the now-vast store of existing documents.[670] A new IFLANET mirror site was announced in August 1999, hosted by the National Library Board of Singapore.[671]

IFLANET was a massive undertaking at a time when the Internet's basic standards and protocols were still nascent; Kuny and his colleagues had to be dedicated and driven, "focusing on developing an international website and breaking new ground with everything we did. There were very few websites at the time and no best practices. It was all HTML 1.0 and then 2.0 stuff by that time (I remember being excited by the introduction of the <table> tag in HTML 3: it was a big deal... you try mark up without ANY layout capability and long before CSS!)."[672] As such, IFLANET represents a concrete and lasting way in which Canadians have contributed to the ongoing growth of IFLA, helping to move the Federation into the digital age with grace and relative ease. The relationship was reciprocally beneficial as well; Kuny states that, ironically, "IFLA's electronic services were actually in operation on NLC's server for quite a period before the NLC got its own web services operational! In many respects, UDT activities not only spurred NLC's own digital library development work, but also that of the Government of Canada in areas such as the adoption of Dublin Core Metadata by the government and in pushing interoperability standards."[673] IFLANET hosting would remain in Canada until the end of 2001.[674]

Meanwhile in IFLA: 1993 to 1999

Throughout the 1990s, as IFLANET was being developed at the National Library of Canada, many other Canadians continued to increase their engagement with the Federation. In 1993, Donna Duncan (McGill University Library) was elected Chair and Treasurer of the Section on Classification and Indexing.[675] During her tenure as Chair, the Section received approval for and published the *Guidelines for Subject Authority and Reference Entities (GSARE)*, "the Section's first international standard."[676] Duncan's position as Chair/Financial Officer was renewed at the next elections in 1995,[677] and she also became Secretary of the Division of Bibliographic Control.[678] In the same year, Paulette Bernhard (EBSI, Université de Montréal) was re-appointed Chair of the Section of School Libraries for a second term,[679] and Frank Kirkwood was appointed Chair of the Section on Government Information and Official Publications.[680] These appointments were in addition to the Chair positions held by Parent, Swain, and Manning at the time.

Kirkwood, by then working at the Library of Parliament, had attended several conferences since first coming into contact with IFLA through Zielinska—but it was Erik Spicer who pushed him to become more meaningfully involved. Kirkwood had been at the pivotal Moscow conference in 1991 with Spicer, and had been inspired by the possibility he saw within IFLA for it to take a more activist stance. He noted that the 1994 conference was taking place in Havana, and "I thought really if I want to do something internationally, which I did as a result of my experiences in Moscow, this is the time to do it. Because Havana is in a country that's under boycott by the Americans, here may be a chance for me to get in and do some useful work instead of being lost in the crowd of librarians from rich countries."[681] Without any prior engagement with the Federation, however, Kirkwood arrived "without any clear plan except to attend meetings and see what I could find that was interesting to do if I was going to be involved internationally."[682] At Spicer's urging, Kirkwood "looked at a couple of meetings and committees" until he found himself in a session "which sort of corresponded with what I did at work: Government Information and Official Publications."[683]

Thanks to the US government's embargo on Cuba, few American IFLA members had made it to the conference; the section's meeting had only two attendees and one of them was the Chair. "And I happened in, and I'm sort of the third person in the room and that kind of made a quorum. So I wasn't a member of the committee but I said 'Well, I'll do this or I'll do that for you.' . . . I did some work when I went home to help them out because it was a very difficult situation when you didn't have your committee there to plan the year's work."[684] Kirkwood corresponded with the members throughout the year, assisting in their work, and then attended the section's meeting at the 1995 IFLA conference in Istanbul the following year.

> And I walked into the meeting 15 minutes late and Al said, "And here's your new Chair!" Turns out his term limit was up, and the Secretary's term limit was up. And I was their golden boy and I didn't even know it! [laughs] The anointed candidate. So I jumped from being a nobody in terms of IFLA organization to Chair of the Section of Government Information and Official Publications.[685]

Spicer, still in attendance at IFLA despite having retired from the Library of Parliament after 34 years of service, apparently said to Kirkwood "with the wry humour that he has, 'I look forward to observing with interest your meteoric rise.' To which I replied, 'And doubtless, my equally meteoric fall.'"[686] Kirkwood would continue as Chair of the section until 1999, and stayed on the Standing Committee until 2003,[687] when he would join the Committee on Freedom of Access to Information and Freedom of Expression (FAIFE).[688]

Réjean Savard (Professor, l'École en bibliothéconomie et sciences de l'information, Université de Montréal) would also begin his real involvement with IFLA at the 1995 conference. Long associated with ASTED, Savard had attended the occasional conference in the 1970s and 1980s, but had found the Federation's size and complexity overwhelming at the time. "I was not feeling very comfortable in that big conference so I said, 'No, IFLA, it's not for me.' But I've been always interested in the international. . . . The first real time that I was involved in IFLA was in '95."[689] Savard was invited to attend the Istanbul conference by several colleagues interested in taking their work on library marketing to an international forum, and "at that time I was really involved in teaching marketing, developing marketing courses here, and also in other countries, French-speaking countries; I was giving courses so they invited me to go there."[690]

In fact, Tees had previously drawn attention to Savard's work on library marketing and management by giving it a strong endorsement in a publication on the topic in the *IFLA Journal* in 1993: "Réjean Savard has prepared *Guidelines for the Teaching of Management in the Training of Librarians, Documentalists and Archivists.* It is invaluable for teachers of management, and should be widely consulted and used."[691] So it was that Savard's experience and the encouragement of his colleagues saw him involved in an effort to transform the Round Table on Management into a Section on Management and Marketing. Being involved in a section changed Savard's perception of IFLA "because going through a section was much more interesting because it was a small group within [the] larger IFLA. So since that time, I've been to IFLA every year."[692] Savard continued to work with the Round Table on Management, and on 10 December 1996, the Professional Board approved the creation of the new section, noting that the "Round Table's activities now rival or exceed those of many Sections" and "in this increasingly competitive environment the marketing of library services . . . is becoming ever more vital."[693] Savard joined the newly formed section as a Standing Committee member in 1997; by 1999, he would be Chair.[694] Says Savard, "I was, in fact, one of the founders of this new Section of Management and Marketing. So it was really fun to work with them. I was there for many, many years. I was the Chair for two terms, I think. I'm still on the Standing Committee."[695]

The *School Library Manifesto*

Another major accomplishment of the 1990s was the creation of the *UNSECO/IFLA School Library Manifesto*, which was ratified by UNESCO in 1999.[696] The *Manifesto* was largely a result of the work of Anne Galler (who in 1993 was Chair of the Section for Libraries Serving Disadvantaged Persons),[697] Gwynneth Evans, who became the Director General of National and International Programmes at the National Library of Canada in 1993,[698] and Paulette Bernhard, who was a Standing Committee member of the Section of School Libraries and Resource Centres from 1991 to 1995.[699]

> In 1993, the International Federation of Library Associations and Institutions (IFLA) organized a pre-conference seminar on school librarianship, sponsored by UNESCO. . . . Anne Galler of Concordia University, Montreal; Paulette Bernhard of the Université de Montréal; and Gwynneth Evans, the National Library of Canada's

Director General of National and International Programs, were part of the group. Ms Galler and Ms Bernhard were active in the IFLA Section on School Libraries and Resource Centres. The three Canadians committed themselves to some tangible results from the pre-conference seminar by identifying the needs of the school library community and by working with the Conference of Directors of National Libraries; Canadian school library associations; IASL [International Association of School Librarians]; IFLA and UNESCO.[700]

Following the pre-conference seminar, a "survey of national policies on school libraries was undertaken by Anne Galler and the National Library of Canada as a practical application of the 1993 IFLA Policy for School Libraries."[701] Galler notes that the survey "was encouraged and supported by both Dr Marianne Scott and Ms Gwynneth Evans . . ."[702] and that "without [their] encouragement and help this research and eventual article would not have been possible."[703] Response to the survey was strong, and "there was general agreement about the importance of school libraries in national development statements;" consequently, "[a]s a result of the survey, the National Library of Canada began working with representatives from the Canadian school library community, IFLA and IASL to test the feasibility of drafting a school library manifesto for UNESCO consideration."[704]

Drafts of the *Manifesto* were produced, circulated, and revised based on the survey's feedback between 1996 and 1998. As this process wrapped up, Evans organized a workshop hosted by the IFLA Section of School Libraries and Resource Centres to review the latest iterations. The *School Library Manifesto* Workshop was held on 17 August 1998 in Amsterdam, and attended by approximately 60 people. After a short introduction, Evans and Bernhard (now as former Chair of the section) traced the *Manifesto*'s chronology[705] and solicited comments from numerous attendees, including Canadian Dianne Oberg, IFLA member and Canadian representative of IASL.[706] At the workshop, Bernhard, Evans, and others including Ross Shimmon (Secretary General of IFLA) gave presentations; when the second part of the workshop broke into groups, two of the English-speaking groups were led by Oberg and Tomy Kjekstad of Norway.[707] By the end of the workshop, having "achieved consensus on the main points, a small drafting committee prepared a version for the consideration of the Professional Board," which, once approved, was forwarded for consideration to UNESCO.[708] The *Manifesto*'s text was approved by the Intergovernmental Council of the UNESCO General Information Programme in December 1998 and was submitted to the UNESCO General Conference in 1999.[709] On 26 November 1999, IFLA announced that the *School Library Manifesto* had been ratified by the 30th UNESCO General Conference.[710] Tragically, on the same day that the announcement was made by IFLA, Galler passed away in Montreal. In its obituary, the National Library of Canada remarked that Galler "will be missed by all those who have worked with her—missed for her tireless work on behalf of all types of libraries and for her passion and care of children and those less advantaged."[711] The *UNESCO/IFLA School Library Manifesto*, still in circulation today and available through UNESCO, represents an enduring contribution to the international community. It highlights in clear terms the importance of the school library as "essential to every long-term strategy for literacy, education, information provision and economic, social and cultural development."[712]

Scott and the IFLA Presidency

In 1997, Scott was coming to the end of her term as a member of the Standing Committee of the Section on National Libraries. When the CLA proposed to nominate her for President at the upcoming conference in Copenhagen, Scott agreed; the IDRC, the Croatian Library Association, and the Russian Library Association all swiftly agreed to back her nomination.[713] "My opponent," Scott soon learned, "was Christine Deschamps from France."[714] Ralph W. Manning, who "worked quite hard with Marianne to get her elected," claims she "had a lot of support for her in a lot of countries."[715] The year was spent writing letters seeking support until the time of the 63rd IFLA Council and General Conference in Copenhagen. The conference that year was large, even by IFLA standards: "attended by 2976 delegates from 141 countries, this Conference was also particularly exciting for all those involved as 1997 was an election year: IFLA was all set to elect its new President, a President to take the organization into the next millennium."[716] The two candidates "were regularly seen canvassing in the registration area during the first few days of the conference, while Robert Wedgeworth, President of IFLA from 1991 to 1997 prepared to step down from office."[717] On 31 August, at the first Council session, the two candidates were "introduced to Council and invited to deliver a three-minute speech."[718] Shortly after, the results were announced: Scott received 567 votes, Deschamps 810.[719]

Reflecting on the election, Scott is light-hearted, claiming she was "saved from six very strenuous years," but she admits that it was "not my happiest moment when the election results were announced! . . . I found out that elections in IFLA were really very political—one large block of votes left me at the very end, presumably thinking of the future?"[720] Manning is less restrained, calling it "a travesty."[721]

> It's interesting that Guy Sylvestre also ran for the IFLA presidency and lost. And the announcement was made in the same city. And the idiot, sorry, the unfortunate person who got up and said "Well, Marianne Scott is a loser. Isn't it interesting that she lost in the same city the last Canadian lost in?" He actually said that to the whole Congress. It was not very tactful.[722]

Despite this, Scott was still highly regarded in the Federation, and when the Council passed a resolution to establish a Committee on Copyright and other Legal Matters (CLM), they proposed that she should become its Chair.[723] Though Scott would jokingly refer to it as her "consolation prize," she was pleased to be "back to one of my other loves—legal issues,"[724] and would Chair the Committee until 2003.[725]

Throughout this time, Scott had continued encouraging other Canadians to join the Federation and to become involved in its work. Barbara Clubb, then the Chief Librarian at the Ottawa Public Library, was one of those who credit Scott with the beginning of her involvement in IFLA:

> She made it part of her mission to get as many Canadians involved in IFLA as possible. I and many others were—I don't want to say dragged—but we were. When she called, it sounded interesting but we . . . initially had no idea what we were getting

into until we got into it. And by the time we got into it, first of all, it looked a little strange, and we went, "What is this beast?" But as you looked around and you got to know both the programs and the politics of IFLA it became, for many of us, a very useful part of our professional and, to some extent, personal life because in IFLA you always make really good friends that you communicate with not only on a professional basis but also on a personal basis, which I do with a couple of them still.[726]

Clubb attended her first IFLA conference that year in Copenhagen and joined the Standing Committee of the Section of Public Libraries.[727] She had also assisted with Scott's campaign for President prior to the conference: "I certainly contacted all the colleagues that I knew and urged them to vote for the Canadians."[728] By 1999, Clubb was Chair and Treasurer of the section,[729] and would remain involved with IFLA for the better part of the next decade.

Paul Whitney was also introduced to IFLA through Scott in 1998. "Marianne was recruiting people to sit on CLM and I had known her from a number of things we had done together nationally in Canada. I had been the chair of the CLA copyright committee . . . and had done a lot of copyright work. I had just finished a term as President of the Canadian Library Association."[730] Although he was unable to attend the 1998 conference, Whitney accepted the appointment to CLM; the next year he would plan his vacation around the conference, and recalls that he has "been to every one since then, with one exception."[731]

Marianne Scott retired in 1999, although she would remain involved with IFLA (through CLM) into the next decade. Her tenure as Canada's National Librarian, and her subsequent involvement with IFLA, would bookend the many accomplishments of Canadians in IFLA throughout the 1980s and 1990s, and her vocal support of IFLA in all of her activities brought a new generation of committed Canadian librarians into the Federation. Whitney recalls:

I spoke at Marianne Scott's retirement party and I think one of the things I acknowledged at that event was [that] one of her key contributions was drawing so many Canadians into IFLA and encouraging people like me who were sort of sitting on the sidelines and getting us involved. You look at the librarians who were directly involved over the last 20 years and it's been a sea change. And I think she was the catalyst.[732]

Ingrid Parent adds, "Marianne Scott was one of the major drivers, talking to directors of libraries, all types of libraries, university libraries, public libraries, across the country."[733] In recognition of her achievements, Scott would be appointed an Honorary Fellow at the 2003 conference, "in recognition of distinguished service to IFLA."[734]

By the end of the decade, Canadians held at least 26 different positions on the Standing or Executive Committees of IFLA's various divisions, sections, and round tables,[735] and 32 different Canadian institutions were registered as institutional members.[736] Ralph W. Manning was Chair of the Professional Board and Ingrid Parent had been elected to the Executive Board,[737] while Barbara Clubb (Chief Librarian, Ottawa Public Library) was Chair and Treasurer of the Section of Public Libraries;[738] Ken Haycock (Director, School of Library, Archival and Information Studies, University of British Columbia) was Chair of the Section on Education and Training;[739] Rosemary Kavanagh (CNIB) was Chair of the Section of Libraries for the Blind;[740] and Richard Paré (Parliamentary Librarian) was the Chair of the Section on Library and Research Services for Parliament.[741] Meanwhile Richard Landon and Marie Zielinska, each having served more than two terms in their respective section's Standing Committees and having both acted as Chairs throughout their involvement, were considered "Special Advisers" to their sections.[742] Over the course of two decades, Canadians had helped to revise IFLA's Medium-Term Programme structures, founded a new Core Programme at the National Library of Canada that would become the birthplace of IFLANET, given the CDNL a formalized structure and improved its communication with IFLA, helped to create the *UNESCO/IFLA School Library Manifesto,* and assisted in the formation of numerous new sections. The next millennium would see, among many other contributions, another IFLA conference held in Canada and even a Canadian IFLA President.

Profile: Guy Sylvestre

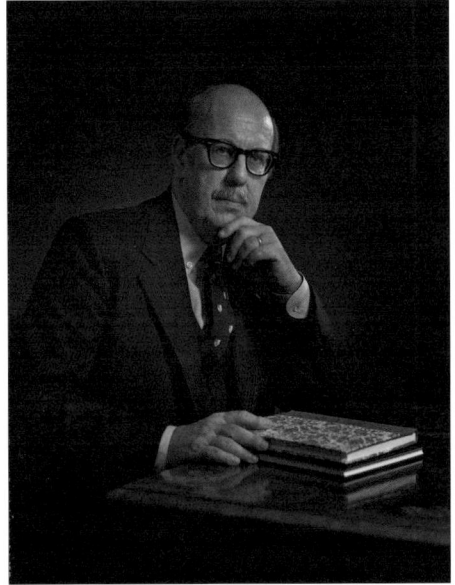

Joseph Jean Guy Sylvestre (b. 17 May 1918, Sorel, Quebec; d. 26 September 2010, Ottawa, Ontario) was an essayist, literary critic, literary historian, and the second National Librarian of Canada (1968–1983).[743] Sylvestre received a classical education at the Collège Sainte-Marie in Montreal and, obtained both a Bachelor of Arts in Philosophy (1941) and a Master's Degree in the Arts (1942) from the University of Ottawa.[744] After completing his postgraduate studies, Sylvestre became a translator for the House of Commons (1943–1947)[745] and then an Editor at the Wartime Information Board[746] (1944–1945).[747] Afterwards, Sylvestre served as the Private Secretary[v] to the Rt. Hon. Louis St-Laurent (1945–1950)[748] during St-Laurent's tenure as Secretary of State for External Affairs[749] and Prime Minister.[750] Sylvestre then worked as an Administration Officer for the Department of Resources and Development (1950–1953). He wrote regularly for *Le Droit* newspaper (1940–1948), *Nouvelle revue canadienne* (1951–1956), and the *University of Toronto Quarterly* (1958–1968),[751] and contributed more than 150 articles to other newspapers, journals, and scholarly publications.[752] In 1943, he founded the *Gants du ciel* journal,[753] also writing under the pseudonyms Jean Bruneau and Blaise Orlier.[754] He was named to the Royal Society of Canada in 1952

Figure 6: Guy Sylvestre, National Librarian of Canada (1968–1983).

Permission courtesy of the Estate of Yousuf Karsh. Yousuf Karsh, Library and Archives Canada, R613-880. © Estate of Yousuf Karsh.

---

[v] This position has also been reported as being called Associate Private Secretary and is also said to have first taken place during St-Laurent's time as Secretary of State. Source: Marianne Scott, e-mail message to the authors, 19 May 2013.

(President, 1973–1974)[755] and to the Académie canadienne-française in 1954.[756] He received various honorary doctorates, the Order of Canada (1982), an Outstanding Public Service Award (1983), and Poland's Order of Merit (1974).[757]

Before becoming the National Librarian, Sylvestre was Assistant Parliamentary Librarian (1953–1956) and Associate Parliamentary Librarian (1956–1968).[758] Throughout his career, Sylvestre "celebrated the literature of French and English Canada and sought throughout his career to build bridges between Canada's literary communities."[759] During his term as National Librarian, he also worked to revise the National Library Act and oversaw the establishment of several special-ized collections and services, including multilingual publications.[760] He belonged to several library associations, including the Canadian Library Association and the Library Association of Ottawa.

Sylvestre was an active Canadian force in IFLA. In 1974, he helped create the Conference of Directors of National Libraries (Chair, 1974–1978). During his time in IFLA, Sylvestre worked towards common standards and the strengthening of library services, including the engagement of national libraries worldwide.[761] He saw a strong link between IFLA and the work he viewed as necessary in Canada.[762] In 1979, Sylvestre ran against Else Granheim from Norway for the presidency of IFLA and lost by what former IFLA President Herman Liebaers recalls as an "historic difference of one vote."[763] However, while the election results were very close, Marianne Scott remembers the difference as being slightly larger than Liebaers.[764] Fellow Canadian IFLA member, Erik Spicer, recalls campaigning for Sylvestre, as he was bilingual, cultured, and "would fit in very easily with the Europeans and the other people who would be around."[765] Sylvestre also served on IFLA's Executive Board.[766] During his time as National Librarian, he visited 26 countries and retained close links to many national libraries around the world.[767] He received the IFLA Medal in 1985.[768] He was also a representative of Canada to UNESCO,[769] for which he prepared the *Guidelines for National Libraries* in 1987.[770]

Spotlight: National Library of Canada

T he idea of a Canadian national library dates back at least to the 19th century, when Sir John A. Macdonald called for the creation of an institution "containing every book worthy of being kept on the shelves of a library" in a speech to the House of Commons on 16 April 1883.[771] These words were motivated by Macdonald's observation that the Parliamentary Library of his day was witnessing a dramatic expansion of its collections far beyond what would be expected of a library of its type; Macdonald, among others, felt that the Parliamentary Library was not only fulfilling its stated role but also serving as a de facto national library, and as a consequence, neither mandate was being served especially well.[772] Despite these concerns, it was another 70 years before the official creation of a separate National Library of Canada; in the meantime, the stopgap measure of appointing both a General Librarian and a Parliamentary Librarian was established in 1885.[773] In the early 20th century, Lawrence J. Burpee of the Ottawa Public Library[774] (and President of the Ontario Library Association)[775] campaigned strongly for the creation of a national library; a cornerstone of this effort was his 1911 speech entitled "A Plea for a National Library," which was subsequently reproduced in print.[776] Despite this and other supporting voices over the years, "it was becoming evident to librarians that before a national library could emerge, there was needed the professional and moral support of a *national* library association."[777] The Canadian Library Association (CLA) became a strong advocate for the creation of a national library "through articles, radio speeches, and interviews and by soliciting support from library enthusiast and soon-to-be [G]overnor [G]eneral Vincent Massey,"[778] which culminated in the creation of a President's Advisory Committee on the National Library and a *Joint Brief* submitted to the government of Canada in 1946 from the CLA, the Royal Society of Canada, the Canadian Historical Association, the Canadian Political Science Association, and the Canadian Social Science Research Council, which further included "resolutions from 16 national and provincial organizations."[779]

On the heels of these efforts, the Canadian Bibliographic Centre was formally created on 1 May 1950.[780] This paved the way for the National Library to be formed shortly afterwards by way of Bill 245, which was introduced in the House of Commons on 20 May 1952, proclaimed on 22 December of the same year, and brought into effect on 1 January 1953 when Dr. William Kaye Lamb became the first official National Librarian of Canada.[781] The National Library began its existence in the old Public Archives building, and despite several short-term moves, "it would be another 14 years before a building would be erected for the National Library's collections and services," on Wellington Street in Ottawa, in 1967.[782] Meanwhile, the National Library expanded on the national bibliography begun by its predecessor, the Canadian Bibliographic Centre, established an interlibrary loan program, began its music library with the acquisition of the Scholes collection in late 1957,[783] and first implemented what is known today as *Theses Canada* in 1965.[784] When Guy Sylvestre took over as the National Librarian in 1968, he established the Rare Books and Music divisions, Children's Literature and Multilingual Services, and was the first to move the National Library towards automation with the creation of electronic catalogues in the 1970s.[785] Marianne Scott, who succeeded Sylvestre as National Librarian in 1984, not only managed to see the library through a nationwide recession without a significant reduction in services, but also increased the National Library's early web presence, developed "a program for the preservation and conservation of titles printed on paper,"[786] and was instrumental in increasing Canada's involvement in IFLA. Sylvestre and Scott were both heavily involved with the Conference of Directors of National Libraries,[787] which is held in partnership with IFLA. Other prominent Canadian IFLA members who at one time worked for the National Library include Ingrid Parent,[788] Mijin Kim,[789] Hope Clement,[790] Cynthia Durance,[791] and Tom Delsey.[792] The National Library of Canada also hosted IFLANET, IFLA's first website, from 1994 until 2001, with National Library staff leading its development and management.[793] In 2004, the National Library merged with the National Archives,[794] becoming Library and Archives Canada.[795]

Profile: Marianne Scott

Marianne Florence Scott (b. 4 December 1928, Toronto, Ontario) is recognized for being not only Canada's first female National Librarian (1984–1999) but also the "first professionally educated librarian to hold the post."[796] After completing a Bachelor of Arts in 1949 and a Bachelor of Library Science in 1952 from McGill University, Scott began her career in librarianship as an Assistant Librarian for the Bank of Montreal (1952–1955).[797] She then returned to McGill University to work as a Law Librarian (1955–1973), a Lecturer in legal bibliography (1964–1974), the Law Area Librarian (1973–1974), and finally as Director of McGill Libraries (1975–1984).[798] Reflecting on her time at McGill, Scott says that she "really loved every minute of it."[799] In recognition of her achievements, Scott received honorary degrees from York University (LL.D., 1985), Dalhousie University (LL.D., 1989), and Laurentian University (D.Litt., 1990).[800] In addition to these honours, she received the Queen's Silver Jubilee Medal (1977), the Queen's Golden Jubilee Medal (2002), and was appointed an Officer in the Order of Canada (1995).[801] Scott is also the author of numerous articles and Co-Founder of the *Index to Canadian Legal Periodical Literature* (which began in 1963).[802]

Figure 7: Marianne Scott, National Librarian of Canada (1984–1999).

Permission courtesy of the Estate of Yousuf Karsh. © Estate of Yousuf Karsh.

Scott has been involved with library associations throughout her career, including the International Association of Law Libraries, the American Association of Law Libraries, the Canadian Association of Law Libraries (President, 1963–1969), the Corporation of Professional

Librarians of Quebec (Vice President, 1975), the Canadian Association of Research Librarians (President, 1978–1979), and the Canadian Library Association (President, 1981–1982).[803] In a 1985 *American Libraries* interview, Scott states that her "involvement with a variety of library organizations was invaluable" and helped in her role as the National Librarian.[804]

It was during her time with McGill Libraries and through her membership with various other library associations that Scott first became involved with IFLA.[805] She was on the Honour Committee at the 1982 Montreal IFLA conference and was involved with IFLA's committees on national libraries and on preservation during her tenure as National Librarian.[806] In 1997, Scott ran unsuccessfully for the office of President of IFLA.[807] Scott chaired IFLA's Committee on Copyright and Other Legal Matters (1998–2003) and was named an Honorary Fellow by IFLA in 2003.[808]

Throughout her membership in IFLA, Scott encouraged her fellow Canadians to join the organization—particularly her colleagues at the National Library (now Library and Archives Canada): "I reviewed the list of Standing Committees and identified the committees where I thought NL [the National Library] should be. In fact for a number of years we had had someone on certain committees. In my opinion the National Library really contributed a lot to IFLA during [Guy] Sylvestre's and my time."[809] In 1996, Scott received the IFLA Medal in recognition of the National Library's work on developing the IFLA UDT Core Programme.[810]

Chapter 5

Canadian Memories of the 1991 Moscow IFLA Conference

Figure 8: Boris Yeltsin, President of the Russian Federation, speaking near the building of the Council of Ministers of the Russian Soviet Federative Socialist Republic, 19 August 1991, Krasnopresnenskaia Naberezhnaia, Moscow.

Photograph from the website of the President of Russia, www.kremlin.ru. Author: ITAR-TASS. Used under the Creative Commons Attribution 3.0 Unported Licence.

D uring the 57th IFLA Conference held in Moscow from 18 to 24 August 1991, Canadian and international IFLA members were unanticipated witnesses to a pivotal moment in history. While the conference was in session, the world's eyes were fixed on Moscow as anti-Revisionist Communist elements attempted to wrest power from Mikhail Gorbachev in a coup d'état that would come to be known as the August Putsch. Spanning three days, from 19 to 21 August, the event cast a long shadow over the IFLA conference and had a lasting impact on the Canadian members who attended—even, some have suggested, serving to increase Canadian IFLA participation in subsequent years. Barbara Clubb, former City Librarian for the Ottawa Public Library, mentioned that one of the reasons she became aware of IFLA was that "colleagues would come back from IFLA [with talk . . .] of tanks rolling into Moscow."[811] Frank Kirkwood, Reference Librarian and Information Consultant for the Canadian Library of Parliament, credited the conference with making him a dedicated IFLA member: "The . . . early formative thing that made me a convinced IFLA activist for life was the conference in '91 in Moscow."[812]

IFLA has always been a nominally apolitical and neutral organization which aims to bring together librarians from across the world without prejudice, but tensions between the United States and the USSR meant that an undercurrent of stress was present in IFLA from the post–Second World War era until the 1990s. As stated by Donald G. Davis in *With Malice toward None: IFLA and the Cold War*, IFLA "suffered from the verbal darts and political skirmishes of an international community undergoing tremendous postwar changes and of the stifling Cold War."[813] To try to create a balance in opinions during these troubled years, the IFLA Executive Board deliberately included Vice Presidents from both North America and Eastern Europe.[814] Several political events and protests stemming from the Cold War would coincide with IFLA conferences, leading up to the 1991 Moscow conference. The 1968 session in Frankfurt took place while Soviet troops invaded Czechoslovakia, with delegates listening to their transistor radios and anxiously awaiting news of the Prague Spring. This gave rise to a debate as to whether the following year's gathering should still take place in Moscow.[815] As former Canadian Parliamentary Librarian Erik Spicer recalls, "The Russians moved into Czechoslovakia when IFLA was meeting in Frankfurt. . . . We decided to show our displeasure by not going to Moscow in the following year."[816] Ultimately, the 1969 meeting was moved to Copenhagen, and the Moscow conference was postponed to 1970.[817] Tensions between US and Soviet members were still high during the 1970 IFLA conference, owing largely to its provocative theme, "Lenin and Libraries."[818] As former National Librarian of Canada Marianne Scott recalls, "there was a time . . . in the '70s and '80s when there was a sort of a balancing act [in IFLA] and maybe it had something to do with the Cold War."[819]

In addition to the Cold War predicaments, the 1970s and 1980s also saw tensions rise over what to do with South African delegates who supported apartheid. Davis notes that the 1974 conference in Washington, DC, saw troubles when "[u]nder the strong influence of UNESCO [the United Nations Educational, Scientific, and Cultural Organization], IFLA dropped members that were viewed as troublesome for the entire international community," including South Africa.[820] The 1985 IFLA Conference in Chicago was also controversial; American Library Association President E. J. Josey openly protested the inclusion of South African delegates at the session.[821] Jeffrey M. Wilhite, author of *IFLA 85 Years*, notes that "[m]ilestones in the 90s for IFLA occurred mainly in the political realm."[822] The 1990 conference in Stockholm saw IFLA picketed by two separate groups of protestors—one group opposing the attendance of "South African librarians who had not renounced apartheid" and another speaking out against the "presence of the Iranian delegation."[823]

The 1991 conference saw delegates from 74 countries, including Canada, "having to make their way past road blocks, soldiers, and tanks to reach the Conference center each morning."[824] Frank Kirkwood recalls the turn of events as being completely unexpected: "Unfortunately or fortunately, depending on your point of view, I thought [before leaving for the conference], 'Nothing ever happens in Moscow in August.'"[825] The leader of the IFLA 1991 Organizing Committee was Nikolaj Gubenko, the Minister of Culture of the USSR, who told the audience at the official opening, "I find myself in an equal position with you on the state of emergency that exists in the Soviet Union."[826] Shortly after, IFLA President Hans-Peter Geh of the Württemberg State Library in Stuttgart, Germany, assured attendees that after "having discussed the present coup situation with a number of organizing members that the Conference would indeed go on."[827]

The conference was held at the Congress Center of the Center for International Trade and Scientific and Technical Cooperation with Foreign Countries.[828] The opening session was in the Rossiya Concert Hall, which was located close to Red Square, where the majority of the action of the failed coup took place. [829] At the Rossiya Concert Hall, during the height of the coup, a performance of the ballet *Romeo and Juliet* took place.[830] When asked how the attempted coup changed the atmosphere of the opening ceremony, Marianne Scott recalls:

> Oh it definitely had a very chilling effect on it. . . . They had a beautiful ballet, part of a cultural opening. . . . The ballerinas were crying; they were dancing with tears streaming down their faces. It was just so emotional. Then some countries called their people home.[831] She continues: The sessions . . . went on. And it was amazing. I mean people went and other people stepped in and did whatever needed to be done. . . . People were very innovative about how they handled it.[832]

Around this time, Erik Spicer took action to secure the safety of the Canadians and told a fellow countryman to: "Get all the names you can of Canadians and their telephone numbers. I will do the same, and then I'll take both lists and call them in to the duty officer when I get home."[833] Scott says the Canadians were "concerned for some of the Eastern country people that were there [at the conference] . . . because we had no idea what the scope of it was."[834]

In the Secretariat notes from the *IFLA Journal*, Paul Nauta wrote the following:

> The IFLA Conference . . . will hold a special place in the hearts of all who attended. Rarely in a lifetime does one have the opportunity to be present at the turning point in a nation's history; even more rarely is one fully aware of the significance of events as they unwind.[835]

Despite being aware of the importance of the moment, Western attendees were left in the dark as to what was happening outside their windows. English-language newspapers were difficult to obtain and television news feeds were unreliable.[836] Scott remembers staying together with other Canadians, awaiting any news:

> A few of us Canadians were together and I said "Let's go up to my room and watch the television." So we got up there and we were all sitting on the beds watching the tanks rumbling down

the street. And one of our members had gone over to the window. He said "My, those tanks are interesting!" We were watching the television, but they were rumbling by our window.[837]

During this time, rumours were starting to grow "that Gorbachev had been assassinated; that all airports had been closed; that communication outside the Soviet Union was impossible."[838] The IFLA Executive Board gave the following message to attendees:

> Delegates are urged to stay in contact with their embassies with regard to their own personal decisions, and to keep their tickets, passports and money with them at all times. The Minister of Culture and Mr. Gennady Yanayev [who had assumed the role of Acting President of the Soviet Union] have guaranteed the safety of all delegates as far as possible.[839]

Scott recalled the Canadian Embassy being "cautious and low-keyed" and that they "did not foresee a problem" for the Canadian IFLA delegates if they kept a low profile.[840]

One Canadian who did not follow the Canadian Embassy's advice was Spicer. Scott recalls the following story with a sense of humour:

> Because Erik is an ex-military man . . . he went out, and, . . . in his good military style, as I recall, sort of crept forward and found a couple of the soldiers that were in front of the White House, the Parliament building, and I think he was offering them a cigarette. And he came back and told us this story, and I said "Erik! What are you doing? You could have got killed!" [laughs][841]

Spicer, who served in the military during the Second World War, remembers the event this way:

> I also went out on the barricade, because I'm fascinated by this sort of thing. I was handing out cigarette packages. . . . I then reached in my pocket for one of those ubiquitous Canadian flags . . . and just as I was going to hand one to one of the people, I thought, "Wait! Some damned TV camera is going to zoom in. People are going to be able to identify me. 'What does he look like?'" And I would go to jail! . . . So I put it back in my pocket,

but I also watched the performance. I got as close as I could and I walked through. One thing that really upset me a bit was they were giving instruction with gasmasks for the people in that area. Then I climbed up on a wall to get a better view, and then I looked around carefully and there was a group of thugs, you know, everybody dressed in black with peculiar bulges in their costumes that I took to be submachine guns . . . and I thought, "If anything happens, they're going to be spraying bullets all over the place, and one place is the top of this wall." So I got off there . . . promptly and nearly hid behind a bush and thought, "That's equally stupid because a bush will hide you from view, but it won't hide you from bullets." These were things an infantryman learns. I got behind a thicker wall where I didn't have quite as good a view, but at least I could look up and see the President come out and smile or something.[842]

Spicer's story highlights how "an absurd sense of unreality permeated the conference," as observed in Nauta's Secretariat report from the *IFLA Journal*.[843]

While Kirkwood was less venturesome than Spicer, he does recall seeing the action firsthand with several international colleagues:

I came out of the opening ceremony heading back across that central axis, past the White House. Two-and-a-half hours before it was deserted. . . . Now there was a big crowd and Boris Yeltsin was standing on a tank. Actually, he had just gotten down from the tank. So people from my group who were just ahead of me said, "Did you see that? I think it was Yeltsin on top of a tank!" So talk about being a witness to history.[844]

Receptions occurred at the Lenin State Library and the Kremlin Palace of Congresses on the day the coup collapsed. Kirkwood recalls that "[t]he people who occupied the Kremlin on the night of the flight of the coup were the world's librarians."[845] He continues:

> And we took over a couple of halls of the Palace of Congress. . . .
> We didn't actually take over anything administrative, but there
> was this one bemused-looking guard, and all these people
> started marching in and he didn't know what to do. So we all
> came in and we had one hell of a party![846]

When it was over, Scott says that the Canadian Embassy threw a "very
small reception" for the "relieved" Canadian IFLA delegates.[847]

The 1991 conference is remembered in an essay by Carol Henry
and Donald G. Davis commemorating the 75th Anniversary of IFLA as
"a milestone in international professional solidarity and . . . a symbol of
fresh possibilities that lay ahead."[848] As stated by Kirkwood,

> This [event] shaped a generation of IFLA activism. . . . I think that
> the experience of being in Moscow in '91 changed the perspec-
> tive of a lot of librarians and made them want to be part of
> this profession . . . [that was] making a difference in the world
> because they could see the role that the librarians had played
> during the coup.[849]

The theme of the Moscow Conference was "Libraries and Culture:
Their Relationship," foreshadowing the lasting impact this cultural and
historical event would have on IFLA members from Canada and around
the world.

Profile: Ingrid Parent

ngrid Parent was born in Graz, Austria, and arrived in Canada as a one-year-old child after a "long ship ride from Europe to Quebec City and then [a] train to Vancouver."[850] She was the first Canadian to become president of IFLA (2011–2013). She received a Bachelor of Arts with Honours in History (1970) and a Bachelor of Library Science (1971), both from the University of British Columbia.[851] The year that she completed her degree in library science, Parent joined the National Library of Canada (1971–1975),[852] going on to become a Team Leader and Systems Specialist for the University of Laval Library's Technical Services Division (1975–1983). Parent returned to

Figure 9: Ingrid Parent, University Librarian, University of British Columbia (2009–Present) and IFLA President (2011–2013).

Permission courtesy of University of British Columbia Library.

the National Library of Canada (now Library and Archives Canada) in 1983 and stayed until 2009. During her tenure at the National Library, she served as Assistant Director (Systems), Cataloguing Branch (1983–1987); Assistant Director, Acquisitions & Bibliographic Services Branch (1987–1990); Acting Director (1990–1993), and Director General (1994–2004), culminating in an appointment as Assistant Deputy Minister for Library and Archives Canada's Documentary Heritage Collection Sector (2004–2009).[853] In 2009, she was appointed University Librarian of the University of British Columbia. Throughout her time with Library and Archives Canada and the University of British Columbia, Parent has shown an enduring interest in the digital milieu and has "led activities to develop national standards and policies for managing digital material."[854]

Parent is "recognized nationally and internationally for her out-standing contributions to libraries and to the library profession."[855] In 2009, she was the recipient of the Canadian Association of Research Libraries (CARL) award for Distinguished Service to Research Librarianship, and in 2011, she received an honorary doctorate from the University of Ottawa. She has been involved in several Canadian information organizations, including the Canadian Research Knowledge Network (CRKN), l'Association pour l'avancement des sciences et techniques de la documentation (ASTED), and the Canadian Library Association.[856] Internationally, Parent has been affiliated with the United Nations Educational, Scientific, and Cultural Organization (UNESCO), the International Publishers Association,[857] the ISSN International Network (Vice-Chair, 1992–1994; Chair, 1994–1996),[858] the World Intellectual Property Organization, and the Association of Research Libraries.[859]

Parent has been actively involved in IFLA since the early 1990s, starting with a seat on the Cataloguing Committee at the 1993 meeting in Barcelona; she would become Chair of the committee in 1995.[860] She sat on the IFLA Professional Board in the late 1990s[861] and subsequently served on IFLA's Board of Governors from 1999 to 2005 (during which time, she served as Treasurer and held a seat on the Executive Committee from 2003 to 2005).[862] Following on from this, she was Chair of the Section on National Libraries from 2005 to 2009.[863] She returned to the Governing Board from 2007 to 2009, and during that period, she also served as Vice-Chair of the IFLA Professional Committee.

Like Marianne Scott before her, Parent has been enthusiastic in her efforts to get more Canadians involved with the Federation. She asserts, "You almost feel like this is a mission in life to have Canadians more involved in IFLA. And you feel that need to be there."[864] With a total of 895 votes,[865] Parent became the President-Elect of IFLA from 2009 to 2011, and served as IFLA President from 2011 to 2013.[866] Parent's presidential theme was "Libraries—A Force for Change."[867] Of her experience with the organization, Parent remarks, "You bring your own values; you bring your own sense of vision, not just for IFLA, but for libraries and for users, and how we function in the world today.

So I'm coloured by my environment here [in Canada]. I'm coloured by diversity. I wasn't born in Canada. I'm multilingual. I promote those values in whatever I do."[868]

Spotlight: CNIB

The CNIB (formerly known as the Canadian National Institute for the Blind)[869] describes itself as a "registered charity, passionately providing community-based support, knowledge and a national voice to ensure Canadians who are blind or partially sighted have the confidence, skills and opportunities to fully participate in life."[870] Officially established through a federal charter on 30 March 1918, the organization's founding document was signed[871] by seven men, five of whom were blind and all of whom were involved in advocacy work before the creation of the CNIB.[872]

Although several schools, associations, and institutions for the blind had been established in Canada prior to CNIB's founding (including the Canadian Free Library for the Blind, founded in 1906 in Toronto, which later changed its name and merged with the CNIB in 1919[873]), existing approaches to both education and advocacy had been described as "patchwork,"[874] and were often at odds with one another. A united voice was needed to ensure continued support for education, rehabilitation, and employment programs for the blind and vision-impaired. Events such as the return of blinded veterans from the First World War and the Halifax Harbour explosion of 1917, as well as the near-closure of the Canadian National Library for the Blind in 1917, helped to bring the need for an organization such as the CNIB into focus.[875]

By the time of its first annual general meeting in 1919, the organization had 734 members and "27 employees serving 1,521 people who are blind;" by 1920, the organization had both a job placement program and a series of purchased "factories, broom shops and concession stands" to employ its members.[876] Françoise Hébert, the CNIB's Director of Library Services, was an active IFLA member; she co-authored IFLA's *Copyright and Library Materials for the Handicapped* with Wanda Noel in 1982, which led to a pre-conference meeting before the 1982 General Council in Montreal where Hébert was selected to represent IFLA at a 1982 UNESCO/WIPO (United Nations Educational, Scientific, and Cultural Organization/World Intellectual Property Organization) Working Group meeting later that year.[877] Hébert also worked with IFLA's Round Table of Libraries for the Blind to draft a statement in support of national and international access to materials for the handicapped.[878] CNIB members were actively involved in the creation of IFLA's *Guidelines for Library Service to Braille Users* (developed in Toronto in 1998),[879] and the *Manifesto for Libraries Serving Persons with a Print Disability;*[880] they were also prominent advocates for and early adopters of the DAISY (Digital Accessible Information System) format for audio books.[881] Rosemary Kavanagh, Chair of IFLA's Libraries for the Blind Section from 1999 to 2003,[882] also co-edited IFLA's *Libraries for the Blind in the Information Age—Guidelines for Development* in 2005.[883]

Today, the organization is "one of the world's largest private agencies committed to vision health issues," and is composed of nine provincial and territorial divisions with more than 10,000 volunteers and 1,100 full-time staff.[884] The CNIB's national office is located in Toronto, and provides community-based support, advocacy, rehabilitation, and resources to visually impaired Canadians. The organization works "hand-in-hand with Canadians who are blind or partially sighted to advocate for a barrier-free society, and [strives] to eliminate avoidable sight loss with world-class research and by promoting the importance of vision health through public education."[885]

Chapter 6

2000 to 2012

Building on the foundation laid by Canadian IFLA members in the 1990s and earlier, the new millennium saw more Canadians taking on important leadership roles in the Federation, and saw Canada play host to its third IFLA conference (Quebec City, 2008). Canadians were also continuing to be leaders in international initiatives for libraries in areas such as multiculturalism, multilingualism, technology, legal matters, and copyright. In 2000, IFLA's political structures underwent significant change through revisions of the *Statutes and Rules of Procedure*—the first such revision since 1976—which brought a "new structure and progressive changes" to IFLA, including a shortened two-year Presidential term and the creation of the President-Elect position.[886] Kelly Moore, current Executive Director of the Canadian Library Association and former IFLA Membership Manager from 2000 to 2007, remembers the changes:

> [IFLA] has changed dramatically since I started there, and all for the better. . . . I think the changes that they made in 2000 to the governance structure really opened up possibilities for countries who previously couldn't participate. . . . And we've seen that in the composition of the Governing Board over recent years, for those directly elected members of the Governing Board particularly, but also for the Presidents.[887]

Decades of increasing Canadian involvement with IFLA culminated in the election of Ingrid Parent, University Librarian of the University of British Columbia, to the IFLA Presidency. In 2009, she became the President-Elect, taking up the office in 2011 as the first Canadian IFLA President.

2000 to 2002: A Growth in Confidence and Rumours of Another Conference

The new millennium saw Canadians maintain and increase their involvement in projects they had started working on in the late 1990s. Scott, now retired as the National Librarian of Canada, continued as Chair of the Copyright and Other Legal Matters Committee (CLM).[888] Paul Whitney, then the Chief Librarian of the Burnaby Public Library and an emerging influential Canadian voice within IFLA, also continued his work as a member of the CLM, and presented at the 66th IFLA conference in Jerusalem. Whitney, who had represented IFLA the year before at the 1999 Seattle World Trade Organization Ministerial meeting, noted in his presentation that it is "imperative that library organizations support the emerging movement advocating the preservation and encouragement of cultural identity and diversity. Canada, France and a number of other countries from the European Union are in the forefront of this movement."[889]

In 2000, the *IFLA Journal* printed a special thanks to Canadian members for their role in the development of the *IFLA/UNESCO School Library Manifesto*: "IFLA is grateful for the support that colleagues throughout the world have given to the development of the School Library Manifesto. Many professionals were involved in this, but special reference should be made to the library community of Canada for the role it played in this process."[890] Canadians designed and printed the text "as an attractive brochure in English, French and Spanish versions."[891] The National Library of Canada was also thanked by IFLA for its role in directing the United Nations Educational, Scientific, and Cultural Organization (UNESCO)–sponsored revision of 1981's *Guidelines for Legal Deposit Legislation* by Jules Larivière, Director of the Law Library at the University of Ottawa, in 2000.[892] Marianne Scott served as Chair of the Conference of Directors of National Libraries (CDNL) Advisory Committee on the Revision of the Guidelines,[893] which also included Paul McCormack and Ingrid Parent.[894] One major downturn in Canadian IFLA support, however, was the National Library's December 2000 decision to stop hosting IFLA's website. In a terse announcement, the National Library informed the public that due to "changing priorities resulting from government policy, it was withdrawing as host of the [IFLA]'s website IFLANET from the end of 2001."[895]

The Boston conference in 2001 was the largest IFLA conference to date, with 108 Canadian delegates attending—the sixth largest delegation at the conference.[896] Canadians were also well represented on the Standing Committees, with 14 delegates being elected for the 2001 to 2005 term: Frances Groen (University Libraries and Other General Research Libraries);[897] Richard Paré (Library and Research Services for Parliaments);[898] Barbara Clubb (Chair/Treasurer, Public Libraries);[899] Rosemary Kavanagh (Chair, Libraries for the Blind);[900] Susan Henderson (Libraries for Children and Young Adults);[901] Carol Smale (Document Delivery and Interlending);[902] Bruno Gnassi (Chair, Government Information and Official Publications);[903] Johanna Wellheiser (Preservation and Conservation);[904] Claude Bonnelly (Information Technology);[905] Pierre Meunier (Statistics);[906] Ken Haycock (Education and Training);[907] Jo Beglo (Art Libraries);[908] Réjean Savard (Chair, Management and Marketing);[909] and Gwyneth Evans (Secretary, Reading).[910] Moreover, Ingrid Parent became a member of the 2001 to 2003 Governing Board, a member of the Executive Committee,[911] Co-Chair of the IFLA/IPA Steering Group,[912] and Chair of the Conference Planning Committee.[913]

The Canadian Caucus meeting at the 2001 Boston conference hinted that the Canadian Library Association (CLA) wanted to place a bid to host the 2008 conference. As Margaret Law, Associate Director of Libraries (Science, Technology, and Health Sciences) at the University of Alberta and CLA President from 2001 to 2002, remarked in *Feliciter*: "One of the issues discussed was whether CLA will make a bid to host the IFLA conference in 2008. This is on the CLA Executive Council agenda."[914] Law also commented on Canada's achievements in international librarianship: "Many other library associations are using the Canadian library community's work on the General Agreement on Trade in Services (GATS) as a foundation for their work and their thinking. We are a significant contributor to international initiatives for libraries."[915] Further hinting at Canada's ability to host a future conference, a satellite meeting for the Boston conference was held in Quebec City, which was sponsored by the Management and Marketing Section and the Education and Training Section. Underscoring Canada's longstanding commitment to multilingualism, this meeting "succeeded in attracting independent funding to enable the participation of about fifteen francophone colleagues from the developing world."[916] Another satellite meeting in Washington, DC, was sponsored by the Section on Libraries for the Blind in collaboration with the Library of Congress and the Canadian National Institute for the Blind (now CNIB). At this meeting, Canada and Sweden were honoured with the first IFLA Best Practices Award.[917]

The 68th IFLA General Conference and Council was held in Glasgow from 18 to 24 August 2002, celebrating 75 years since IFLA's 1927 founding in Edinburgh. At the conference, it was announced that the Institute of Science and Technology (INIST) in Vandoeuvre-les-Nancy, France, had agreed to take over the hosting of IFLANET from the National Library of Canada; IFLA commented that the move was "so smooth that most users would not have realized it had taken place."[918] Special thanks was given to "all colleagues in the National Library of Canada who developed and maintained IFLANET to the stage it has now reached; an essential and integral part of the professional activities, communications and management of the Federation."[919] At the same conference, IFLA's Management and Marketing Section awarded the Calgary Public Library an IFLA Marketing Award for the "Rediscover Your Library" project.[920] Canadian IFLA members were also heavily invested in a fringe meeting at the conference called "The Profit Virus: Globalization, Libraries, and Education," which "aimed to raise awareness about the General Agreement on Trade in Services (GATS) and its implications for libraries."[921] Canadians had received several requests the previous year for their "report on GATS."[922] Paul Whitney once again represented Canadian libraries at the meeting, presenting on "International Trade Treaties and Libraries: A Canadian Perspective."[923]

2003 to 2007: The Road to Quebec City, Two Canadians on the Governing Board, and an Increase in National Pride

In 2003, Canada made a successful bid to hold the 2008 IFLA conference in Quebec City, overcoming Rome as the top choice, after a May 2003 site visit from an IFLA delegation headed by then-President Alex Byrne.[924] The proposal team was led by l'Association pour l'avancement des sciences et des techniques de la documentation (ASTED); both Roch Carrier (then the National Librarian of Canada) and Lise Bissonnette (President and General Director of the Bibliothèque Nationale du Québec) supported the bid.[925] After a formal presentation to the IFLA Governing Board during the 2003 Berlin conference, Quebec City was officially announced as the location of the 2008 conference.[926] Kelly Moore recalls the reaction of Canadian IFLA members to the announcement:

> The whole Canadian contingent was getting up and cheering, and going onto the stage. Well, bless him, Harry Campbell . . . managed somehow in Berlin, in August, to track down hockey sticks, and he and Roch Carrier . . . stick-handled their way across the stage at the Berlin conference centre with a big Canadian flag following them across the room when they were awarded the conference. It was quite a fun, funny moment.[927]

The Federation's decision would usher in many years of hard work from Canadians to make the conference a success.

The 2003 conference also saw Canadian delegates take more significant leadership roles in IFLA itself. Both Ingrid Parent and Réjean Savard, Professor at the School of Library and Information Science at the University of Montreal, ran for the Governing Board to serve for the 2003 to 2005 term. Savard received 316 votes (14th place) and Parent received 606 votes (sixth place),[928] but since just the first 10 candidates in order of the most votes cast could be appointed, only Parent was successful in her campaign. She was also elected to become the 2004 to 2006 IFLA Treasurer and would chair the National Association Members Fees Working Party.[929]

The 2004 IFLA conference in Buenos Aires marked Parent's first year as Treasurer. During this time, she proposed amendments to the *Statutes* to establish a membership category for "Other Associations," and recommended that membership should rise by a minimum of one percent due to the rate of inflation in the Netherlands.[930] Parent also noted that there were concerns regarding the financial health of IFLA owing to unexpected expenses incurred during 2004.[931] Her report was adopted.[932]

After the Buenos Aires conference, preparations for 2008 began in earnest. Autumn saw ASTED strike a formal Conference Organizing Committee. This was comprised of three subcommittees: the Organization Committee, the Honorary Committee, and the Advisory Committee.[333] The Organization Committee (also known as the National Committee),[334] was composed of representatives from the National Library of Canada (later Library and Archives Canada) and la Bibliothèque nationale du Québec (later Bibliothèque et Archives nationales du Québec),[335] and professional associations from Quebec.[336] The Honorary Committee, by contrast, was comprised of the Directors of the National Library and la Bibliothèque nationale du Québec, with "select personalities from political institutions and private business,"[937] including Michel Bissonnet, President of the Assemblée nationale du Québec.[938] Lastly, the Advisory Committee was made up of representatives from major Canadian library associations, such as the CLA, ASTED, and the Canadian Urban Libraries Council.[939]

Excitement for the Quebec City conference grew across Canada in 2005. In the *Feliciter* article "IFLA Comes Back to Canada," ASTED Executive Director Louis Cabral remarked on the honour of hosting two conferences in less than 30 years:

> Few countries have enjoyed such a privilege in such a short period of time. Perhaps the nation's influential role in this prestigious organization explains the honour. Canada has received worldwide recognition for its contributions to several IFLA committees and work groups, including the Governing Board. Individuals such as Marianne Scott and Ingrid Parent have helped Canada earn a reputation for achievement and progress.[940]

Adding to this reputation, more than 60 Canadian delegates attended the 2005 IFLA conference in Oslo.[941] Barbara Clubb, the 2005 to 2006 CLA President, explained in *Feliciter* why Canadians were becoming so actively involved in IFLA:

> Some are involved because IFLA offers the best forum for their area of work (e.g., the Parliamentary Libraries section, the National Libraries section or the Services for the Blind

section). Others (such as myself) were mentored onto the international scene by the former National Librarian, Marianne Scott; others have worked abroad and find that IFLA helps to continue that interest, while some Canadian librarians work abroad and find that IFLA is a way of connecting back home.[942]

Corroborating this idea, Gwynneth Evans (then the Chair of IFLA's Reading Section and a member of the 2005 to 2007 Professional Committee and Governing Board) wrote that "[a]t the moment, more than 40 Canadians are actively involved at all levels: HQ staff; section Standing Committees and divisions; and in the elected positions on the Professional Committee and Governing Board."[943] These members included Réjean Savard, who was successfully elected into the IFLA Governing Board in 2005 with more than twice the votes he received in 2003.[944]

Canadian engagement slowed somewhat in 2006. That year's conference was held in Seoul, increasing travel costs for Canadians wishing to attend, and Parent was no longer on the Governing Board nor serving as Treasurer. She recalls thinking to herself, "'Well, that's it. I've finished with IFLA. I'm just going to say goodbye.' I got a nice certificate and so that was it. In 2005, I said, 'Well, I'll still be involved but just as a regular member,' so I was just a member of the National Library Section of IFLA [in 2006]."[945] In spite of this comparative decrease in engagement, Canadians did win the second-place IFLA Marketing Award for the Public Library of Quebec for its "Follow the Stream" project.[946] Canadians also made contributions to the IFLA HQ Core Activity Fund, with Library and Archives Canada ranking as the seventh largest contributor to the fund.[947] Advertisements for the 2008 Quebec City conference began appearing in the *IFLA Journal* by this time, proudly declaring its theme: "Libraries without Borders: Navigating toward Global Understanding."[948]

At the 2007 IFLA conference in Durban, Réjean Savard was elected to a second term on the Governing Board with 1,131 votes;[949] he also served on IFLA's Executive Committee and as Chair of its PAC Advisory Board.[950] In Savard's words: "I served on the board for two terms, and in the second term, I was on the Executive Committee of IFLA so . . . [I] was really 'in the action.' . . . There was also the IFLA [conference] in Quebec City in 2008, so I was there at about the same time, and I worked on the organization of the IFLA Quebec conference."[951] No longer just a member, Ingrid Parent was re-elected to the Governing Board for the 2007 to 2009 term and served concurrently as Chair/Treasurer of the Section on National Libraries,[952] Chair of the Division of General Research Libraries, and Vice-Chair of the Professional Committee.[953] Other Canadians involved at this time included Victoria Owen (Copyright and Other Legal Matters);[954] Frank Kirkwood (Freedom of Access to Information and Freedom of Expression);[955] Mijin Kim (Chair, Library Services to Multicultural Populations);[956] Jackie Druery (Chair, Government Information and Official Publications);[957] and Johanna Wellheiser (Preservation and Conservation).[958] This was also Kelly Moore's last year working for IFLA, and she announced in the *IFLA Journal*: "It has been a pleasure to work with you all over the past seven years, and a privilege to have been part of the IFLA HQ staff."[959]

A *Final Announcement* (an 80-page, fully bilingual bulletin) giving details of the upcoming conference was launched at the May 2007 CLA conference in St. John's, Newfoundland. In the *Final Announcement*, experienced IFLA member and National Committee Chair Claude Bonnelly of the Bibliothèque de l'Université Laval stated the following in his official invitation to IFLA members around the world:

> August 2008, Quebec City, Canada: This is indeed a 'rendez-vous' that you do not want to miss! All members of the National Committee and of the National Advisory Committee are working hard to make this Conference a memorable event that you will find both entertaining and stimulating.[960]

The National Committee, consisting largely of librarians from Quebec, comprised Claude Bonnelly (Chair), Jocelyne Dion, Jean-Eudes Bériault, Louis Cabral, Francis Farley-Chevrier, Monique Désormeaux, Benoît Ferland, Céline Gendron, Lucie Gobeil, Judith Mercier, Aline Néron, Suzanne Payette, Jean Payeur, Ghislain Roussel, Phillippe Sauvageau, and Réjean Savard.[961] The National Advisory Committee's membership included Pam Bjornson, Michel Bonneau, Don Butcher, Louis Cabral, Bernard Clavel, Barbara Clubb, Madeleine Lefebvre, Laurette Mackey, Ingrid Parent, Diane Poinicky, Liz Kerr, Hélène Roussel, Philippe Sauvageau, Paul Whitney, and William R. Young.[962]

Another project inspired by the run-up to the conference was a joint ASTED–CLA effort that established a charitable organization called "Bibliomondialis: Canadian Partners for Library Bridge-Building," which would be officially launched during the conference itself.[963] The goal of Bibliomondialis was to "promote and encourage the participation of delegates from developing countries in IFLA conferences, to increase participation in national and international library science seminars, and to support and encourage research that focuses on international library science issues."[964] By 2007, $45,000 had been collected for this purpose; ASTED, CLA, the Ontario Library Association, l'ABCDEF internationale, Bibliothèque et Archives nationales du Québec, Réseau Biblio du Québec, la Corporation des bibliothécaires professionnels du Québec, and les Bibliothèques publiques du Québec all participated in fundraising for this initiative.[965]

2008 Satellite Meetings: Multiculturalism, Bilingualism, and Technology

Figure 10: Attendees of the Library and Research Services for Parliaments Section's Satellite Meeting, "Legislative Libraries: Partners in Democracy," at the Library of Parliament, Ottawa, 7 August 2008.

Permission courtesy of Ross Becker.

A total of 15 satellite meetings occurred throughout Canada and the United States prior to the Quebec City conference, providing international IFLA members with a preview of what the Canadian library community had to offer.[966] Eight satellite sessions were held in the province of Quebec alone; these included the Academic and Research Libraries Section's meeting, "Consortia and Cooperative Programmes" (7 August, Laval University, Quebec City); the Statistics and Evaluation Section's meeting, "Library Statistics for the 21st-century World" (18– 19 August, Concordia University, Montreal); IFLA Action for Development through Libraries Programme (ALP)'s meeting, "Francophonies et bibliothèques: innovations, changements et réseautage (Libraries and the French-Speaking Communities of the World: Innovation, Change and Networking)" (5–7 August, Grande Bibliothèque du Québec, Montreal); the Knowledge Management Section's meeting, "Knowledge Management—Best Practices and Lessons Learned in Web 2.0 Environment" (8 August, Montreal); the Science and Technology Libraries Section and Government Information and Official Publications Section's meeting, "National Science Policies and Science Portals" (8 August, École Polytechnique de Montréal, Montreal); the Health and Biosciences Section's meeting, "The Role of Evidence Based Research in Medical Libraries" (9 August, Quebec City); the Cataloguing Section and Joint Steering Committee for the Development of RDA's meeting, "RDA: Resource Description and Access: Foundations, Changes and Implementation" (8 August, Quebec City);[967] and the Public Libraries Section, Libraries for Children and Young Adults Section, and Management and Marketing Section's meeting, "In these days of technology, how can public libraries attract and keep youth patrons?" (5–7 August, McGill University, Montreal).[968] Suzanne Payette (Director, Bibliothèque de Bossard, member of the National Committee, and member of IFLA Standing Committee of Public Libraries) was Chair of the Public Libraries Section meeting, which was also called "Navigating with Youth."[969] Réjean Savard was Chair of the IFLA ALP's meeting.[970] These meetings emphasised Canada's post-IFLANET engagement in the relationship between technology and librarianship.

Four additional satellite sessions were held in Ontario. These included the Library and Research Services for Parliaments Section's meeting, "Legislative Libraries: Partners in Democracy" (5–7 August, The Library of Parliament, Ottawa); the Social Science Libraries Section's meeting, "Disappearing Disciplinary Borders in the Social Science Library—Global Studies or Sea Change?" (6–7 August, University of Toronto); the Genealogy and Local History Section and Reference and Information Services Section's meeting, "Genealogy and Local History for All—Services for Multi/cultural Communities" (6–7 August, Canadian Centre for Genealogy, Library and Archives Canada, Ottawa); and the Preservation and Conservation Section and National Libraries Section's meeting, "Preserving Cultural Heritage: The Canadian View" (6–8 August, Ottawa).[971] Many tours of Library and Archives Canada also took place during these meetings, providing the institution an opportunity to proudly showcase Canada's cultural heritage to the world.

In Western Canada, one satellite session was held in British Columbia by the Section on Library Services to Multicultural Populations. This meeting was called "Multicultural to Intercultural: Libraries Connecting Communities," and ran from 5 to 7 August 2008 in

Vancouver.[972] Paul Whitney (who was also on the National Advisory Committee for the Quebec City conference) was the Co-Chair of the Vancouver satellite meeting alongside Library and Archives Canada's Mijin Kim, who also served as Chair of IFLA's Library Services to Multicultural Populations.[973] According to Whitney, the initial plan of some Canadians was to write a proposal for an IFLA conference to occur in Vancouver, but this was scrapped in favour of a satellite meeting due to political changes in the provincial government, and decreased funding and marketing opportunities.[974] Whitney and Kim shared a belief that Vancouver would be the perfect environment to showcase Canada's multiculturalism, notwithstanding its distance from Quebec City, and Whitney remembers that the "satellite meeting was a lot of fun to do."[975] This would not be the last IFLA meeting to take place in Vancouver.

Quebec City 2008: A Dynamic and Diverse Conference

Figure 11: A presentation during the Opening Session of the 2008 IFLA Conference, Quebec City, 10 August 2008.

Permission courtesy of Yves Tessier, photographe conseil and retired Head of the Map Library of Laval University Library in Quebec City, and colleague of Claude Bonnelly, the 2008 IFLA conference organizer in Quebec City.

Figure 12: Press Conference for the 2008 IFLA Conference in Quebec City on the day before the Opening Ceremony, 11 August 2008, given by Claude Bonnelly (Chair of the National Committee), Claudia Lux (IFLA President, 2007–2009), and Philippe Sauvageau (President of ASTED, 2008), in presence of members of the Honorary Committee and their representatives. Top row, left to right: Ingrid Parent, Pierre Morency, Philippe Sauvageau, Silvie Delorme, and Ernie Ingles. Bottom row, left to right: Lise Bissonnette, Claudia Lux, and Claude Bonnelly.

Permission courtesy of Yves Tessier, photographe conseil and retired Head of the Map Library of Laval University Library in Quebec City, and colleague of Claude Bonnelly, the 2008 IFLA conference organizer in Quebec City.

The Quebec City conference, which happened to coincide with the city's 400th anniversary,[976] ran from 10 to 14 August 2008.[977] Over 3,000 participants representing 118 countries attended, giving rise to a dizzying array of meetings and presentations. These included 224 professional meetings (102 sessions and 122 business meetings), 245 paper presentations, 137 poster sessions, 15 satellite meetings, and a trade show with 120 exhibitors.[978] Approximately 275 volunteers participated in the 2008 IFLA conference; about 40 were from the Salon international du livre de Québec, with the rest being drawn from organizations and institutions across Quebec, the rest of Canada, the United States, and Europe.[979] In her opening address, IFLA President Claudia Lux complimented Canadians for their historically hard work in the Federation:

Canada, a country and a government that puts libraries on its agenda with its strong support of this Congress. Canada, a country with a high professional level of library work. Canada, a country with new library buildings as outstanding models. Canada, a country with remote libraries in isolated rural communities connected by satellite technology to the world's knowledge. Canada, a country whose librarians have played an important role in the International Federation of Library Associations and Institutions for decades and have given us professional help of great value—and still do.[980]

This opening was also graced by the Right Honourable Michaëlle Jean, who served as Governor General of Canada from 2005 to 2010; this was a testament to the importance of the conference to Canada and to Canadians. In her address, she reaffirmed the importance of libraries in preserving and promoting cultural heritage: "Like you, I believe that any space dedicated to sharing humanity's great adventure and knowledge enlightens and enriches our collective heritage. That is why you, as guardians of the world's memories, have always played an essential role in human development."[981] Other notable guests included the 27th Lieutenant Governor of Ontario and a member of the Mnjikaming First Nation, the Honourable James K. Bartleman; artist and philosopher Hervé Fischer;[982] the Chief Executive Officer of Brill Publishing, Herman Pabbruwe;[983] and writer Danny Laferriere, the keynote speaker.[984]

A quintessentially Canadian feature of the Quebec City conference was the simultaneous translation of sessions into English and French throughout the event. Bibliothèque et Archives nationales du Québec (BAnQ), which co-sponsored the conference with ASTED and Library and Archives Canada, bore most of the costs of translation; a Quebec City firm called "Bilingua" was hired to oversee this effort.[985] This service was not without obstacles, however. Devices to listen to live translation were available, but those wishing to use them had to produce visas or driver's licences; this was a problem for some members from developing countries, who did not have access to either and, therefore, could not access any mode of translation services. In other cases, translators were unable to understand the specialized vocabulary of sessions; there were incidences of translators halting translation entirely partway through sessions.[986]

Réjean Savard remembers: "There was some part of the opening ceremony that was not translated because it was a kind of artistic work, so some people were a little bit disappointed with that, but it was impossible to translate everything."[987] Savard also mentions some international guests' surprise at Canada's bilingualism: "Well, [perhaps] people came here and did not know that Quebec City was mainly French. . . . It's still a . . . mainly French-speaking city, so people were surprised by that, but anyway, that's Canada. It's a bilingual country, where we speak French and English."[988] While the prominence of the French language may have been unexpected at an IFLA conference, which had historically been dominated by English, this experience did highlight the leadership role of French-Canadian libraries among francophone libraries around the world. Paul Whitney remarks that "Quebec has always seen its role in the francophonie as being really important, and that carries over most definitely to the library community."[989] Likewise, Ralph Manning (now retired from Library and Archives Canada) thought that "Quebec City was a good opportunity for IFLA to demonstrate that it is not just an anglophone organization."[990]

The difficulty encountered by non–visa-holding delegates in obtaining translation services highlighted another significant problem with the otherwise successful conference. Peter Johan Lor, who retired as IFLA Secretary General during the conference, wrote in the *IFLA Journal* about serious difficulties with the provision of Canadian travel visas to delegates:

> Unfortunately I have to express deep disappointment about the problems many participants, particularly colleagues from developing countries, have experienced in obtaining visas to enter Canada. In spite of all the efforts of IFLA Headquarters, Concorde Services Ltd, and the Canadian National Committee, which worked really hard to assist the affected persons, this has unfortunately prevented some 40 pre-registered participants from joining us here. The visas were refused in violation of assurances that had been given when Quebec City was selected as our congress venue in 2003.[991]

Several speakers, Standing Committee members, and Arabic-speaking participants who had intended to serve as translators were denied visas, possibly as a result of the governmental tightening of visas to Canada after the major terrorist attacks in the United States on 11 September 2001. Lor's commentary went on: "It is ironic that the visa issue has cast a cloud over a congress held under the slogan of 'Libraries without Borders.'"[992] Both the Canadian National Committee and Library and Archives Canada attempted to redress this and "generously stepped in to help by providing interpreters for the opening session."[993]

Despite these problems surrounding language and documentation issues, the Quebec City conference had some remarkable outcomes: the Quebec Chamber of Commerce presented the conference with the prestigious "'Fideide' award, recognizing it as the 'business event of the Year'; the event was also awarded the 'Grand Prix du Tourisme Québécois' from the Quebec Tourism Bureau."[994] Both prizes recognized the 2008 IFLA conference as the "the most important conference being held in Quebec in 2008,"[995] which was impressive considering how many events took place during Quebec City's 400th anniversary celebrations that year. According to the 2008 *IFLA Annual Report,* the conference and Quebec satellite meetings were estimated to generate $8.8 million in economic impact.[996] IFLA was deeply appreciative of these prizes, stating, "The increased visibility offered through these awards to libraries, IFLA and national associations and institutions, among politicians, business people, tourism industry and the general public, is a great achievement."[997]

The event also generated substantial press coverage. ASTED had hired the public relations firm HKPD to handle media relations; the firm suggested that approximately 17 million people were reached through the cumulative media promotions surrounding the conference.[998] IFLA's Communications Sub-Committee alone released eight issues of the "IFLA Express" throughout the conference—a testament to the dedication and hard work of its Chair, Céline Gendron.[999] A local firm, Octopus,[1000] created webcasts of the opening ceremonies; this was the first IFLA conference where blogs and tweets were formally tracked and archived on the Federation's website.[1001] Lastly, through the CLA–ASTED charitable organization, Bibliomondialis, 10 people from developing countries were assisted in attending the conference.[1002]

Figure 13: Participants at the 35th Conference of Directors of National Libraries, 13 August 2008, Quebec City.

Permission courtesy of Yves Tessier, photographe conseil and retired Head of the Map Library of Laval University Library in Quebec City, and colleague of Claude Bonnelly, the 2008 IFLA conference organizer in Quebec City.

Figure 14: Claude Bonnelly, of the Quebec City National Committee, and Claudia Lux, IFLA President (2007–2009), at the Closing Session of the 2008 IFLA conference, Quebec City, 14 August 2008.

Permission courtesy of Yves Tessier, photographe conseil and retired Head of the Map Library of Laval University Library in Quebec City, and colleague of Claude Bonnelly, the 2008 IFLA conference organizer in Quebec City.

2008 to 2012: A Canadian Presidency, Copyright, and Indigenous Knowledge

Also in 2008, Canadians won two IFLA Marketing Awards. The Richmond Public Library won second place for its "Go Anywhere, Learn Anything; Read Every Day©" project; third place went to the Calgary Public Library for its "The Neatest People Have a Library Card" initiative.[1003] The National Library of Canada (i.e., Library and Archives Canada), along with other national libraries, was thanked by IFLA for its "valuable contribution . . . [to] IFLA Core Activities."[1004] All this added to the buzz of anticipation surrounding the upcoming IFLA Presidential election; it was at this time that Ingrid Parent began to seriously consider running for the position. After various Canadian colleagues encouraged her to run, Parent recalls thinking, "Let's do it."[1005]

These efforts bore fruit the following year at the 2009 IFLA conference in Milan. On 28 August of that year, Ingrid Parent was elected to "serve as President-Elect by postal election for the 2009 to 2011 term and to serve as President for the 2011 to 2013 term," with Ellen Tise, Senior Director, Library and Information Services at the University of Stellenbosch, South Africa, becoming IFLA President for 2009 to 2011.[1006] Parent won the President-Elect position with 895 votes; Jesús Lau, Academic Librarian at the University of Veracruz in Mexico, came in second place with 844 votes.[1007] Parent commented on how tight the election was:

> I was fortunate enough to win the election, which was pretty close. It was very, very political. IFLA never had had a Spanish-speaking president, and my opponent was Jesús Lau, from Mexico. He had a lot of support, especially from the European countries who thought, "Maybe it's time for a Spanish-speaking [President]." I had, I think, more support from individual institutions, because I worked a lot with . . . [them] on standards and other things [in relation to] . . . being Treasurer.[1008]

The 2009 to 2011 term also saw Paul Whitney elected to the Governing Board.[1009] The conference recognized the Edmonton Public Library, which won a third-place IFLA International Marketing Award for their "Books and Beyond" campaign.[1010] Library and Archives Canada was once again thanked by IFLA in 2008, along with other institutions and organizations, for its contributions to the Federation's "core and regional activities and development projects."[1011] The year concluded with Parent and Whitney helping IFLA by drafting an ambitious new Strategic Plan for 2010 to 2015; its stated aim was to "not only provide access to information but . . . also enrich access (value-added information) and play . . . an active (strong, dynamic and inclusive) role in (the knowledge/information) society by creating meeting places and arenas for creativity."[1012]

After a devastating 2010 earthquake in Haiti, IFLA collaborated with a number of non-governmental organizations and inter-governmental organizations to help safeguard Haiti's cultural heritage, working to "set up a treatment centre where damaged archive and library materials [could] be cleaned, preserved, catalogued and if necessary digitised."[1013] Outgoing IFLA President Ellen Tise wrote about a trip she and Parent took to Haiti after the disaster:

> In June President-elect Ingrid Parent and I visited Port au Prince and saw firsthand the devastation. At the same time it was heartwarming to meet with Françoise Thybulle, the National Librarian and Elizabeth Pierre-Louis, Director of FOKAL, and to experience their empowering will to enter a new future—a future in which libraries will play an important role.[1014]

The efforts IFLA and its members made to preserve the world's cultural heritage demonstrated the compassion of the international library community.

In addition to humanitarian efforts, 2010 also saw IFLA's Copyright and Legal Matters Committee issue a "statement expressing its concern about the ongoing negotiations for the Anti-Counterfeiting Trade Agreement (ACTA)."[1015] Delegates from Canada joined other IFLA representatives in Mexico City for the seventh round of ACTA negotiations.[1016] As Chair/Treasurer of IFLA's Library Services to Multicultural Populations Section, Mijin Kim once again was involved in a satellite session on multiculturalism, which was called "Libraries in a Multicultural Society—Possibilities for the Future" and was held in Copenhagen.[1017]

Ellen Tise's last IFLA Presidential meeting was held on 14–15 April 2011 in the Koninklijke Bibliotheek in Den Haag; attendees included Paul Whitney, Kelly Moore, and Ingrid Parent.[1018] Strategic tactics under discussion included access to information as a human right, copyright, and open access.[1019] The Presidential meeting also launched two key IFLA documents that come from Whitney and Parent's strengths in legal matters; these were the "IFLA Statement on Open Access" and the "Draft Treaty on Copyright Exceptions and Limitations for Libraries and Archives."[1020] Later in the same year, IFLA President Tise participated alongside Parent and other members of an IFLA delegation (including Copyright and Legal Matters' Chair Victoria Owen) in the "22nd meeting of the World Intellectual Property Organisation (WIPO) Standing Committee on Copyright and Related Rights (SCCR)."[1021] Toward the end of the year, in November, Parent spoke at the World Intellectual Property Organization Standing Committee on Copyright and Related Rights on behalf of IFLA, delivering the following words on the importance of libraries in copyright considerations:

> Libraries enable and encourage creativity and innovation, a major WIPO goal. By collecting, organising, preserving and providing access to information, libraries support society in general and the cultural and scientific sectors in particular. Libraries foster the sharing of ideas and knowledge, while stimulating and enabling creativity and innovation around the world; they are distinctive guardians of the public trust.[1022]

Owen commented on the importance of such matters to Canadian and international libraries: "[T]he biggest challenge for Libraries, Archives and Museums . . . is to ensure that the laws are flexible enough to allow libraries to be able to fulfill their mission . . . to provide access to knowledge and . . . they have a mission to preserve cultural heritage."[1023] She continued, saying that in order to achieve this goal, libraries "need to ensure that the laws are there to allow for that to take place."[1024]

Ingrid Parent began her IFLA Presidency on 18 August 2011 at the IFLA conference in San Juan.[1025] In the introduction to the 2011 *IFLA Annual Report*, Parent wrote about her priorities as President:

> I feel very honoured and humbled in taking on the Presidency. I intend to build on the successes of the past several years through my theme of 'Libraries—A Force for Change' encompassing the principles and practices of inclusion, transformation, innovation and convergence. Libraries can be a true force for positive change in a world where nations are increasingly facing social and economic challenges.[1026]

Paul Whitney was also re-elected to the 2011 to 2013 Governing Board.[1027] Canada had the fourth largest delegation at the conference, with over 60 participants.[1028] In support of Parent's inauguration, Library and Archives Canada, CLA, ASTED, BAnQ, the Canadian Association of Research Libraries, the Canadian Urban Libraries Council, and the Association of Parliamentary Libraries in Canada jointly hosted an exhibition at the conference entitled "Discover Canada/Découvrir le Canada."[1029] Canadian delegates involved with the exhibition included Diane Beattie, F. Benoit-Plamondon, Guy Bertiaume, Lynn Brodie, Barbara Clubb, Benoit Ferland, Hélène Galarneau, Daniel Godon, Susan Haigh, Mijin Kim, Sonia L'Heureux, Kelly Moore, Pat Riva, Brent Roe, Réjean Savard, Marg Stewart, and Leslie Weir.[1030] This year also saw the sixth time a Canadian library had won an IFLA Marketing Award, this time going to the Edmonton Public Library, which came in second place with its project "Rebranding the Edmonton Public Library—from Research to Implementation to Results."[1031]

"Indigenous Knowledges: Local Priorities, Global Contexts," Parent's first President's Meeting—a small, focused conference—was held in Vancouver from 12 to 14 April 2012. She cites this meeting as one of her proudest moments:

> It was incredibly moving to witness the empowerment experienced by all the participants at this international gathering on the topic of Indigenous Knowledge: local priorities, global contexts. It was an amazingly informative and heartfelt two days of discussion with indigenous speakers from Canada, Finland, the United States, New Zealand, and Australia.[1032]

Paul Whitney comments that this topic for a Presidential Meeting was critically important, given that "the subject of both the multicultural and the Indigenous Knowledge is indicative of where a number of us would like to see Canada as being a world leader."[1033] Mijin Kim was also involved in the meeting, providing the welcome and introduction on the final day of the conference.[1034] Whitney and Owen also worked in 2012 on an eLending Working Group intended to "contribute to the preparation of an IFLA strategy regarding libraries and eBooks for the period of 2013–2014."[1035] In the run-up to the 2012 Helsinki conference, Jo-Anne Belair of the Université Laval helped organize the IFLA Classification and Indexing Section's satellite meeting; Frank Kirkwood was involved in several groups, including the IFLA Access to Information Network—Africa (ATINA) Special Interest Group, IFLA Information Literacy Section, and IFLA Africa Section's satellite meeting.[1036] Closer to home, Parent, Owen, and Whitney spoke at the 2012 CLA Conference in Ottawa on "the relationship between IFLA and its association members, advocacy efforts in international fora, and opportunities for CLA members to play a role in international activities."[1037]

These efforts capped off an exciting decade for Canadian participation in international librarianship, paving the way for a vibrant and rich future. Parent sums up the position of Canada within IFLA at this juncture: "Canadians have participated in IFLA since its beginning, and increasingly so now. And I must say that Canadian librarians and other professionals are well respected within IFLA, and the work we do in our libraries and profession often serves as models for other countries."[1038] Efforts such as these by Canadian librarians, from their first engagement with IFLA in 1927 to the present day, have truly helped to shape libraries as a force for change around the world, and Canadian librarians will undoubtedly continue in this tradition into the future, maintaining a strong commitment to international librarianship while expressing their uniquely Canadian values and vision.

Afterword: Looking Forward by Ingrid Parent

As *The Canada IFLA Adventure* illustrates, the International Federation of Library Associations and Institutions survived and thrived over the years despite some tumultuous times. The Second World War, Cold War, and apartheid-era tensions, and a Soviet coup attempt during the 1991 IFLA Conference in Moscow are just a few of the extraordinary events and dynamics that helped define the world during IFLA's development over the decades.

Another trend that stands out is the exponential rate of technological change. In 1927, the year that marks IFLA's beginnings, Charles Lindbergh achieved worldwide fame by completing the first non-stop solo transatlantic flight. Today, air travel is a ubiquitous mode of travel, and planes transport passengers with ease around the globe.

Indeed, technology has connected the world, and the world's libraries, in so many ways. Technology has also impacted IFLA—and as the rise of IFLANET, its debut website, illustrates, Canadians were integral to this process. As noted in *The Canada IFLA Adventure*, "IFLANET represents a concrete and lasting way in which Canadians have contributed to the ongoing growth of IFLA, helping to move the Federation into the digital age with grace and relative ease."

This is one of the many Canadian contributions that are highlighted, and I hope that it serves as an inspiration for all IFLA members —Canadian and otherwise—to continue leading technology-related initiatives that will help us confront the challenges we face as information professionals in a digital world. Doubtless, those challenges are many—as technology advances, so, too, do issues of access, preservation, privacy, copyright, collections management, and more. In the midst of this complex environment, IFLA will need to continue innovating, and Canadians can and should play a key role in fostering this spirit of innovation.

My theme during my presidency is "Libraries—A Force for Change." I truly believe that libraries have the power to change people's lives, and therefore, to help change communities and society. There are countless stories about how libraries have transformed the social, economic, and cultural fabric of societies around the world—and often, the process begins with one person, one book, and one helping hand in a library. As the Nobel Prize–winning writer Doris Lessing said, "With a library you are free, not confined by temporary political climates. It is the most democratic of institutions because no one—but no one at all —can tell you what to read and when and how."

We can magnify such impacts by working closer and working smarter. Indeed, collaboration is key, and libraries have always been good at sharing insights, resources, and expertise. But we are now entering an era of deep and pervasive interdependencies—with each other, and with our communities. The future of libraries and library values—which Canadians have contributed to greatly, in terms of fostering respect, integrity, fairness, and tolerance—will depend on libraries around the world working together at local, regional, national, and international levels.

I first joined IFLA in 1993; it has been an honour to serve this organization in various roles, and fascinating to see how IFLA, libraries, and the world in general have changed over the years. IFLA has grown into a truly global institution; it now boasts 1,500 members in approximately 150 countries. Its challenge and opportunity moving forward will be to maintain its momentum as the global voice of the library and information profession—and in doing so, demonstrate the enduring value of libraries in an age of sound bites, instant messages, and information overload.

I remain confident that IFLA is more than up to the task, and I'm equally confident that Canadians will continue to play vital roles in the organization in the 21st century, enhancing the efforts and honouring the legacies of our colleagues who came before us. The adventure continues!

Ingrid Parent

President of IFLA, 2011–2013,
President-Elect, 2009–2011,
University Librarian, University of British Columbia

Endnotes

[1] Moore, interview.
[2] Owen, interview.
[3] Kirkwood, interview.
[4] Ibid.
[5] Clubb, interview.
[6] Scott, interview.
[7] Clubb, interview.
[8] Parent, interview.
[9] Moore, interview.
[10] Parent, interview.
[11] Clubb, interview.
[12] Scott, interview.
[13] Moore, interview.
[14] IFLA Headquarters Staff, *IFLA Directory 2007–2009*, 34, 36, 93.
[15] Savard, interview.
[16] Shimmon, *IFLA Directory 2000–2001*, 14, 70, 281.
[17] Manning, interview.
[18] Parent, interview.
[19] Wilhite, *85 Years IFLA*, 23.
[20] Ibid.
[21] Byrne, Foreword, 11.
[22] Wilhite, *85 Years IFLA*, 23.
[23] United Nations, "History of the United Nations."
[24] Wieder, "IFLA's First Fifty Years: A Reprise," 107.
[25] Wilhite, *85 Years IFLA*, 26.
[26] L'Association des Bibliothécaires de France. "L'Association des Bibliothécaires de France c'est . . ."
[27] Wieder, "IFLA's First Fifty Years: A Reprise," 107
[28] Ibid.
[29] Ibid.
[30] Ibid.
[31] Wilhite, *85 Years IFLA*, 27.
[32] Ibid.
[33] Ibid.
[34] Ibid.
[35] Ibid.
[36] Ibid.
[37] International Library and Bibliographical Committee, "International Library Co-Operation," n.p.
[38] Wilhite, *85 Years IFLA*, 23.
[39] Ibid.
[40] Ibid.
[41] Henry and Davis, Jr., *IFLA 75th Anniversary*, 2.
[42] Wilhite, *85 Years IFLA*, 36–38.

[43] Ibid., 23.

[44] Wieder, "IFLA's First Fifty Years: A Reprise," 109.

[45] Ibid.

[46] Wilhite, *85 Years IFLA*, 24.

[47] Wieder, "IFLA's First Fifty Years: A Reprise," 110.

[48] Ibid.

[49] Wilhite, *85 Years IFLA*, 32.

[50] Ibid., 39.

[51] Wieder, "IFLA's First Fifty Years: A Reprise," 110.

[52] Ibid.

[53] Wilhite, *85 Years IFLA*, 39.

[54] Ibid., 348.

[55] Ibid., 42.

[56] Wieder, "IFLA's First Fifty Years: A Reprise," 110.

[57] Wilhite, *85 Years IFLA*, 348–349.

[58] Henry and Davis, Jr., *IFLA 75th Anniversary*, 3.

[59] Wilhite, *85 Years IFLA*, 24.

[60] Ranganathan, "IFLA," 183.

[61] Wilhite, *85 Years IFLA*, 24.

[62] Ibid.

[63] Ibid.

[64] Ibid., 54.

[65] Ibid., 349.

[66] Vladimirov, "The Socialist Countries of Europe," 103.

[67] Henry and Davis, Jr., *IFLA 75th Anniversary*, 3.

[68] Wilhite, *85 Years IFLA*, 25.

[69] Henry and Davis, Jr., *IFLA 75th Anniversary*, 3.

[70] Wilhite, *85 Years IFLA*, 60.

[71] Ibid., 59.

[72] Ibid., 60.

[73] Ibid., 25.

[74] Campbell, "IFLA: Library Universality," 119.

[75] Henry and Davis, Jr., *IFLA 75th Anniversary*, 4.

[76] Wilhite, *85 Years IFLA*, 25.

[77] Campbell, "IFLA: Library Universality," 118–119.

[78] Wilhite, *85 Years IFLA*, 25.

[79] Ibid., 349.

[80] Vladimirov, "The Socialist Countries of Europe," 104.

[81] Wilhite, *85 Years IFLA*, 349–350.

[82] Ibid., 25.

[83] Campbell, "IFLA: Library Universality," 119.

[84] Wilhite, *85 Years IFLA*, 25.

[85] Ibid., 242.

[86] Ibid., 25.

[87] Ibid.

[88] Ibid., 288.

[89] Campbell, "IFLA: Library Universality," 120.

[90] Wilhite, *85 Years IFLA*, 350.

[91] Ibid.

[92] Ibid., 297.

[93] Ibid.

[94] Ibid, 26.

[95] Ibid.

[96] Library and Archives Canada, "Elizabeth Morton—Themes."

[97] Ibid.

[98] Ibid.

[99] Tunnell, "Elizabeth Morton," 736.

[100] Ibid.

[101] Library and Archives Canada, "Elizabeth Morton—Themes."

[102] Ibid.

[103] Ibid.

[104] Tunnell, "Elizabeth Morton," 737.

[105] Library and Archives Canada, "Elizabeth Morton—Themes."

[106] Tunnell, "Elizabeth Morton," 737.

[107] Library and Archives Canada, "Elizabeth Morton—Themes."

[108] Ibid.

[109] IFLA Secretariat, "News Section," *IFLA Journal* 4, no. 1 (1978): 73.

[110] Library and Archives Canada, "Elizabeth Morton—Themes."

[111] Ibid.

[112] Howard, "Honorary Degree Citation."

[113] Beacock, Preface, ix.

[114] Ibid.

[115] Canadian Library Association, "History."

[116] Stuart-Stubbs, "1900: As We Were," 131.

[117] Stuart-Stubbs, "1934–46: The Long Last Lap," 112.

[118] Canadian Library Association, "History."

[119] Wikipedia contributors, "Canadian Library Association."

[120] Canadian Library Association, "History."

[121] Stuart-Stubbs, "1927–30: The Muddle Years," 148–149.

[122] Stuart-Stubbs, "1934–46: The Long Last Lap,"113.

[123] Canadian Library Association, "History."

[124] Canadian Library Association Executive Council, *Proposed CLA Future Plan*, 5.

[125] IFLA Secretariat, "News Section," *IFLA Journal* 4, no. 3 (1978): 73.

[126] Spicer to Guy Sylvestre, 20 September 1979.

[127] Lumley, "Scott, Marianne Florence," 1168.

[128] Lumley, "Campbell, Henry Cummings," 205.

[129] Canadian Library Association, "Canadian Library Association Past Presidents."

[130] Ibid.

[131] Canadian Library Association, "Home."

[132] de Costa, "Foundation and Development," 45.

[133] Ibid.

[134] de Vries, "History," 9.

135 Toronto Public Library, "George H. Locke."
136 International Library and Bibliographical Committee, "International Library
 Co-Operation," n.p.
137 IFLA, *Actes* (1931), 17.
138 Ibid., 32.
139 Wilhite, *85 Years IFLA*, 30.
140 de Costa, "Foundation and Development," 46.
141 IFLA, *Actes* (1930), 63.
142 IFLA, *Actes* (1930), 4.
143 IFLA, *Actes* (1932), 114.
144 IFLA, *Actes* (1932), 115.
145 Gifford, "Canadian Participation," 2.
146 Toronto Public Library, "History of Toronto Public Library."
147 IFLA, *Répertoire* (1938), 7.
148 Wilhite, *85 Years IFLA*, 24.
149 Wilhite, *85 Years IFLA*, 41, 129, and Wilhite, "A Chronology of IFLA Sessions
 1927–2009," 29, report that the Canadian Library Association joined IFLA
 in 1946, while Wilhite, "A Chronology of IFLA Sessions 1927–2009," 30,
 reports that the organization joined in 1947. IFLA, *Actes* (1947), 24, reports
 that CLA had become a new member since the IFLA meeting of 1946.
150 Canadian Library Association, "History."
151 Morton to T. P. Sevensma, 21 April 1947.
152 VanBuskirk, *1924 to 2009*, 3.
153 Morton to T. P. Sevensma, 21 April 1947.
154 Moore, "Become a Librarian," 230.
155 Morton to T. P. Sevensma, n.d.
156 Ibid.
157 IFLA, *Repertoire* (1948), 4.
158 Morton to T. P. Sevensma, 27 June 1950.
159 IFLA, *Actes* (1951), 87.
160 Ibid., 88.
161 Morton to T. P. Sevensma, 21 August 1950.
162 Ibid.
163 Ibid.
164 Morton to T. P. Sevensma, 12 December 1950.
165 Campbell, "IFLA: Library Universality," 118.
166 Wilhite, *85 Years IFLA*, 46.
167 Morton to T. P. Sevensma, 29 April 1952.
168 Ibid.
169 Wilhite, "A Chronology of IFLA Sessions 1927–2009," 36.
170 Ibid., 41.
171 Morton to T. P. Sevensma, 7 October 1958.
172 New York Public Library, "John Mackenzie Cory Records."
173 New Westminster Public Library, "Library History."
174 IFLA, "Past IFLA Secretaries General."
175 Hutcheson to Joachim Wieder, 27 May 1959.

176 Canadian Library Association, "Feliciter."

177 Sevensma, "Twenty-Fourth Session."

178 "Twenty-Fifth Session," 15.

179 Wilhite, "A Chronology of IFLA Sessions 1927–2009," 44.

180 Morton to T. P. Sevensma, 7 October 1958.

181 Ibid.

182 Sevensma, "Twenty-Fourth Session," 30.

183 IFLA, "Past IFLA Secretaries General."

184 Wieder to Elizabeth H. Morton, 4 April 1959.

185 IFLA, "Past IFLA Presidents."

186 Hofmann to Elizabeth H. Morton, 6 May 1959.

187 "Twenty-Fifth Session," 15.

188 Wieder, "IFLA's First 50 Years: A Reprise," 109.

189 IFLA,"Past IFLA Conferences and IFLA Presidents."

190 Wilhite, "A Chronology of IFLA Sessions 1927–2009," 48.

191 Lumley, "Erik Spicer," 1241.

192 Ibid.

193 Ibid., 1241–1242.

194 Spicer, interview.

195 Lumley, "Erik Spicer," 1241.

196 Lumley, "Erik Spicer," 1241.

197 Spicer, interview.

198 Ibid.

199 Lumley, "Erik Spicer," 1241.

200 Spicer, interview.

201 Ibid.

202 Peter P. Hallsworth (OLA) to Bernard McNamee (Executive Director, CLA), 25 April 1973.

203 IFLA, "Past Presidents."

204 Browne and Peroni, "Mr. Erik John Spicer."

205 Wijnstroom, *IFLA Directory 1973*, 15; Wijnstroom, *IFLA Directory 1974*, 15; Wijnstroom, *IFLA Directory 1975*, 21.; Wijnstroom, *IFLA Directory 1976*, 20.

206 Wijnstroom, *IFLA Directory 1973*, 11; Wijnstroom, *IFLA Directory 1975*, 17; Wijnstroom, *IFLA Directory 1976*, 19; Wijnstroom, *IFLA Directory 1979–1980*, 19.

207 Wijnstroom, *IFLA Directory 1973*, 11.

208 Wijnstroom, *IFLA Directory 1982–1983*, 44; Nauta, *IFLA Directory 1988–1989*, 53.

209 Voogt, *IFLA Directory 1994–1995*, 39.

210 Wijnstroom, *IFLA Directory 1973*, 14; Wijnstroom, *IFLA Directory 1975*, 18; Wijnstroom, *IFLA Directory 1977*, 16.

211 Browne and Peroni, "Mr. Erik John Spicer."

212 Wijnstroom, *IFLA Directory 1975*, 31; Wijnstroom, *IFLA Directory 1977,* 32.

213 Lumley, "Erik Spicer," 1241.

214 Ibid., 1242.

215 Ibid., 1241–1242.

216 Ibid., 1242.

[217] Ibid.

[218] Government of Canada, Parliament of Canada Act, R.S.C., c. P-1 (1985), R.S., c. L-7, s. 2.

[219] Parliament of Canada, "Officers and Officials of Parliament."

[220] Parliament of Canada, "The Library of Parliament."

[221] Ibid.

[222] Donnelly, *The National Library of Canada*, 9.

[223] Spicer, "Update, Rehabilitate, Conserve," 1.

[224] Donnelly, *The National Library of Canada*, 14.

[225] Ibid., 15, 25.

[226] Parliament of Canada, "The Library of Parliament."

[227] Donnelly, *The National Library of Canada*, 101.

[228] Hillmer, "Library of Parliament."

[229] Donnelly, *The National Library of Canada*, 237.

[230] White, "Librarians in the News," 6.

[231] Shimmon, *IFLA Directory 2000–2001,* 64.

[232] IFLA, "The Association of Parliamentary Libraries in Canada."

[233] Breycha-Vauthier to Pierre Matte (Associate Director of Service des Bibliothèques publiques de Québec), 25 January 1961.

[234] Morrisset, to A.C. Breycha-Vauthier (IFLA Treasurer), 16 August 1961.

[235] Morton to Anthony Thompson, 17 March 1963.

[236] Campbell to Anthony Thompson, 6 May 1963.

[237] de Ronde, "In Memoriam."

[238] Williamson, "Harry Campbell's Association with IFLA," 10.

[239] Campbell to Anthony Thompson, 6 May 1963.

[240] Thompson to H. C. Campbell, 27 October 1964.

[241] Thompson to Jack Dalton (Dean, School of Library Service, Columbia University), 20 February 1964.

[242] Ibid.

[243] Ex Libris Association, "Librarians in the News."

[244] Benoit, "The First Twenty-Five Years," 33.

[245] Spicer, interview.

[246] Ibid.

[247] Arntz et al., "Personal Reflections," 292.

[248] Ibid.

[249] Spicer, interview.

[250] Ibid.

[251] Arntz et al., "Personal Reflections," 293.

[252] Spicer, interview.

[253] Ibid. See also: Arntz et al., "Personal Reflections," 292.

[254] Browne and Peroni, "Mr. Erik John Spicer."

[255] Wijnstroom, *IFLA Directory 1973*, 15; Wijnstroom, *IFLA Directory 1974*, 15; Wijnstroom, *IFLA Directory 1975*, 21; Wijnstroom, *IFLA Directory 1976*, 20.

[256] Wijnstroom, *IFLA Directory 1973*, 11; Wijnstroom, *IFLA Directory 1975*, 17; Wijnstroom, *IFLA Directory 1976*, 19; Wijnstroom, *IFLA Directory 1979–1980*, 19.

[257] Wijnstroom, *IFLA Directory 1973*, 14; Wijnstroom, *IFLA Directory 1975*, 18; Wijnstroom, *IFLA Directory 1977*, 16.

[258] Browne and Peroni, "Mr. Erik John Spicer."

[259] Wijnstroom, *IFLA Directory 1975*, 31; Wijnstroom, *IFLA Directory 1977,* 32.

[260] Lumley, "Erik Spicer," 1241.

[261] Wilhite, *85 Years IFLA*, 228.

[262] Campbell to Louis Cabral (Executive Director, ASTED), 13 January 2006.

[263] Gifford, "Canadian Participation," 2.

[264] IFLA, "News Section," *IFLA Journal* 4, no. 1 (1978): 73.

[265] Koops and Harvard-Williams, *IFLA Annual 1974,* 294.

[266] Wilhite, *85 Years IFLA*, 194.

[267] Ibid.

[268] Plötz, "The History of IFLA as a Research Theme," 351.

[269] Wilhite, *85 Years IFLA,* 194–196.

[270] Ibid, 195.

[271] Harrod, "The IFLA Conference, 1967," *Library Review* 21, no. 3 (1967): 124.

[272] Harrod, "The IFLA Conference, 1967," *Library Review* 21, no. 4 (1967): 176.

[273] Ibid., 177.

[274] Canadian Library Association, "Report to IFLA—1967/68," 251.

[275] Wilhite, *85 Years IFLA,* 195.

[276] Ibid., 198; and Wieder, "An Outline of IFLA's History," 44–45.

[277] Wieder, "An Outline of IFLA's History," 45.

[278] IFLA, "Metropolitan Libraries Section." Note that some sources claim that INTAMEL did not become a Round Table until 1976; see, for example: Wedgeworth, *World Encyclopedia of Library and Information Services*, 371.

[279] Campbell, "International Association of Metropolitan City Libraries (INTAMEL)," 2.

[280] Wijnstroom, *IFLA Directory 1972*, 8.

[281] IFLA, "Metropolitan Libraries Section."

[282] Wilhite, *85 Years IFLA,* 196.

[283] Spicer, interview.

[284] Wilhite, *85 Years IFLA,* 196.

[285] Donnelly, *The National Library of Canada,* 204.

[286] Brown, Thomas C. "Expo 67;" and Wikipedia contributors, "Expo 67."

[287] Wilhite, *85 Years IFLA,* 196.

[288] Randall and Thompson, *Proceedings of the General Council, 34th Session,* 284–285.

[289] Library and Archives Canada, "Sylvestre, Guy."

[290] Randall and Thompson, *Proceedings of the General Council, 34th Session*, 8–20.

[291] Wilhite, *85 Years IFLA*, 197.

[292] Ibid., 201.

[293] Chartrand to Preben Kierkegaard (IFLA President), 21 December 1978.

[294] Harrod, "The IFLA Conference, 1967," *Library Review*, 21, no. 3 (1967): 121.

[295] Wilhite, *85 Years IFLA,* 25.

[296] Ibid.

[297] Ibid., 62.

[298] Ibid.

299 Ibid., 227.

300 Gifford, "Canadian Participation," 2.

301 Wijnstroom to B. McNamee, 12 March 1975.

302 Gifford to Canadian members of IFLA, 9 May 1979.

303 Canadian Library Association, "Canadian Delegation to IFLA Moscow 1970."

304 Canadian Library Association, "CLA Delegates to IFLA—Liverpool," 26 August 1971.

305 Canadian Library Association, "CLA Delegates to IFLA," 2 August 1972.

306 Wilhite, *85 Years IFLA*, 197, 201, 205, 209, 212.

307 Adorian, "IFLA Congress, Budapest 1972," 4.

308 Canadian Library Association, "Delegates/Observers to IFLA Conference '73;" and Canadian Library Association, "IFLA Conference '73—Conferees Attending."

309 Canadian Library Association, "IFLA Conference '73—Sections and Committees."

310 "Summary of Board and Council Action," 7.

311 Koops, Harvard-Williams, and Coops, *IFLA Annual 1974,* 277–304.

312 Ibid., 306–309.

313 Gifford, "Canadian Participation," 2–3.

314 Wilhite, *85 Years IFLA,* 218.

315 Gifford, "Canadian Participation," 6.

316 Rugaas, "Past, Present and Future Relations," 142.

317 Conference of Directors of National Libraries, "Home."

318 Koops, Harvard-Williams, and Coops, *IFLA Annual 1974,* 299.

319 Canadian Library Association, Archives, CLA Headquarters. See also: Hewitt, "International Federation," 363.

320 Canadian Library Association, Archives, CLA Headquarters. See also: Hewitt, "International Federation," 363.

321 Wijnstroom, *IFLA Directory 1972,* 8.

322 "In Memoriam: Henry C. ("Harry") Campbell," 188.

323 Peter P. Hallsworth (OLA) to Bernard McNamee (Executive Director, CLA), 25 April 1973.

324 "In Memoriam: Henry C. ("Harry") Campbell," 188.

325 "In Memoriam: Henry C. ("Harry") Campbell," 188; and Campbell, "CLA Conference Highlights," 5.

326 Wijinstroom, to the voting members of IFLA and the members of IFLA Consultative Committee, 8 July 1974.

327 Sauvé to Margreet Wijnstroom, 9 July 1974. See also: Wijnstroom, to the voting members of IFLA and the members of IFLA Consultative Committee, 8 July 1974.

328 Koops, Harvard-Williams, and Coops, *IFLA Annual 1974,* 21.

329 "In Memoriam: Henry C. ("Harry") Campbell," 188.

330 Peel to Hilda Gifford, 19 September 1978.

331 Wilhite, *85 Years IFLA,* 232.

332 Kitchen (Executive Director, CLA) to Dean Halliwell (CLA Representative to IFLA), 4 July 1979.

333 Kitchen (Executive Director, CLA) to the Association of Canadian Map Libraries and the Association of Parliamentary Librarians in Canada, 10 April 1979.

[334] Wilhite, *85 Years IFLA*, 236.

[335] Spicer to Guy Sylvestre, 20 September 1979.

[336] Lunn, "Canadiana 1867–1900," 59.

[337] Byrum, "The Birth and Re-Birth of the ISBDs," 34.

[338] Ibid.

[339] Lunn, "Canadiana 1867–1900," 59.

[340] Ibid.

[341] Evans, "Homage," 14.

[342] Gifford, "Canadian Participation," 4.

[343] Evans, "Homage," 14; and Ex Libris Association, "Alice Jean Elizabeth Lunn."

[344] Balatti, "The Canadian National Bibliography," 1.

[345] Lunn, quoted in Evans, "Homage," 14.

[346] Spicer, "The International Federation of Library Associations," 17.

[347] Lunn, quoted in Larivière, *Guidelines*, 1.

[348] Anderson to Jack Cain (Head, Catalogue Department, University of Toronto Library), 17 July 1973.

[349] "News Notes," *Feliciter* 21, no. 7–8 (1975): 32.

[350] Ibid.

[351] Stibbe, "Cataloguing Cartographic Materials in Archives," 443.

[352] Gifford, "Canadian Participation," 4.

[353] Stibbe, "Cataloguing Cartographic Materials in Archives," 446.

[354] Ibid., 447.

[355] Ibid., 443.

[356] Wijnstroooom, *IFLA Directory 1975*, 23.

[357] Ibid., 30.

[358] Gifford, "Canadian Participation," 5.

[359] Wijnstroooom, *IFLA Directory 1975*, 17.

[360] Ibid., 8–9, 17–18, 21–22, 28, 31

[361] IFLA Secretariat, "From the Secretariat," *IFLA Journal* 3, no. 2 (1977): 144.

[362] Ibid., 149–150.

[363] Ibid., 152.

[364] Ibid., 153.

[365] Ibid., 152.

[366] Ibid., 157.

[367] Ibid., 155.

[368] Canadian Library Association, "IFLA, International Federation of Library Associations & Institutions, Canadian Committee Members," 11 April 1978.

[369] Williamson, "Harry Campbell's Association with IFLA," 10.

[370] See, for example: Bossuat, "Report by the Treasurer," 192.

[371] Gifford, "IFLA General Council Meeting," 23.

[372] Wilhite, *85 Years IFLA*, 209.

[373] "News Notes and Miscellany," *Feliciter* 19, no. 5 (1973): 10. See also: Wilhite, *85 Years IFLA*, 216.

[374] Gifford, "IFLA, The International Federation of Library Associations," 3.

[375] Parker, "The Developing Countries and IFLA," 145.

[376] Ibid., 146–147.

[377] Williamson, "Harry Campbell's Association with IFLA," 11.

[378] Ex Libris Association, "Harry Campbell."

[379] Wieder, "An Outline of IFLA's History," 55, endnote 76.

[380] Arntz et al., "Personal Reflections," 292.

[381] Ibid., 293.

[382] "In Memoriam: Henry C. ("Harry") Campbell," 188.

[383] Lumley, "Campbell, Henry Cummings," 205.

[384] Canadian Organization for Development through Education, "CODE Remembers."

[385] Williamson, "Harry Campbell's Association with IFLA," 10.

[386] Lumley, "Campbell, Henry Cummings," 205.

[387] Ibid.

[388] Bruce, "Harry C. Campbell."

[389] "In Memoriam: Henry C. ("Harry") Campbell," 188. Note: According to Lumley, "Campbell, Henry Cummings," 216, his start date is 1992.

[390] Lumley, "Campbell, Henry Cummings," 205.

[391] "In Memoriam: Henry C. ("Harry") Campbell," 188.

[392] Williamson, "Harry Campbell's Association with IFLA," 10.

[393] "In Memoriam: Henry C. ("Harry") Campbell," 188.

[394] Peter P. Hallsworth (Ontario Library Association) to Bernard McNamee (Executive Director, Canadian Library Association), 25 April 1973; and Sauvé to Margreet Wijnstroom, 9 July 1974.

[395] Bruce, "Harry C. Campbell."

[396] Williamson, "Harry Campbell's Association with IFLA," 10.

[397] "In Memoriam: Henry C. ("Harry") Campbell," 188.

[398] Williamson, "Harry Campbell's Association with IFLA," 10.

[399] Chartrand, *From ACBLF to Asted*, 12–13.

[400] Gobeil, *Bibliothèque d'aujourd'hui*, 82.

[401] Léveillé, "Les bibliothécaires canadiens français," 720.

[402] Hilda Gifford to Paul Kitchen (Executive Director, CLA), 8 May 1979.

[403] Marianne Scott, e-mail message to the authors, 9 May 2013.

[404] Michel L. Bonneau to Preben Kirkegaard (IFLA President), 21 March 1978.

[405] IFLA Secretariat, "News Section," *IFLA Journal* 4, no. 3 (1978): 281.

[406] Georges-A. Chartrand to Preben Kierkegaard (IFLA President), 21 December 1978.

[407] Guy Cloutier to Erik J. Spicer (President, CLA), 6 November 1979.

[408] McGill Association of University Teachers, "Featured Retiree: Miriam Tees."

[409] Erik J. Spicer to Guy Cloutier (President, ASTED), 5 December 1979.

[410] Canadian Library Association, Archives, CLA Headquarters.

[411] Association pour l'avancement des sciences et des techniques de la documentation, "Preliminary Program," 1.

[412] Marianne Scott, e-mail message to the authors, 9 May 2013.

[413] Wilhite, *85 Years IFLA,* 241.

[414] Kum, "Abstracts of Papers to be Presented at the IFLA Conference in Leipzig," 123.

[415] Rooney, Sieglinde, "IFLA Congress Report: Papers Lack Originality," 9.

[416] Ibid.

[417] Marianne Scott, e-mail message to the authors, 9 May 2013.

[418] Scott, interview.

[419] Wilhite, *85 Years IFLA*, 243.

[420] Ibid.

[421] Koops and Coops, *IFLA Annual 1982*, 225—258.

[422] Wilhite, *85 Years IFLA,* 243.

[423] IFLA International Office for UBC, "The International Cataloguing-in-Publication Meeting," 419.

[424] Adler, "IFLA 1982: A First-Time View," 569.

[425] Wilhite, *85 Years IFLA*, 244.

[426] Coops, "The Main Meetings of the 48th IFLA Conference," 398.

[427] Ibid.

[428] Schobert, "IFLA Focuses on Future," 1.

[429] Coops, "The Main Meetings of the 48th IFLA Conference," 399.

[430] Adler, "IFLA 1982: A First-Time View," 567.

[431] Canadian Librarian Association, "IFLA: What They Were Saying in Montreal," 3.

[432] IFLA, "The 48th General Conference," 198.

[433] Canadian Library Association, "IFLA: What They Were Saying in Montreal," 8.

[434] Ibid.

[435] IFLA, "The 48th General Conference," 203.

[436] Canadian Library Association, "IFLA: What They Were Saying in Montreal," 8.

[437] IFLA, "The 48th General Conference," 199.

[438] Ibid., 200.

[439] Ibid.

[440] Ibid., 201.

[441] Ibid., 202.

[442] Ibid., 203.

[443] Ibid., 205.

[444] Wilhite, *85 Years IFLA,* 243.

[445] Adler, "IFLA 1982: A First-Time View," 567.

[446] IFLA, "From the Divisions, Sections and Round Tables," *IFLA Journal* 8, no. 4 (1982): 433, 432.

[447] IFLA Executive Board, "Summary Record of the Meetings," *IFLA Journal* 8, no. 4 (1982): 413.

[448] Coops, "The Main Meetings of the 48th IFLA Conference," 398.

[449] IFLA Secretariat, "Montreal – 1982," 397.

[450] Ibid.

[451] IFLA Executive Board, "Summary Record of the Meetings," *IFLA Journal* 8, no. 4 (1982): 413.

[452] IFLA Secretariat, "Professional Resolutions of the 48th IFLA General Conference," 405.

[453] Ibid.

[454] Ibid.

[455] Denis, "Libraries and Librarianship in Canada," 11.

[456] IFLA, "The 48th General Conference," 205.

[457] Wilhite, *85 Years IFLA,* 71.

[458] Wijnstroom, *IFLA Directory 1982–1983*.

[459] Koops and Coops, *IFLA Annual 1983*, 271.

460 Wijnstroom, *IFLA Directory 1982–1983*, 58, 10.
461 IFLA "IFLA Publications," 7.
462 Koops and Coops, *IFLA Annual 1983*, 245–275.
463 Wijnstroom, *IFLA Directory 1984–1985,* 32.
464 Ibid., 55.
465 Ibid., 46, 207.
466 Wijnstroom, *IFLA Directory 1982–1983,* 52.
467 Ibid., 35.
468 Clement, interview.
469 Ibid.
470 Clement, "An International MARC Network," 257.
471 Clement, "International MARC Programme (IMP)," 296.
472 Wijnstroom, *IFLA Directory 1984–1985,* 6, 10, 38.
473 Wijnstroom, *IFLA Directory 1986–1987*, 8, 13, 18, 20, 21, 26, 42.
474 IFLA Professional Board, "Summary Record of the Meeting of the Professional
    Board," 274.
475 Clement, interview.
476 Nauta, *IFLA Directory 1988–1989*, 13, 19, 29, 45, 46.
477 Clement, interview.
478 IFLA Executive Board, "Summary Record of the Meeting of the Executive Board,"
    IFLA Journal 16, no. 1 (1990): 151.
479 Clement, interview.
480 Kirkwood, "IFLA Moscow 1991," 4.
481 Clement, interview.
482 Clement, interview.
483 Clement, "Planning IFLA's Professional Programmes," 332.
484 Ex Libris Association, "Cynthia Jean Durance."
485 IFLA Secretariat, "From the Secretariat," *IFLA Journal* 3, no. 2 (1977): 152.
486 IFLA, *Guidelines for the Applications of the ISBDs*, viii.
487 Wijnstroom, *IFLA Directory 1984–1985*, 37.
488 McCallum, "40 Years of Technology in Libraries," 4.
489 Durance, "Exploiting Technology," 312.
490 Ex Libris Association, "Cynthia Jean Durance."
491 Durance and McLean, "Libraries and Access to Information," 138.
492 Ex Libris Association, "Cynthia Jean Durance."
493 IFLA, "From the IFLA Core Programmes," *IFLA Journal* 15, no. 2 (1989): 164.
494 Manning, "Cynthia Durance," 389.
495 Delsey, interview.
496 Ibid.
497 Delsey, introduction to *Guidelines for the Application of the ISBDs*, vii.
498 Thomas J. Delsey, e-mail message to the authors, 1 May 2012.
499 Ibid.
500 Ibid. Note that Delsey's position at NLC evolved significantly throughout his
    23-year term of employment. See also: Jean Whiffin, ed., *International
    Directory of Serials Specialists*, (New York: Haworth Press, 1995): 10–11.
501 Whiffin, *International Directory of Serials Specialists*, 10.

[502] Thomas J. Delsey, e-mail message to the authors, 1 May 2012.
[503] Delsey, interview.
[504] Ibid.
[505] Thomas J. Delsey, e-mail message to the authors, 1 May 2012.
[506] Delsey, interview.
[507] IFLA Study Group on the Functional Requirements for Bibliographic Records, *Functional Requirements for Bibliographic Records,* vii.
[508] Nauta, *IFLA Directory 1992–1993*, 31.
[509] IFLA Study Group on the Functional Requirements for Bibliographic Records, *Functional Requirements for Bibliographic Records.*
[510] Riva, "Introducing the Functional Requirements," 8, 10.
[511] IFLA Meetings of Experts on an International Cataloguing Code (IME-ICC): *Statement of International Cataloguing Principles*, 1.
[512] OCLC Research, "OCLC Research Activities."
[513] Oliver, *FRBR and RDA*, 2.
[514] Joint Steering Committee for Development of RDA, "Tom Delsey appointed as AACR3 Editor."
[515] Zielinska, *Celebrating 20 Years,* 1–2.
[516] Ibid., 2.
[517] Zielinksa, "Report of the First Open Meeting," 68.
[518] Zielinksa, "IFLA's Section on Library Services," 303.
[519] Ibid., 303.
[520] Ibid.
[521] Ibid., 304.
[522] Ibid.
[523] IFLA, "Reports of Meetings," *IFLA Journal* 13, no. 1 (1987): 70.
[524] Nauta, *IFLA Directory 1990–1991*, 51.
[525] Zielinksa and Kirkwood, *Multicultural Librarianship: An International Handbook.*
[526] Kirkwood, interview.
[527] Ibid.
[528] Ibid.
[529] Ibid.
[530] Kirkwood, "Ethnic Services Seminar," 6.
[531] Kirkwood, interview.
[532] Zielinska, *Celebrating 20 Years*, 7–8.
[533] Voogt, *IFLA Directory 1996–1997,* 55.
[534] Shimmon, *IFLA Directory 2000–2001*, 66, 289.
[535] Scott, interview.
[536] Marianne Scott, e-mail message to the authors, 9 May 2013.
[537] Wijnstroom, *IFLA Directory 1984–1985*, 41.
[538] Ibid.
[539] Ibid., 32.
[540] Ibid., 29, 203.
[541] Ibid., 29, 206.
[542] Ibid., 34.
[543] Ibid., 51.

544 Ibid., 45.
545 Ibid., 41.
546 Ibid., 41.
547 Ibid., 31.
548 Ibid., 39.
549 Ibid., 53, 206.
550 Koops and Henry, *IFLA Annual 1984*, 167–186.
551 Wilhite, *85 Years IFLA*, 247.
552 Ibid, 248.
553 Marianne Scott, e-mail message to the authors, 9 May 2013.
554 Marianne Scott, e-mail message to the authors, 14 January 2013.
555 Marianne Scott, e-mail message to the authors, 9 May 2013.
556 Wijnstroom, *IFLA Directory 1986–1987*, 39.
557 Patricia Scarry to Beth Miller, 30 July 1985.
558 Koops and Henry, *IFLA Annual 1986*, 194–222.
559 Ibid., 194.
560 Koops and Henry, *IFLA Annual 1986*, 196.
561 Ibid.
562 Ibid., 198.
563 Ibid., 206.
564 Ibid., 220.
565 Ibid., 222.
566 Aman, "IFLA Section on Library Education and Training," 234.
567 Nauta, *IFLA Directory 1988–1989,* 13, 31, 41, 42.
568 Aman, "IFLA Section on Library Education and Training," 234.
569 Ibid., 235.
570 McGill Association of University Teachers, "Featured Retiree: Miriam Tees."
571 Galler, "International Librarianship," 6.
572 IFLA, "Publications of International Relevance," *IFLA Journal* 17, no. 4 (1991): 448. See: Blanche Woolls, *Continuing Professional Education: An IFLA Guidebook,* München; New York: K.G. Saur, 1991.
573 Galler, "International Librarianship," 8.
574 Galler, "Indigenous Publishing, 1981–1992," 419.
575 Galler, "International Librarianship," 8.
576 Nauta, *IFLA Directory 1990–1991*, 12, 30, 49.
577 Galler, "International Librarianship," 8.
578 Galler, "International Librarianship," 7.
579 Marianne Scott, e-mail message to the authors, 9 May 2013.
580 Scott, "Conference of Directors of National Libraries," 38.
581 Ibid., 39.
582 IFLA Secretariat, "IFLA Annual Report 1988," 142.
583 Scott, "Conference of Directors of National Libraries," 38.
584 Ibid., 39.
585 Rugaas, "Past, Present and Future Relations," 144.
586 Scott, "Conference of Directors of National Libraries," 39.
587 Manning, interview.

588 Marianne Scott, e-mail message to the authors, 14 January 2013.
589 Nauta, *IFLA Directory 1990–1991*, 41, 72.
590 Ibid., 42.
591 Ibid., 48–49.
592 Ibid., 56.
593 Ibid., 66.
594 Ibid., 23, 47.
595 Ibid., 31.
596 Ibid., 73, 79, 104–107, 175.
597 Henry, *IFLA Annual 1990*, 201–240.
598 Nauta, *IFLA Directory 1992–1993*, 33, 63.
599 Voogt, *IFLA Directory 1994–1995*, 38.
600 Marianne Scott, e-mail message to the authors, 9 May 2013.
601 Manning, interview.
602 Ibid.
603 IFLA, "From the Divisions, Sections and Round Tables." *IFLA Journal* 19, no. 4 (1993): 460.
604 IFLA, "From the Divisions, Sections and Round Tables." *IFLA Journal* 21, no. 4 (1995): 316.
605 IFLA Professional Board, "Summary Report," *IFLA Journal* 22, no. 1 (1996): 57.
606 IFLA Secretariat. "Istanbul 1995 – An Overview," 304.
607 Voogt, *IFLA Directory 1996–1997*, 14, 35, 45.
608 Shimmon, *IFLA Directory 2000–2001*, 14, 70, 281.
609 IFLA, "Publications of International Relevance," *IFLA Journal* 26, no. 4 (2000): 322.
610 Ibid.
611 Wilhite, *85 Years IFLA*, 82. Wilhite further adds that in 2006, "Arabic and Chinese were added to the list of five official IFLA languages (English, French, German, Russian, and Spanish)."
612 Manning, interview.
613 Ibid.
614 IFLA, "From the Divisions, Sections and Round Tables," *IFLA Journal* 23, no. 1 (1997): 71.
615 Manning, interview.
616 Ibid.
617 Ibid.
618 Ibid.
619 Wilhite, *85 Years IFLA*, 82.
620 Ingrid Parent, e-mail message to the authors, 18 March 2013.
621 Ingrid Parent, interview.
622 Ibid.
623 Ibid.
624 IFLA, "From the Divisions, Sections and Round Tables," *IFLA Journal* 21, no. 4 (1995): 315.
625 IFLA Secretariat, "IFLA Annual Report 1999," 216.
626 IFLA, "From the Divisions, Section and Round Tables," *IFLA Journal* 23, no. 5–6 (1997): 404.

⁶²⁷ Parent, interview.

⁶²⁸ IFLA Secretariat, "IFLA Annual Report 1999," 215.

⁶²⁹ IFLA, "65th IFLA Council," 286.

⁶³⁰ Parent, interview.

⁶³¹ IFLA Secretariat, "Summary Report of Meetings of the Professional and Executive Boards," *IFLA Journal* 26, no. 1 (2000): 57.

⁶³² Nauta, *IFLA Directory 1988–1989*, 21.

⁶³³ Swain,"Annual Report 1992," 235.

⁶³⁴ Swain and Cleveland, "Overview of the Internet," 16.

⁶³⁵ See for example: Swain, "Annual Report 1991," 168.

⁶³⁶ Terry Kuny, e-mail message to the authors, 14 January 2013.

⁶³⁷ Terry Kuny, e-mail message to the authors, 16 January 2013.

⁶³⁸ Ibid.

⁶³⁹ Terry Kuny, e-mail message to the authors, 14 January 2013.

⁶⁴⁰ Terry Kuny, e-mail message to the authors, 16 January 2013.

⁶⁴¹ Wilhite, *85 Years IFLA*, 73.

⁶⁴² Terry Kuny, e-mail message to the authors, 14 January 2013.

⁶⁴³ Wedgeworth, "The Virtual IFLA," 23.

⁶⁴⁴ Kirkwood, "An IFLA in the Sun," 25.

⁶⁴⁵ Terry Kuny, e-mail message to the authors, 16 January 2013.

⁶⁴⁶ Kuny and Lantaigne, "NOTE: IFLA Mailing Lists are Closed for the Holidays."

⁶⁴⁷ Lantaigne, "Press Release: First mirror of IFLANET. "

⁶⁴⁸ Cleveland, "New IFLANET address." See also: Voogt, *IFLA Directory 1996–1997*, 26.

⁶⁴⁹ Kuny, "IFLANET Statistics and Update (November, 1995)."

⁶⁵⁰ Kuny, "IFLA-L has moved."

⁶⁵¹ Terry Kuny, e-mail message to the authors, 16 January 2013. See also: Kuny, "NEW LIST: LIBJOBS."

⁶⁵² Kuny, "WWW Access to IFLANET."

⁶⁵³ IFLA, "From the Divisions, Sections and Round Tables," *IFLA Journal* 21, no. 4 (1995): 316.

⁶⁵⁴ Voogt, *IFLA Directory 1994–1995*, 39.

⁶⁵⁵ McGarry, "IFLA 1995: Libraries of the Future."

⁶⁵⁶ Kuny, "IFLANET Statistics– September 1995 (correction)."

⁶⁵⁷ Swain, "Annual Report 1996," 227.

⁶⁵⁸ Kuny, "FYI: IFLANET Statistics."

⁶⁵⁹ Swain, "Annual Report 1996," 227.

⁶⁶⁰ Ibid., 227–228.

⁶⁶¹ Ibid., 228.

⁶⁶² IFLA Secretariat, "From the Secretariat," *IFLA Journal* 23, no. 2 (1997): 145.

⁶⁶³ Ibid.

⁶⁶⁴ Marianne Scott, e-mail message to the authors, 9 May, 2013.

⁶⁶⁵ Kuny, "Curriculum Vitae," 9, 10.

⁶⁶⁶ Kuny, "1996 UDT Core Programme."

⁶⁶⁷ Terry Kuny, e-mail message to the authors, 14 January 2013.

⁶⁶⁸ Cleveland, "New IFLANET address."

[669] Swain, Cleveland, and Lantaigne, "Annual Report 1999," 228.

[670] Ibid., 229.

[671] Cleveland, "IFLANET mirror site is now available."

[672] Terry Kuny, e-mail message to the authors, 16 January 2013.

[673] Terry Kuny, e-mail message to the authors, 14 January 2013.

[674] IFLA Secretariat, "From the Secretariat," *IFLA Journal* 27, no. 1 (February 2001): 41.

[675] Duncan, "Section on Classification and Indexing Review of Activities, 1993–1994."

[676] Ibid.

[677] Ibid.

[678] IFLA, "From the Divisions, Sections and Round Tables." *IFLA Journal* 21, no. 4 (1995): 315.

[679] Ibid., 314.

[680] Ibid., 315.

[681] Kirkwood, interview.

[682] Ibid.

[683] Ibid.

[684] Ibid.

[685] Ibid.

[686] Ibid.

[687] Shimmon, *IFLA Directory 2002–2003*, 108.

[688] IFLA Headquarters Staff, *IFLA Directory 2005–2007*, 36, 96.

[689] Savard, interview.

[690] Ibid.

[691] Tees, "Teaching Management," 297.

[692] Savard, interview.

[693] IFLA, "From the Divisions, Sections and Round Tables," *IFLA Journal* 23, no. 1 (1997): 70.

[694] Voogt, *IFLA Directory 1998–1999*, 64.

[695] Savard, interview.

[696] Lor, "The IFLA-UNESCO Partnership," 275.

[697] Nauta, *IFLA Directory 1992–1993*, 38.

[698] Evans and Savard, "Canadian Libraries on the Agenda," 158.

[699] Nauta, *IFLA Directory 1992–1993*, 48.

[700] Evans, "Report on the Development of the School Library Manifesto," 56.

[701] Ibid.

[702] Galler, "National School Library Policies," 292.

[703] Ibid., 297.

[704] Evans, "Report on the Development of the School Library Manifesto," 57.

[705] Ibid.

[706] ibid.

[707] IFLA Section of School Libraries and Resource Centers, "Annual Report 1998–1999."

[708] Evans, "Report on the Development of the School Library Manifesto," 57.

[709] IFLA, "From the Divisions, Sections and Round Tables," *IFLA Journal* 25, no.2 (1999): 116.

[710] IFLA, "School Library Manifesto Ratified by UNESCO."
[711] National Library of Canada. "Obituary."
[712] UNESCO, "UNESCO/IFLA School Library Manifesto."
[713] Canadian Library Association, Archives, CLA Headquarters.
[714] Marianne Scott, e-mail message to the authors, 17 January 2013.
[715] Manning, interview.
[716] IFLA, "63rd IFLA Council," 383.
[717] Ibid.
[718] Ibid., 387.
[719] Ibid.
[720] Marianne Scott, e-mail message to the authors, 17 January 2013.
[721] Manning, interview.
[722] Manning, interview.
[723] IFLA, "63rd IFLA Council," 383.
[724] Marianne Scott, e-mail message to the authors, 17 January 2013.
[725] Shimmon, *IFLA Directory 2002–2003,* 68.
[726] Clubb, interview.
[727] Voogt, *IFLA Directory 1998–1999*, 67.
[728] Clubb, interview.
[729] IFLA, "From the Divisions, Sections and Round Tables," *IFLA Journal* 25, no. 5–6 (1999): 306.
[730] Whitney, interview.
[731] Ibid.
[732] Ibid.
[733] Parent, interview.
[734] Scott, e-mail message to the authors, 9 May 2013.
[735] Shimmon, *IFLA Directory 2000–2001.*
[736] Voogt, *IFLA Directory 1998–1999*, 143–147.
[737] Shimmon, *IFLA Directory 2000–2001,* 14.
[738] Ibid., 71.
[739] Ibid., 56.
[740] Ibid., 62.
[741] Ibid., 64.
[742] Ibid., 72, 66.
[743] Library and Archives Canada, "Sylvestre, Guy."
[744] Ibid.
[745] Bruce, "Guy Sylvestre."
[746] Wyczynski, "Joseph Jean Guy Sylvestre."
[747] Marianne Scott, e-mail message to the authors, 19 May 2013.
[748] Wyczynski, "Joseph Jean Guy Sylvestre."
[749] McCormick, "Dr. Guy Sylvestre—Prime Mover," 5.
[750] Bruce, "Guy Sylvestre."
[751] Library and Archives Canada, "Sylvestre, Guy."
[752] Bruce, "Guy Sylvestre."
[753] Library and Archives Canada,"Sylvestre, Guy."
[754] Bruce, "Guy Sylvestre."

755 Library and Archives Canada,"Sylvestre, Guy."
756 Wyczynski, "Joseph Jean Guy Sylvestre."
757 Bruce, "Guy Sylvestre."
758 Ibid.
759 McCormick, "National Librarian Guy Sylvestre, 1918–2010," 237.
760 Bruce, "Guy Sylvestre."
761 Marianne Scott, e-mail message to the authors, 19 May 2013.
762 Ibid.
763 Liebaers, "The Dutch Tea Party," 16.
764 Marianne Scott, e-mail message to the authors, 19 May 2013.
765 Spicer, interview.
766 Parent, Interview.
767 McCormick, "Dr. Guy Sylvestre—Prime Mover," 5.
768 Bruce, "Guy Sylvestre."
769 "Jean-Guy Sylvestre," *Ottawa Citizen.*
770 McCormick, "Dr. Guy Sylvestre—Prime Mover," 2.
771 Sylvestre, Foreword, ix.
772 Donnelly, *The National Library of Canada*, 19.
773 Ibid., 23.
774 Clayton, "Answering a Nation's Call," 126.
775 Donnelly, *The National Library of Canada*, 31.
776 Burpee, "A Plea for a Canadian National Library," 191.
777 Donnelly, *The National Library of Canada*, 44.
778 Clayton, "Answering a Nation's Call," 126.
779 Donnelly, *The National Library of Canada*, 60.
780 Ibid., 83.
781 Ibid., 101.
782 Clayton, "Answering a Nation's Call," 128.
783 Donnelly, *The National Library of Canada*, 131.
784 Library and Archives Canada, "About Theses Canada."
785 Clayton, "Answering a Nation's Call," 128.
786 Ibid.
787 Conference of Directors of National Libraries, "Past Executives."
788 Parent, interview.
789 IFLA, "Standing Committee Members of the Reference and Information Services Section."
790 Clement, interview.
791 Durance and McLean, "Libraries and Access to Information," 148.
792 Delsey, interview.
793 Terry Kuny, e-mail message to the authors, 14 January 2013.
794 Parliament of Canada, "Bill C-8."
795 Library and Archives Canada, "Home."
796 Veaner, "Woman at the Top," 18.
797 Lumley, "Scott, Marianne Florence," 1168.
798 Ibid.
799 Scott, interview.

800 Lumley, "Scott, Marianne Florence," 1168.
801 Ibid.
802 Ibid.
803 Ibid.
804 Veaner, "Woman at the Top," 18.
805 Scott, interview.
806 Ibid.
807 Parent, interview.
808 Lumley, "Scott, Marianne Florence," 1177.
809 Marianne Scott, e-mail message to the authors, 19 May 2013.
810 Ibid.
811 Clubb, interview.
812 Kirkwood, interview.
813 Davis, Jr., "With Malice toward None," 14.
814 Ibid., 15.
815 Ibid., 17.
816 Spicer, interview.
817 Wilhite, *85 Years IFLA*, 201.
818 Davis, Jr., "With Malice toward None," 17.
819 Scott, interview.
820 Davis, Jr., "With Malice toward None," 17.
821 Ibid., 18.
822 Wilhite, *85 Years IFLA*, 74.
823 Ibid.
824 Ibid.
825 Kirkwood, interview.
826 Kniffel, "Caught in a Coup," 846.
827 Wilhite, *85 Years IFLA*, 76.
828 Wilhite, *85 Years IFLA*, 269.
829 Ibid.
830 Ibid.
831 Marianne Scott, e-mail message to the authors, 9 May 2013.
832 Ibid.
833 Spicer, interview.
834 Scott, interview.
835 Nauta, "From the IFLA Secretariat," 401.
836 Ibid.
837 Marianne Scott, e-mail message to the authors, 9 May 2013.
838 Kniffel, "Caught in a Coup," 847.
839 Ibid.
840 Scott, interview.
841 Ibid.
842 Spicer, interview.
843 Nauta, "From the IFLA Secretariat," 401.
844 Kirkwood, interview.
845 Ibid.

846 Ibid.

847 Scott, interview.

848 Henry and Davis, Jr., *IFLA 75th Anniversary*, 4.

849 Kirkwood, interview.

850 Parent, e-mail message to the authors, 4 June 2013.

851 Browne and Peroni, "Ms. Ingrid Parent."

852 Ibid.

853 Ibid.

854 National Taiwan University Library, "Keynote 1."

855 Ibid.

856 Browne and Peroni, "Ms. Ingrid Parent."

857 National Taiwan University Library, "Keynote 1."

858 Browne and Peroni, "Ms. Ingrid Parent."

859 National Taiwan University Library, "Keynote 1."

860 Parent, interview.

861 Ibid.

862 Browne and Peroni, "Ms. Ingrid Parent."

863 Ibid.

864 Parent, interview.

865 Nicholson, "Results of the Election."

866 Browne and Peroni, "Ms. Ingrid Parent."

867 Wilhite, *85 Years IFLA,* 338.

868 Parent, interview.

869 CNIB, "CNIB."

870 CNIB, "About Us."

871 Herie, *Journey to Independence,* 15.

872 CNIB, "CNIB Founders."

873 Herie, *Journey to Independence,* 70.

874 Ibid., 30.

875 Ibid., 48–52.

876 CNIB, "Historic Timeline."

877 IFLA, "Reports of Meetings: Copyright and Library Materials for the Handicapped," 436.

878 Ibid.

879 IFLA, "Guidelines for Library Service to Braille Users."

880 IFLA Libraries Serving Persons with Print Disabilities Section, *Manifesto.*

881 Freeze, "The Impact of the Integrated Digital Library System."

882 Shimmon, *IFLA Directory 2000–2001*, 62.

883 IFLA Libraries Serving Persons with Print Disabilities Section, "Libraries for the Blind in the Information Age."

884 CNIB, "How We Are Structured."

885 CNIB, "About Us."

886 Wilhite, *85 Years IFLA*, 26.

887 Moore, Interview.

888 Shimmon, *IFLA Directory 2000–2001, 20.*

889 Whitney, "Libraries and the WTO," n.p.

890 IFLA, "News Section," *IFLA Journal* 26, no. 1 (2000): 68.

891 Koopman, *Annual Report 2000*, 7.

892 IFLA, "From Other Organizations," *IFLA Journal* 27, no. 1 (2001): 53–54.

893 Ibid.

894 Marianne Scott, e-mail message to the authors, 19 May 2013.

895 IFLA Secretariat, "From the Secretariat," *IFLA Journal* 27, no. 1 (2001): 41.

896 Wilhite, *85 Years IFLA*, 301.

897 IFLA, "News Section," *IFLA Journal* 27, no. 3 (2001): 182.

898 Ibid., 183.

899 IFLA, "News Section," *IFLA Journal* 27, no. 5–6 (2001): 345.

900 Ibid., 345.

901 IFLA, "News Section," *IFLA Journal* 27, no. 3 (2001): 183.

902 Ibid., 183.

903 IFLA, "News Section," *IFLA Journal* 27, no. 3 (2001): 183.

904 Ibid., 184.

905 Ibid.

906 Ibid.

907 Ibid.

908 Ibid.

909 Ibid., 185.

910 IFLA, "News Section," *IFLA Journal* 27, no. 5–6 (2001): 348.

911 Ibid., 343.

912 Ibid., 344.

913 Ibid., 343.

914 Law, "@ your library eh?," 221.

915 Ibid., 222.

916 IFLA, "News Section," *IFLA Journal* 27, no. 5–6 (2001): 349.

917 Ibid., 349.

918 IFLA, "News Section," *IFLA Journal* 28, no. 2 (2002): 85.

919 Ibid., 85.

920 Gupta, Koontz, and McAdam, "In Search of," 180.

921 IFLA, "Other Events in Glasgow," 341.

922 Law, "@ your library eh?,"222.

923 IFLA, "Other Events in Glasgow," 342.

924 Cabral, "IFLA Comes Back," 285.

925 Ibid., 284.

926 Ibid.

927 Moore, interview.

928 IFLA, "IFLA 69–2003: Minutes."

929 IFLA, "IFLA Policies and Programme," 260.

930 IFLA, "IFLA 70–2004: Minutes."

931 Ibid.

932 Ibid.

933 Cabral, "IFLA Comes Back," 284.

934 IFLA, "IFLA and Its Officials," *Final Announcement,* 11.

935 Cabral, "IFLA Comes Back," 284.

[936] Association pour l'avancement des sciences et des techniques de la documentation, "Annexe A – Comités."

[937] Cabral, "IFLA Comes Back," 284.

[938] Association pour l'avancement des sciences et des techniques de la documentation, "Comité d'Honneur du 74th."

[939] Association pour l'avancement des sciences et des techniques de la documentation, "Annexe A – Comités."

[940] Cabral, "IFLA Comes Back," 284.

[941] Clubb, "Globally Speaking," 201.

[942] Ibid.

[943] Evans, "IFLA: Just Another Acronym," 237.

[944] IFLA. "News." *IFLA Journal* 31, no. 3 (2005): 274.

[945] Parent, interview.

[946] Gupta, Koontz, and McAdam, "In Search of,"180.

[947] IFLA Secretariat, "From the Secretariat," *IFLA Journal* 33, no. 3 (2007): 277.

[948] IFLA, "News," *IFLA Journal* 32, no. 3 (2006): 255.

[949] IFLA Secretariat, "From the Secretariat," *IFLA Journal* 33, no. 3 (2007): 276.

[950] IFLA Headquarters, *IFLA Annual Report 2007,* 18.

[951] Savard, interview.

[952] IFLA, "From IFLA Headquarters," *IFLA Journal* 33, no. 4 (2007): 378.

[953] IFLA Headquarters, *IFLA Annual Report 2007,* 17.

[954] IFLA Secretariat, "From the Secretariat," *IFLA Journal* 33, no. 3 (2007): 276.

[955] IFLA, "From the Divisions and Sections," *IFLA Journal* 33, no. 3 (2007): 277.

[956] IFLA, "Officers of IFLA 2007–2009," *IFLA Journal* 33, no. 4 (2007): 380.

[957] Ibid.

[958] Ibid.

[959] Moore, "Au Revoir from Kelly Moore," 64.

[960] Bonnelly, "Official Invitation," 4.

[961] IFLA, "IFLA and its Officials," 11.

[962] Ibid.

[963] Gendron, "74th IFLA General Conference," 132.

[964] Ibid.

[965] Ibid.

[966] IFLA, "Satellite Meetings. . . . 2008."

[967] Ibid.

[968] Ibid.

[969] Association pour l'avancement des sciences et des techniques de la documentation, ASTED Records. See also: Yarrow, "IFLA 2008."

[970] IFLA, "Satellite Meetings. . . . 2008."

[971] Ibid.

[972] Ibid.

[973] Whitney, interview.

[974] Ibid.

[975] Ibid.

[976] Bonnelly, "Official Invitation," 4.

[977] Wilhite, *85 Years IFLA,* 323.

[978] Ibid., 87; Association pour l'avancement des sciences et des techniques de la documentation, ASTED Records.

[979] Association pour l'avancement des sciences et des techniques de la documentation, ASTED Records. See also: Bradley, "2008 IFLA Congress."

[980] Lux, "Opening Address," 333.

[981] Jean, "Opening Address," 330.

[982] Wilhite, *85 Years IFLA*, 324.

[983] IFLA Headquarters, *IFLA Annual Report 2008*, 9.

[984] Wilhite, *85 Years IFLA*, 324.

[985] Association pour l'avancement des sciences et des techniques de la documentation, ASTED Records.

[986] Ibid.

[987] Savard, interview.

[988] Ibid.

[989] Whitney, interview.

[990] Manning, interview.

[991] Lor, "Secretary General's Report," 365.

[992] Ibid.

[993] Ibid.

[994] IFLA Headquarters, *IFLA Annual Report 2008*, 10.

[995] Ibid.

[996] Ibid.

[997] Ibid.

[998] Association pour l'avancement des sciences et des techniques de la documentation, ASTED Records.

[999] IFLA Express, "IFLA Express."

[1000] Association pour l'avancement des sciences et des techniques de la documentation, ASTED Records.

[1001] Wilhite, *85 Years IFLA*, 325.

[1002] IFLA Express, "Bibliomondialis,"2.

[1003] Gupta, Koontz, and McAdam, "In Search of," 180.

[1004] IFLA Headquarters, *IFLA Annual Report 2008*, 20.

[1005] Parent, interview.

[1006] Wilhite, *85 Years IFLA*, 326.

[1007] IFLA, "News," *IFLA Journal* 35, no. 3 (2009): 274.

[1008] Ingrid Parent, interview.

[1009] IFLA Headquarters, *IFLA Annual Report 2009*, 20.

[1010] Gupta, Koontz, and McAdam, "In Search of," 180.

[1011] IFLA Headquarters, *IFLA Annual Report 2009*, 9.

[1012] IFLA Strategic Plan Committee, "Strat. Plan Mar 31, 2010."

[1013] Tise, "Introduction," 3.

[1014] Ibid.

[1015] IFLA, "News," *IFLA Journal* 36, no. 2 (2010): 187.

[1016] Ibid.

[1017] Ibid., 190.

[1018] IFLA, "IFLA Presidential Meeting 2011."

[1019] IFLA Headquarters, *IFLA Annual Report 2011*, 3.

[1020] Ibid.

[1021] Ibid.

[1022] Parent, "Remarks, Speeches and Presentations."

[1023] Owen, interview.

[1024] Ibid,

[1025] IFLA Headquarters, *IFLA Annual Report 2011*, 6.

[1026] Parent, "Introduction," 3.

[1027] IFLA Headquarters, *IFLA Annual Report 2011*, 6.

[1028] Canadian Library Association, "IFLA 2011 List of Participants."

[1029] Canadian Library Association, CLA Records. See also: Adams, "Renewing CLA."

[1030] Ibid.

[1031] IFLA, "News," *IFLA Journal* 37, no. 2 (2011): 173.

[1032] Parent, "Libraries – A Force for Change," 323.

[1033] Whitney, interview.

[1034] IFLA "Indigenous Knowledges: Local Priorities, Global Contexts Programme," 1.

[1035] IFLA, "Document nr GB 12–12–2.4.3."

[1036] IFLA World Library and Information Congress, "Satellite Meetings," 2011.

[1037] Moore, "For the Times They Are A-changin," 8.

[1038] Parent, "Speaking Notes," 7.

Bibliography

Interviews

Clement, Hope E.A. Interview by Dan Gillean. Telephone, 5 April 2013.

Clubb, Barbara. Interview by J Jack Unrau. Ottawa, ON, 19 June 2012.

Delsey, Thomas J. (Tom). Interview by J Jack Unrau. Ottawa, ON, 20 June 2012.

Kirkwood, Francis T. (Frank). Interview by J Jack Unrau. Ottawa, ON, 19 June 2012.

Manning, Ralph. Interview by J Jack Unrau. Ottawa, ON, 18 June 2012.

Moore, Kelly. Interview by J Jack Unrau. Ottawa, ON, 20 June 2012.

Owen, Victoria. Interview by J Jack Unrau. Toronto, ON, 25 June 2012.

Parent, Ingrid. Interview by Dan Gillean, Myron Groover, Judith Saltman, and J Jack Unrau. Vancouver, BC, 26 April 2012.

Savard, Réjean. Interview by J Jack Unrau. Montreal, QC, 21 June 2012.

Scott, Marianne. Interview by Dan Gillean, Myron Groover, Judith Saltman, and J Jack Unrau. Vancouver, BC, 29 March 2012.

Spicer, Erik. Interview by J Jack Unrau. Ottawa, ON, 17 June 2012.

Whitney, Paul. Interview by Dan Gillean, Myron Groover, Judith Saltman, and J Jack Unrau. Vancouver, BC, 8 May 2012.

Williamson, Nancy. Interview by J Jack Unrau. Toronto, ON, 26 June 2012.

Primary and Secondary Sources

Adams, Karen. "Renewing CLA." *Feliciter* 57, no. 5 (2011): 174.

Adler, Anne G. "IFLA 1982: A First-Time View: Sampling an International Conference and the Joie de Montréal." *American Libraries* 13, no. 9 (October 1982): 567–569. Accessed 11 December 2012. http://www.jstor.org/stable/25626102.

Adorian, Madeleine. "IFLA Congress, Budapest 1972." *Feliciter* 19, no. 1 (1973): 4.

Aman, Mohammed M. "IFLA Section on Library Education and Training: 1987 Report." *Journal of Education for Library and Information Science* 28, no. 3 (Winter 1988): 234–237.

Anderson, Dorothy. Letter to Jack Cain, 17 July 1973. Canadian Library Association fonds. Library and Archives Canada, Ottawa, ON.

Arntz, Helmut, I. Ju. Bagrova, Helmut Bansa, Sabine Barral, I. Bettembourg, W. Boyd Rayward, Laura de Felice Olivieri Sangiacomo, et al. "Personal Recollections." *IFLA Journal* 3, no. 3 (1977): 273–299. doi: 10.1177/034003527700300317.

L'Association des Bibliothécaires de France. "L'Association des Bibliothécaires de France c'est . . ." L'Association des Bibliothécaires de France. Last modified 26 December 2011. Accessed 21 April 2013. http://www.abf.asso.fr/1/113/228/ABF/l-association-des-bibliothecaires-de-france-cest?p=0.

Association pour l'avancement des sciences et des techniques de la documentation. "Annexe A –Comités." Association pour l'avancement des sciences et des techniques de la documentation. Archives. ASTED Headquarters, Montreal, QC.

———. ASTED Records. Archives, ASTED Headquarters, Montreal, QC.

———. *Bibliothèques d'aujourd'hui: Lignes directrices pour les bibliothèques publiques du Québec*. Montreal: ASTED, 2011.

———. "Comité d'honneur du 74th Congrés international de l'information et des bibliothéques Québec 2008 01/06/2005." Association pour l'avancement des sciences et des techniques de la documentation. Archives. ASTED Headquarters, Montreal, QC.

———."Preliminary Program to the 48th General Conference of the International Federation of Library Associations and Institutions, Montréal, Québec, August 22–28 1982." Montreal: International Federation of Library Associations and Institutions, 1982.

Association of Canadian Map Libraries and Archives. "Awards." Association of Canadian Map Libraries and Archives. Last updated 8 January 2013. Accessed 15 February 2013. http://www.acmla.org/awards.html.

Balatti, David. "The Canadian National Bibliography: 50 years of continuity and change." Presentation at the 67th IFLA Council and General Conference, Boston, MA, 16–25 August 2001. Accessed 8 February 2013. http://archive.ifla.org/IV/ifla67/papers/075-133e.pdf.

Bartleman, James. "Libraries and the First Nations People of Canada." *IFLA Journal* 34, no. 4 (2008): 337–340. doi: 10.1177/0340035208099267.

Beacock, E. Stanley. Preface to *The Morton Years: The Canadian Library Association 1946–1971*, by Elizabeth Hulse. Toronto: Ex Libris Association, 1995.

Benoit, Barbara. "The First Twenty-Five Years: Erik Spicer, Parliamentary Librarian." *Canadian Parliamentary Review* 8, no. 4 (Winter 1985): 33–36. Accessed 11 February 2013. http://www.revparl.ca/8/4/08n4_85e_zinterview.pdf.

Bonneau, Michel L. Letter to Preben Kirkegaard, 21 March 1978. IFLA Headquarters, The Hague, Netherlands.

Bonnelly, Claude. "Official Invitation." *Final Announcement: World Library and Information Congress: 74th IFLA General Conference and Council – 10–14 August 2008.* International Federation of Library Associations and Institutions: 4.

Bossuat, M.-L. "Report by the Treasurer, Mlle M.-L, Bossuat, Concerning the IFLA Accounts 1980 and Financial Guidelines for 1981–82." *IFLA Journal* 7, no. 2 (1981): 184–199. doi: 10.1177/034003528100700214.

Bradley, Fiona. "2008 IFLA Congress in Quebec City." *Libraries Interact.* Last modified 18 August 2008. Accessed 21 June 2013. http://librariesinteract.info/2008/08/18/2008-ifla-congress-in-quebec-city/.

Breycha-Vauthier, A.C. Letter to Pierre Matte, 25 January 1961. Archives, IFLA Headquarters, The Hague, Netherlands.

Brown, Thomas C. "Expo 67." *The Canadian Encylopedia*. Historica-Dominion, 2011. Accessed 9 June 2013. http://www.thecanadianencyclopedia.com/articles/emc/expo-67.

Browne, Lynn N., and Gwen Peroni. "Ms. Ingrid Parent." *Canadian Who's Who: 2011.* Orillia: Third Sector Publishing, 2011. Accessed 22 December 2012. http://canadianwhoswho.ca/.

———. "Mr. Erik John Spicer." *Canadian Who's Who: 2011.* Orillia: Third Sector Publishing, 2011. Accessed 22 December 2012. http://canadianwhoswho.ca/.

Bruce, Lorne. "Elizabeth Homer Morton." *Libraries Today* (Wiki). Accessed 17 February 2013. http://librariestoday.pbworks.com/w/page/36565008/Elizabeth%20Homer%20Morton.

———. "Guy Sylvestre." Ex Libris Association. Last modified December 2011. Accessed 20 December 2012. http://exlibris.pbworks.com/w/page/48252212/Guy%20Sylvestre.

———. "Harry C. Campbell." Ex Libris Association. Last modified June 2011. Accessed 10 December 2012. http://exlibris.pbworks.com/w/page/36143425/Harry%20Campbell.

Bureau of Canadian Archivists. *Rules for Archival Description.* Revised Edition. Ottawa: Bureau of Canadian Archivists, Canadian Committee on Archival Description, July 2008. Accessed 15 February 2013. http://www.cdncouncilarchives.ca/RAD/RADComplete_July2008.pdf.

Burpee, Lawrence J. "A Plea for a Canadian National Library." *Canadian Historical Review* 1, no. 2 (1920): 191–194.

Byrne, Alex. Foreword to *85 Years IFLA: A History and Chronology of Sessions 1927–2012*, by Jeffrey M. Wilhite. Edited by Louis Takács and Ingeborg Verheul. Berlin: De Gruyter Saur, 2012. PDF e-book. Accessed 31 January 2013. http://lib.myilibrary.com?id=394131.

Byrum, John D. "The Birth and Re-birth of the ISBDs: Process and Procedures for Creating and Revising the International Standard Bibliographic Descriptions." *IFLA Journal* 27, no. 1 (2001): 34–37. doi: 10.1177/034003520102700107.

Cabral, Louis. "IFLA Comes Back to Canada." *Feliciter* 51, no. 6 (2005): 284–285.

Campbell, Henry C. "CLA Conference Highlights." *Feliciter* 19, no. 5 (1973): 5.

———. "IFLA: Library Universality in a Divided World." *IFLA Journal* 28, no. 3 (2002): 118–135. doi: 10.1177/034003520202800304.

———. "International Association of Metropolitan City Libraries (INTAMEL)," April 1973. Harry Campbell Papers. Archives, Toronto Public Library, Toronto, ON.

———. Letter to Anthony Thompson, 6 May 1963. Archives, IFLA Headquarters, The Hague, Netherlands.

———. Letter to Edwin Castagna, Dr. F. Andrae, C.W. Black, and Guy Baudin, 26 June 1972. Harry Campbell Papers. Archives, Toronto Public Library, Toronto, ON.

———. Letter to Louis Cabral, 13 January 2006. ASTED Headquarters, Montreal, QC.

Canadian Library Association. Archives. Canadian Library Association Headquarters, Ottawa, ON.

——— "Canadian Delegation to IFLA Moscow 1970." Archives, Canadian Library Association Headquarters, Ottawa, ON.

———."Canadian Library Association Past Presidents." Last modified 2011. Accessed 2 May 2013. http://www.cla.ca/Content/NavigationMenu/AboutCLA/History/PastPresidents/default.htm.

———. "CLA Delegates to IFLA," 2 August 1972. Archives, Canadian Library Association Headquarters, Ottawa, ON.

———. "CLA Delegates to IFLA – Liverpool, England, 1971," 26 August 1971. Archives, Canadian Library Association Headquarters, Ottawa, ON.

———. CLA Records. Canadian Library Association Headquarters, Ottawa, ON.

———. "Delegates/Observers to IFLA Conference '73." ca. August 1973. Archives, Canadian Library Association fonds. Library and Archives Canada, Ottawa, ON.

———. "Feliciter." Accessed 15 January 2013. http://www.cla.ca/AM/Template.cfm?Section=Feliciter1.

———. "History." 2011. Accessed 18 August 2012. http://www.cla.ca/AM/Template.cfm?Section=History&Template=/CM/HTMLDisplay.cfm&ContentID=9948.

———. "Home." 2012. Accessed 19 August 2012. http://www.cla.ca//AM/Template.cfm?Section=Home.

———. "IFLA 1975." Archives, Canadian Library Association Headquarters, Ottawa, ON.

———. "IFLA 2010 - List of Participants as at 8th July 2010." Archives, Canadian Library Association Headquarters, Ottawa, ON.

———. "IFLA 2011 List of Participants as at 3/06/2011." Archives, Canadian Library Association Headquarters, Ottawa, ON.

———. "IFLA Conference '73 – Conferees Attending but Not Canadian Library Association Delegates or Observers." ca. August 1973. Canadian Library Association fonds. Library and Archives Canada, Ottawa, ON.

———. "IFLA Conference '73 – Sections and Committees." 21 August 1973. Canadian Library Association fonds. Library and Archives Canada, Ottawa, ON.

———. "IFLA, International Federation of Library Associations & Institutions, Canadian Committee Members," 11 April 1978. Archives, Canadian Library Association Headquarters, Ottawa, ON.

———. Report to IFLA – 1967/68." In *Proceedings of the General Council, 34th Session, Frankfurt, 1968, August 18–24*, edited by S. Randall and A. Thompson, 250–251. The Hague: Martinus Nijhoff, 1969.

———. "World Library and Information Congress List of Participants as at 22nd July 2009." Archives, Canadian Library Association Headquarters, Ottawa, ON.

Canadian Library Association Executive Council. *Proposed CLA Future Plan Draft 2.* December 2010. Accessed 25 May 2013. http://www.cla.ca/Content/NavigationMenu/AboutCLA/Governance/AnnualGeneralMeetings/AGM2011/CLA_Future_Plan_final_dec10.pdf.

Cardinal, Louis. "In Memoriam: Hugo L. P. Stibbe, 1934–2003." 26 June 2003. Accessed 8 February 2013. http://www.wien2004.ica.org/en/node/595.

Chartrand, Georges-Aimé. "From ACBLF to Asted." *Feliciter* 20, no. 7 (1974): 12–13.

———. Letter to Preben Kierkegaard, 21 December 1978. Archives, IFLA Headquarters, The Hague, Netherlands.

Clayton, Trevor. "Answering a Nation's Call: A Brief History as the National Library Celebrates 50 Years." *Feliciter* 49, no. 3 (2003): 126–129

Clement, Hope E.A. "An International MARC Network." *IFLA Journal* 8, no. 3 (1982): 257–264. doi: 10.1177/034003528200800306

———. "International MARC Programme (IMP)." *IFLA Journal* 12, no. 4 (1986): 296–297. doi: 10.1177/034003528601200409.

———. "Planning IFLA's Professional Programmes: Background." *IFLA Journal* 19, no. 3 (1993): 327–332. doi: 10.1177/034003529301900312.

Cleveland, Gary. "IFLANET mirror site is now available in the Asia Pacific Region." E-mail message to IFLA-L listserv, 23 August 1999. Accessed 26 February 2013. http://infoserv.inist.fr/wwsympa.fcgi/arc/ifla-l/1999-08/msg00035.html.

———. "New IFLANET address - www.ifla.org." E-mail message to IFLA-L listserv, 17 June 1998. Accessed 23 April 2013. http://infoserv.inist.fr/wwsympa.fcgi/arc/ifla-l/1998-06/msg00014.html.

Cloutier, Guy. Letter to Erik J. Spicer, 6 November 1979. Canadian Library Association fonds, Library and Archives Canada, Ottawa, ON.

Clubb, Barbara. "Globally Speaking." *Feliciter* 51, no. 5 (2005): 201–202.

CNIB. "About Us." Accessed 19 August 2012. http://www.cnib.ca/en/about/Pages/default.aspx.

———. "CNIB - Canadian National Institute for the Blind Changes Name to CNIB." 14 January 2010. Accessed 6 June 2013. http://www.cnib.ca/en/news/archive/pages/cnib.aspx.

———. "CNIB Founders." Accessed 6 June 2013. http://www.cnib.ca/en/about/who/history/founders/Pages/default.aspx.

———. "Historic Timeline." 2012. Accessed 25 August 2012. http://www.cnib.ca/en/about/who/history/timeline/Pages/default.aspx.

———. "How We Are Structured." 2012. Accessed 25 August 2012 http://www.cnib.ca/en/about/who/structure/Pages/default.aspx.

CODE. "CODE Remembers Co-Founder Henry Campbell." Last modified 20 November 2009. Accessed 10 December 2012. http://www.codecan.org/media-room/press-releases-code-news/code-remembers-co-founder-henry-campbell.

Conference of Directors of National Libraries. "Home." Accessed 8 February 2013. http://cdnl.info/.

———. "Past Executives." Last modified 2011. Accessed 2 May 2013. http://cdnl.info/index.php?option=com_content&view=article&id=82&Itemid=55.

Coops, W.E.S. "The Main Meetings of the 48th IFLA Conference." *IFLA Journal* 8, no. 4 (1982): 398–402. doi: 10.1177/034003528200800408.

Davis Jr., Donald G. "With Malice toward None: IFLA and the Cold War." *IFLA Journal* 26, no. 1 (2000): 13–20. Accessed 9 December 2012. http://www.ifla.org/files/assets/hq/history/malice-davis.pdf.

de Costa, Serpil. "Foundation and Development of IFLA, 1926–1939." *The Library Quarterly* 52, no. 1 (1982): 41–58. Accessed 13 December 2012. http://www.jstor.org/stable/4307433.

de Ronde, Paula. "In Memoriam: Henry Cummings Campbell." *Access* 16, no. 1 (Winter 2010). Accessed 5 June 2013. http://www.accessola.com/accessonline/onlineonly/archives/winter2010/Memoriam.php.

de Vries, Johanna L. "The History of the International Federation of Library Associations: From Its Creation to the Second World War: 1927–1940." Master's thesis, Loughborough University of Technology, 1976.

Delsey, Tom. Introduction. In *Guidelines for the Application of the ISBDs to the Description of Component Parts.* London: IFLA UBCIM Programme, 1988. Accessed 22 March 2013. http://www.ifla.org/files/assets/cataloguing/isbd/component-parts.pdf.

Denis, Laurent-G., ed. "Libraries and Librarianship in Canada." *IFLA Journal* 8, no. 1 (1982): 11–41. doi: 10.1177/034003528200800107.

Donnelly, Francis Dolores. *The National Library of Canada: A Historical Analysis of the Forces which Contributed to Its Establishment and to the Identification of Its Role and Responsibilities*. Ottawa: Canadian Library Association, 1973.

Duncan, Donna. "Section on Classification and Indexing Review of Activities, 1993–1994." *60th IFLA General Conference - Conference Proceedings - August 21–27, 1994.* Accessed 28 February 2013. http://archive.ifla.org/IV/ifla60/60-dund.htm.

———. "Section on Classification and Indexing Review of Activities, 1995–1996." *62nd IFLA General Conference - Conference Proceedings - August 25–31, 1996.* Accessed 28 February 2013. http://archive.ifla.org/IV/ifla62/ 62-dund.htm.

Durance, Cynthia J. "Exploiting Technology to Build a Canadian Library and Information Network." *IFLA Journal* 11, no. 4 (1985): 299–312. doi: 10.1177/034003528501100407.

Durance, Cynthia J., and Neil McLean. "Libraries and Access to Information in an Open Systems Environment." *IFLA Journal* 14, no. 2 (1988): 137–148. doi: 10.1177/034003528801400206.

Evans, Gwynneth. "Homage to Alice Jean Elizabeth Lunn, 1910–1998." *National Library News* 30, no. 7–8 (1998): 13–14. Accessed 5 January 2013. http://epe.lac-bac.gc.ca/100/202/301/nlnews/nlnews-pdf/1998/3007-e.pdf.

———. "IFLA: Just Another Acronym or a Dynamic Network and Community?" *Feliciter* 51, no. 5 (2005): 235–237.

———. "Report on the Development of the School Library Manifesto and the IFLA Workshop, 17 August 1998." *IFLA Journal* 25, no. 1 (1999): 56–57. doi: 10.1177/034003529902500114.

———, and Réjean Savard. "Canadian Libraries on the Agenda: Their Accomplishments and Directions." *IFLA Journal* 34, no. 2 (2008): 127–159. doi: 10.1177/0340035208092173.

Ex-Libris Association. "Alice Jean Elizabeth Lunn." Last modified 20 October 2011. Accessed 5 January 2013. http://exlibris.pbworks.com/w/page/36147267/Alice%20Elizabeth%20 Jean%20Lunn.

———. "Cynthia Jean Durance." Last modified 19 September 2010. Accessed 16 April 2013. http://exlibris.pbworks.com/w/page/30052634/Cynthia%20Jean%20 Durance.

———. "Harry Campbell." Last modified 7 June 2011. Accessed 15 January 2013. http://exlibris.pbworks.com/w/page/36143425/Harry%20Campbell.

———. "Librarians in the News." *Ex Libris News* 16 (1994): 4–9. Accessed 26 February 2013. http://exlibris.ischool.utoronto.ca/PDF/elan_Issue_16_fall_1994.pdf.

Freeze, Barbara. "The Impact of the Integrated Digital Library System on the CNIB Library." *The Free Library* (22 March 2007). Accessed 14 March 2013. http://www.thefreelibrary.com/The impact of the Integrated Digital Library System on the CNIB...-a0165309864.

Galler, Anne M. "Indigenous Publishing, 1981–1992: An IFLA Pilot Project." *IFLA Journal* 20, no. 4 (1994): 419–427. doi: 10.1177/034003529402000405.

———. "International Librarianship and Its Impact on the Profession." *Education Libraries* 20, no. 1–2 (1996): 5–9. Accessed 30 March 2013. http://units.sla.org/division/ded/educationlibraries/20-1-2.pdf.

———. "National School Library Policies: An International Survey." *IFLA Journal* 22, no. 4 (1996): 292–298. doi: 10.1177/034003529602200410.

Gendron, Céline. "World Library and Information Congress: 74th IFLA General Conference and Council." *Feliciter* 54, no. 3 (2008): 132.

Gifford, Hilda. "Canadian Participation in the International Federation of Library Associations." 15 January 1975. Canadian Library Association fonds, Library and Archives Canada, Ottawa, ON.

———. "IFLA General Council Meeting." *Feliciter* 21, no. 11–12 (November-December 1975): 23–24

———. "IFLA, The International Federation of Library Associations." 4 February 1976. Canadian Library Association fonds. Library and Archives Canada, Ottawa, ON.

———. Letter to Canadian members of IFLA, 9 May 1979. Canadian Library Association fonds, Library and Archives Canada, Ottawa, ON.

———. Letter to Paul Kitchen, 8 May 1979. Canadian Library Association fonds, Library and Archives Canada, Ottawa, ON.

Gobeil, Lucie, Bibliothèques publiques du Québec, et Réseau BIBLIO du Québec. *Bibliothèque d'aujourd'hui: lignes directrices pour les bibliothèques publiques du Québec.* Montréal: Éditions ASTED, 2011.

Government of Canada. Parliament of Canada Act, R.S.C., c. P-1 (1985). Accessed 14 April 2013. http://laws-lois.justice.gc.ca/eng/acts/P-1/.

Gupta, Dinesh K., Christie Koontz, and Daisy McAdam. "In Search of Marketing Excellence in Libraries: The IFLA International Marketing Award." *IFLA Journal* 36, no. 2 (2010): 176–183. doi: 10.1177/0340035210369882.

Hallsworth, Peter P. Letter to Bernard McNamee, 25 April 1973. Canadian Library Association fonds, Library and Archives Canada, Ottawa, ON.

Harrod, L.M. "The IFLA Conference, 1967." *Library Review* 21, no. 3 (1967): 121–125. doi: 10.1108/eb012475.

———."The IFLA Conference, 1967." *Library Review* 21, no. 4 (1967): 175–177. doi: 10.1108/eb012482.

Henry, Carol, ed. *IFLA Annual 1990: Proceedings of the 56th General Conference, Stockholm, 1990. Annual Reports.* Munich: K.G. Saur, 1991.

Henry, Carol, and Donald G. Davis, Jr. *IFLA 75th Anniversary.* Austin, Texas: Morgan Printing, 2002.

Herie, Euclid. *Journey to Independence: Blindness, the Canadian Story*. Toronto: The Dundurn Group, 2005.

Hewitt, Vivian D. "International Federation of Library Associations and Institutions." *Special Libraries* 68, no. 9 (1977): 363–364.

Hillmer, Norman. "Library of Parliament." With revisions by Jasmin H. Cheung-Gertler. *The Canadian Encylopedia*. Historica-Dominion, 2011. Accessed 6 June 2013. http://www.thecanadianencyclopedia.com/articles/library-of-parliament.

Hofmann, Gustav. Letter to Elizabeth H. Morton, 6 May 1959. Canadian Library Association fonds, Library and Archives Canada, Ottawa, ON.

Howard, Helen. "Honorary Degree Citation – Elizabeth Homer Morton – November 1970." Archives, Concordia University. Accessed 9 December 2012. http://archives.concordia.ca/morton.

Hutcheson, Amy M. Letter to Joachim Wieder, 27 May 1959. Archives. IFLA Headquarters, The Hague, Netherlands.

Rooney, Sieglinde. "IFLA Congress Report: Papers Lack Originality." *Feliciter* 27, no. 12 (1981): 9.

IFLA Executive Board. "Summary Record of the Meeting of the Executive Board Held on 29–30 November 1989 in The Hague, Netherlands." *IFLA Journal* 16, no. 1 (1990): 150–151. doi: 10.1177/034003529001600133.

———. "Summary Record of the Meetings of the Executive Board, Held in Montreal, Canada on 19 and 25 August 1982." *IFLA Journal* 8, no. 4 (1982): 413–415. doi: 10.1177/034003528200800410.

IFLA Express. "IFLA Express - World Library and Information Congress Québec, Canada, August 2008." IFLA. Accessed 20 March 2013. http://archive.ifla.org/IV/ifla74/IFLA-express2008-en.htm.

———. "Bibliomondialis" *IFLA Express* no.3 (2008): 6. Accessed 20 March 2013. http://archive.ifla.org/IV/ifla74/xpress2-en-2008.pdf.

IFLA Headquarters, ed. *IFLA Annual Report 2007*. The Hague: IFLA Headquarters, 2009. Accessed 14 February 2013. http://www.ifla.org/files/assets/hq/annual-reports/2007.pdf.

IFLA Headquarters, ed. *IFLA Annual Report 2008*. The Hague: IFLA Headquarters, 2009. Accessed 14 February 2013. http://www.ifla.org/files/assets/hq/annual-reports/2009.pdf.

IFLA Headquarters, ed. *IFLA Annual Report 2009*. The Hague: IFLA Headquarters, 2010. Accessed 14 February 2013. http://www.ifla.org/files/assets/hq/annual-reports/2010.pdf.

IFLA Headquarters, ed. *IFLA Annual Report 2011*. The Hague: IFLA Headquarters, 2012. Accessed 14 February 2013. http://www.ifla.org/files/assets/hq/annual-reports/2011.pdf.

IFLA Headquarters Staff, comp. and ed. *IFLA Directory 2005–2007*. The Hague, Netherlands: International Federation of Library Associations and Institutions, 2006.

IFLA Headquarters Staff, comp. and ed. *IFLA Directory 2007–2009.* The Hague, Netherlands: International Federation of Library Associations and Institutions, 2007. Accessed 20 June 2013. http://www.ifla.org/files/assets/hq/membership/ifla-directory-2007-2009.pdf.

IFLA Headquarters Staff, comp. and ed. *IFLA Directory 2009–2011*. The Hague, Netherlands: International Federation of Library Associations and Institutions, 2010. Accessed 20 June 2013. http://www.ifla.org/files/assets/hq/membership/ifla-directory-2009-2011.pdf.

IFLA International Office for UBC. "The International Cataloguing-in-Publication Meeting, Ottawa, 16–19 August 1982, with Recommendations." *IFLA Journal* 8, no. 4 (1982): 419–420. doi: 10.1177/034003528200800413.

IFLA Libraries Serving Persons with Print Disabilities Section. "Libraries for the Blind in the Information Age - Guidelines for Development." Accessed 13 April 2013. http://www.ifla.org/publications/ifla-professional-reports-86.

———. *Manifesto for Libraries Serving Persons with a Print Disability: Final Draft*. Last modified 5 October 2012. Accessed 13 April 2013. http://www.ifla.org/publications/manifesto-for-libraries-serving-persons-with-a-print-disability-final-draft.

IFLA Meetings of Experts on an International Cataloguing Code (IME-ICC). *Statement of International Cataloguing Principles*. 10 April 2008 version. Accessed 19 April 2013. http://archive.ifla.org/VII/s13/icc/imeicc-statement_of_principles-2008.pdf.

IFLA Professional Board. "Summary Record of the Meeting of the Professional Board, in The Hague, Netherlands on 11–12 April 1988." *IFLA Journal* 14, no. 3 (1988): 273–274. doi: 10.1177/034003528801400315.

———. "Summary Report of the Meeting of the Professional Board Held in The Hague on 4–5 December 1995." *IFLA Journal* 22, no. 1 (1996): 56–57. doi: 10.1177/034003529602200111.

IFLA Secretariat. "From the Secretariat." *IFLA Journal* 3, no. 2 (1977): 133–158. doi: 10.1177/034003527700300207.

———. "From the Secretariat." *IFLA Journal* 23, no. 2 (1997): 145–148. doi: 10.1177/034003529702300213.

———. "From the Secretariat." *IFLA Journal* 27, no. 1 (2001): 41–45. doi: 10.1177/034003520102700109.

———. "From the Secretariat." *IFLA Journal* 33, no. 3 (2007): 276–277. doi: 10.1177/03400352070330030902.

———. "IFLA Annual Report 1988." *IFLA Journal* 15, no. 2 (1989): 139–155. doi: 10.1177/034003528901500211.

———. "IFLA Annual Report 1999." *IFLA Journal* 26, no. 3 (2000): 215–220. doi: 10.1177/034003520002600310.

———. "Istanbul 1995 – An Overview." *IFLA Journal* 21, no. 4 (1995): 303–313. doi: 10.1177/034003529502100413.

———. "Montreal – 1982." *IFLA Journal* 8, no. 4 (1982): 397–398. doi: 10.1177/034003528200800407.

———. "News Section." *IFLA Journal* 4, no. 1 (1978): 47–76. doi: 10.1177/034003527800400109.

———. "News Section." *IFLA Journal* 4, no. 3 (1978): 279–319. doi: 10.1177/034003527800400317.

———. "Professional Resolutions of the 48th IFLA General Conference." *IFLA Journal* 8, no. 4 (1982): 403–412. doi: 10.1177/034003528200800409.

———. "Summary Report of Meetings of the Professional and Executive Boards, 29 November – 3 December 1999." *IFLA Journal* 26, no. 1 (2000): 57–58. doi: 10.1177/034003520002600109.

IFLA Section of School Libraries and Resource Centers. "Annual Report 1998–1999." IFLANET archive. Accessed 22 March 2013. http://archive.ifla.org/VII/s11/annual/ann99.htm.

IFLA Strategic Plan Committee. "IFLA: Strat. Plan Mar 31, 2010 Mexico - April 2011." Office of Ingrid Parent, University of British Columbia Library. Vancouver, BC. Accessed 14 February 2013.

IFLA Study Group on the Functional Requirements for Bibliographic Records. *Functional Requirements for Bibliographic Records: Final Report*. Munich: K.G. Saur, 1998. Accessed 19 April 2013. http://www.ifla.org/files/assets/cataloguing/frbr/frbr.pdf.

"IFLA: What They Were Saying in Montreal." *Feliciter* 28, no. 10 (1982): 3; 8.

IFLA World Library and Information Congress. "Satellite meetings." World Library and Information Congress. Accessed 20 March 2013. http://conference.ifla.org/past/ifla78/satellite-meetings.htm.

"In Memoriam: Henry C. ("Harry") Campbell (1919–2009)." *Feliciter 55*, no. 5 (2009): 188.

International Federation of Library Associations. *Actes du Comité International des Bibliothèques*. Uppsala, Sweden: Almquist and Wiksells Boktryckeri, 1930.

———. *Actes du Comité International des Bibliothèques*. Uppsala, Sweden: Almquist and Wiksells Boktryckeri, 1931.

———. *Actes du Comité International des Bibliothèques*. The Hague, Netherlands: Martinus Nijhoff, 1932.

———. *Actes du Comité International des Bibliothèques*. The Hague, Netherlands: Martinus Nijhoff, 1947.

———. *Actes du Comité International des Bibliothèques*. The Hague, Netherlands: Martinus Nijhoff, 1951.

———. *Répertoire des Associations de Bibliothécaires Membres de la Fédération Internationale*. Geneva, Switzerland: Albert Kundig, 1931.

———. *Répertoire des Associations de Bibliothécaires Membres de la Fédération Internationale*. The Hague, Netherlands: Martinus Nijhoff, 1938.

———. *Répertoire des Associations de Bibliothécaires Membres de la Fédération Internationale*. The Hague, Netherlands: Martinus Nijhoff, 1948.

———. *Répertoire des Associations de Bibliothécaires Membres de la Fédération Internationale*. The Hague, Netherlands: Martinus Nijhoff, 1955.

———. *Répertoire des Associations de Bibliothécaires Membres de la Fédération Internationale*. The Hague, Netherlands: Martinus Nijhoff, 1961.

———. *Répertoire des Associations de Bibliothécaires Membres de la Fédération Internationale*. The Hague, Netherlands: Martinus Nijhoff, 1963.

———. *Repertoire of the Associations of Librarians Members of the International Federation*. The Hague, Netherlands: Martinus Nijhoff, 1948.

International Federation of Libraries Associations and Institutions. "The 48th General Conference: Montreal – 1982." *IFLA Journal* 8, no. 2 (1982): 198–205. doi: 10.1177/034003528200800213.

———. "63rd IFLA Council and General Conference Copenhagen." *IFLA Journal* 23, no. 5–6 (1997): 383–392. doi: 10.1177/034003529702300510.

———. "65th IFLA Council and General Conference Bangkok." *IFLA Journal* 25, no. 5–6 (1999): 283–304. doi: 10.1177/034003529902500506.

———. "The Association of Parliamentary Libraries in Canada / L'Association des bibliothèques parlementaires au Canada (APLIC/ABPAC)." Last modified 16 November 2012. Accessed 3 May 2013. http://www.ifla.org/node/6443.

———. "Committees of the 74th World Library and Information Congress" *Final Announcement: World Library and Information Congress: 74th IFLA General Conference and Council – 10–14 August 2008.* International Federation of Library Associations and Institutions: 7.

———. "From IFLA Headquarters." *IFLA Journal* 33, no. 4 (2007): 375–378. doi: 10.1177/03400352070330041402.

———. "From Other Organizations." *IFLA Journal* 27, no. 1 (2001): 53–54. doi: 10.1177/034003520102700115.

———. "From the Core Programmes." *IFLA Journal* 28, no. 5–6 (2002): 348–349. doi: 10.1177/034003520202800530.

———. "From the Divisions, Sections and Round Tables." *IFLA Journal* 8, no. 4 (1982): 432–434. doi: 10.1177/034003528200800415.

———. "From the Divisions, Sections and Round Tables." *IFLA Journal* 19, no. 4 (1993): 457–463. doi: 10.1177/034003529301900416.

———. "From the Divisions, Sections and Round Tables." *IFLA Journal* 21, no. 4 (1995): 313–318. doi: 10.1177/034003529502100414.

———. "From the Divisions, Sections and Round Tables." *IFLA Journal* 23, no. 1 (1997): 70–71. doi: 10.1177/034003529702300115.

———."From the Divisions, Section and Round Tables." *IFLA Journal* 23, no. 5–6 (1997): 402–408. doi: 10.1177/034003529702300513.

———. "From the Divisions, Sections and Round Tables." *IFLA Journal* 25, no.2 (1999): 115–119. doi: 10.1177/034003529902500211.

———. "From the Divisions, Sections and Round Tables." *IFLA Journal* 25, no. 5–6 (1999): 306–318. doi: 10.1177/034003529902500507.

———. "From the Divisions and Sections." *IFLA Journal* 33, no. 3 (2007): 277–278. doi: 10.1177/03400352070330030903.

———. "From the IFLA Core Programmes." *IFLA Journal* 15, no. 2 (1989): 156–166. doi: 10.1177/034003528901500212.

———. "Guidelines for Library Service to Braille Users." Accessed 13 April 2013. http://www.ifla.org/publications/guidelines-for-library-service-to-braille-users.

———. *Guidelines for the Applications of the ISBDs to the Description of Component Parts.* London: IFLA UBCIM Programme, 1988. Accessed 14 March 2013. http://www.ifla.org/files/assets/cataloguing/isbd/component-parts.pdf.

———. "IFLA 69 – 2003: Minutes." IFLANET. Accessed 15 November 2012. http://ifla.queenslibrary.org/IV/ifla69/minutes.htm.

———. "IFLA 70 – 2004: Minutes." IFLANET. Accessed 15 November 2012. http://ifla.queenslibrary.org/IV/ifla70/Minutes-08-2004.pdf.

———. "IFLA and its Officials" *Final Announcement: World Library and Information Congress: 74th IFLA General Conference and Council – 10–14 August 2008.* International Federation of Library Associations and Institutions: 11.

———. "IFLA Policies and Programmes." *IFLA Journal* 29, no. 3 (2003): 245–267. doi: 10.1177/034003520302900309.

———. "IFLA Presidential Meeting 2011, 14–15 April, List of Participants." *International Federation of Library Associations and Institutions.* Accessed 21 June 2013. http://www.ifla.org/files/assets/hq/news/documents/participants.pdf.

———. "IFLA Publications" (advertisement). *Feliciter* 28, no. 2 (1982): 7.

———. "Indigenous Knowledges: Local Priorities, Global Contexts. Programme. Vancouver, British Columbia." Accessed 4 June 2013. http://iflaindigenous knowledges2012.ok.ubc.ca/IFLA_Program_Guide_FINAL.pdf.

———. "International Federation of Library Associations and Institutions (IFLA) Document nr GB 12–12–2.4.3." Office of Ingrid Parent, University of British Columbia Library. Vancouver, BC. Accessed 14 February 2013.

———. "Metropolitan Libraries Section." Last modified September 21, 2012. Accessed 8 February 2013. http://www.ifla.org/metropolitan-libraries.

———. "News." *IFLA Journal* 31, no. 3 (2005): 271–284. doi: 10.1177/0340035205059436.

———. "News." *IFLA Journal* 32, no. 3 (2006): 251–260. doi: 10.1177/0340035206070210.

———. "News." *IFLA Journal* 33, no. 1 (2007): 59–69. doi: 10.1177/0340035207076412.

———. "News." *IFLA Journal* 35, no. 3 (2009): 274–282. doi: 10.1177/0340035209346218.

———. "News." *IFLA Journal* 36, no. 2 (2010): 187–193. doi: 10.1177/0340035210370105.

———. "News." *IFLA Journal* 37, no. 2 (2011): 168–177. doi: 10.1177/0340035211409852.

———. "News Section." *IFLA Journal* 4, no. 1 (1978): 47–76. doi: 10.1177/034003527800400109.

———. "News Section." *IFLA Journal* 26, no. 1 (2000): 57–83. doi: 10.1177/034003520002600109.

———. "News Section." *IFLA Journal* 27, no. 3 (2001): 177–198. doi: 10.1177/034003520102700311.

———. "News Section." *IFLA Journal* 27, no. 5–6 (2001): 339–370. doi: 10.1177/034003520102700510.

———. "News Section." *IFLA Journal* 28, no. 2 (2002): 81–95. doi: 10.1177/034003520202800212.

———. "Officers of IFLA 2007–2009." *IFLA Journal* 33, no. 4 (2007): 378–383. doi: 10.1177/03400352070330041403.

———. "Other Events in Glasgow." *IFLA Journal* 28, no. 5–6 (2002): 339–342. doi: 10.1177/034003520202800525.

———. "Past IFLA Conferences and IFLA Presidents." Last modified 18 October 2012. Accessed 15 January 2013. http://conference.ifla.org/past-ifla-conferences-and-ifla-presidents.

————. "Past IFLA Presidents." Last modified 16 May 2013. Accessed 4 June 2013. http://www.ifla.org/history/past-ifla-presidents.

————. "Past IFLA Secretaries General." Last modified 5 October 2012. Accessed 15 December 2012. http://www.ifla.org/history/past-ifla-secretaries-general.

————. "Publications of International Relevance." *IFLA Journal* 17, no. 4 (1991): 448–450. doi: 10.1177/034003529101700418.

————. "Publications of International Relevance." *IFLA Journal* 26, no. 4 (2000): 322–326. doi: 10.1177/034003520002600419.

————. "Reports of Meetings." *IFLA Journal* 13, no. 1 (1987): 70–77. doi: 10.1177/034003528701300117.

————. "Reports of Meetings: Copyright and Library Materials for the Handicapped. *IFLA Journal* 8, no. 4 (1982): 435–438. doi: 10.1177/034003528200800416.

————. "Satellite Meetings Related to the IFLA World Library and Information Congress August 2008, Québec, Canada." Internet Archive. Accessed 20 March 2013. http://web.archive.org/web/20080208070608/http://www.ifla.org/IV/ifla74/satellite-en.htm.

————. "School Library Manifesto Ratified by UNESCO." 26 November 1999. Reprinted in *National Library News* 32, no. 1–2 (2000): 6. Accessed 26 April 2013. http://epe.lac-bac.gc.ca/100/202/301/nlnews/nlnews-pdf/2000/3201-e.pdf.

————. "Standing Committee Members of the Reference and Information Services Section." Last modified 20 May 2013. Accessed 6 June 2013. http://www.ifla.org/reference-and-information-services/standing-committee.

International Library and Bibliographical Committee. "International Library Co-Operation." 30 September 1927. Uppsala: Almqvist & Wiksells Boktryckeri-A.-B., 1928. Accessed May 8, 2013. http://www.ifla.org/files/assets/hq/history/1927-resolution.pdf.

Jean, Michaëlle. "World Library and Information Congress, Québec, 2008: Opening Address by the Governor General of Canada." *IFLA Journal* 34, no. 4 (2008): 330–332. doi: 10.1177/0340035208099263.

"Jean-Guy Sylvestre," *Ottawa Citizen*, 29 September 2010. Accessed 18 June 2013. http://www.legacy.com/obituaries/ottawacitizen/obituary.aspx?page=lifestory&pid=145715759#fbLoggedOut.

Joint Steering Committee for Development of RDA. "Tom Delsey Appointed as AACR3 Editor." 17 September 2004. Last modified 1 July 2009. Accessed 19 April 2013. http://www.rda-jsc.org/aacr3editor.html.

Kirkwood, Francis T. "Ethnic Services Seminar Focuses on Minority Problems." *Feliciter* 37, no. 10 (1991): 5–7.

————. "An IFLA in the Sun – Poverty and Pride Greet the World's Librarians." *Feliciter* 41, no. 1 (1995): 24–25.

————. "IFLA Moscow 1991: A Conference Like None Other." *Feliciter* 37, no. 10 (1991): 3–4.

Kitchen, Paul. Letter to Dean Halliwell, 4 July 1979. Canadian Library Association fonds, Library and Archives Canada, Ottawa, ON.

———. Letter to the Association of Canadian Map Libraries and the Association of Parliamentary Librarians in Canada, 10 April 1979. Canadian Library Association fonds, Library and Archives Canada, Ottawa, ON.

Kniffel, Leonard. "Caught in a Coup D'Etat, Librarians Witness History at IFLA in Moscow." *American Libraries* 22, no. 9 (1991): 846–917.

Koopman, Sjoerd, ed. *IFLA Annual Report 2000*. The Hague: IFLA Headquarters, 2003.

Koops, Wilhelm R. H., and Carol Henry, eds. *IFLA Annual 1984: Proceedings of the 50th General Conference, Nairobi, 1984. Annual Reports.* Munich: K.G. Saur, 1984.

Koops, Wilhelm R. H., and W.E.S. (Milisa) Coops, eds. *IFLA Annual 1982: Proceedings of the 48th General Conference, Montreal, 1982. Annual Reports.* Munich: K.G. Saur, 1983.

Koops, Wilhelm R. H., and W.E.S. (Milisa) Coops, eds. *IFLA Annual 1983: Proceedings of the 49th Council Meeting, Munich, 1983. Annual Reports.* Munich: K.G. Saur, 1984.

Koops, Wilhelm R. H., and W.E.S. (Milisa) Coops, eds. *IFLA Annual 1986: Proceedings of the 52nd General Conference, Tokyo, 1986. Annual Reports.* Munich: K.G. Saur, 1986.

Koops, Wilhelm R. H., Peter Harvard-Williams, and W.E.S. Coops, eds. *IFLA Annual 1974: Proceedings of the 40th General Council Meeting, Washington, 1974. Annual Reports*. Munich: Saur K.G., 1975.

Koops, Wilhelm R. H., ed. *IFLA Annual 1975: Proceedings of the 41st General Council Meeting, Oslo, 1975. Annual Reports.* Munich: Saur K.G., 1976.

Kum, Ilhan. "Abstracts of Papers to be Presented at the IFLA Conference in Leipzig, 17–22 August 1981." *IFLA Journal* 7, no. 2 (1981): 113–132. doi: 10.1177/034003528100700206.

Kuny, Terry. "1996 UDT Core Programme/Section on Information Technology Workshops." E-mail message to IFLA-L listserv, 28 April 1997. Accessed 25 January 2013. http://infoserv.inist.fr/wwsympa.fcgi/arc/ifla-l/ 1997-04/msg00068.html.

———. "Curriculum Vitae." *Terribly Cuneiform* (personal website), 2012. Accessed 25 January 2013. http://www.kuny.ca/resume/TerryKuny-CV.pdf.

———. "FYI: IFLANET Statistics (October 1995 – September 1996) and September Top Ten." E-mail message to IFLA-L listserv, 31 October 1996. Accessed 25 January 2013. http://infoserv.inist.fr/wwsympa.fcgi/arc/ifla-l/ 1996-10/msg00032.html.

———. "IFLA-L has moved." E-mail message to IFLA-L listserv, 17 August 1995. Accessed 25 January 2013. http://infoserv.inist.fr/wwsympa.fcgi/arc/ ifla-l/1995-08/msg00008.html.

———. "IFLANET Statistics – September 1995 (correction)." E-mail message to IFLA-L listserv, 2 October 1995. Accessed 25 January 2013. http://infoserv.inist.fr/wwsympa.fcgi/arc/ifla-l/1995-10/msg00001.html.

———. "IFLANET Statistics and Update (November, 1995)." E-mail message to IFLA-L listserv, 4 December 1995. Accessed 25 January 2013. http://infoserv.inist.fr/wwsympa.fcgi/arc/ifla-l/1995-12/msg00001.html.

———. "NEW LIST: LIBJOBS – Library and Information Science Jobs list." E-mail message to IFLA-L listserv, 18 August 1995. Accessed 25 January 2013. http://infoserv.inist.fr/wwsympa.fcgi/arc/ifla-l/1995-08/msg00013.html.

———. "WWW access to IFLANET mailing lists now available." E-mail message to IFLA-L listserv, 18 August 1995. Accessed 25 January 2013. http://infoserv.inist.fr/wwsympa.fcgi/arc/ifla-l/1995-08/msg00014.html.

Kuny, Terry, and Louise Lantaigne. "NOTE: IFLA Mailing Lists are Closed for the Holidays." E-mail message to IFLA-L listserv, 20 December 1995. Accessed 23 April 2013. http://infoserv.inist.fr/wwsympa.fcgi/arc/ifla-l/1995-12/msg00011.html.

Lantaigne, Louise. "Press Release: First mirror of IFLANET now launched." E-mail message to IFLA-L listserv, 25 February 1997. Accessed 23 April 2013. http://infoserv.inist.fr/wwsympa.fcgi/arc/ifla-l/1997-02/msg00027.html.

Larivière, J. *Guidelines for Legal Deposit Legislation*. UNESCO, Paris, 2000. Accessed 5 January 2013. http://unesdoc.unesco.org/images/0012/001214/121413eo.pdf.

Law, Margaret. "@ your library eh?" *Feliciter* 47, no. 5 (2001): 221–222.

Léveillé, Jean-Bernard. "Les bibliothécaires canadiens français et leurs trente-deux ans de vie en association (ACBI ACBLF-Asted)." In *Livre Bibliothèque et culture québécoise*. Mélanges offerts à Edmond Desrochers, edited by Georges Aimé Chartrand, 720. Montréal: Asted 1977.

Library and Archives Canada. "About Theses Canada." Last modified 24 October 2008. Accessed 8 October 2012.http://www.collectionscanada.gc.ca/thesescanada/027007-5000-e.html.

———. "Elizabeth Morton—Themes—Celebrating Women's Achievements." Last modified 16 September 2010. Accessed 9 December 2012. http://www.collectionscanada.gc.ca/women/030001-1357-e.html.

———. "Home." Last modified 31 October 2012. Accessed 6 June 2013. http://www.collectionscanada.gc.ca/index-e.html.

———. "Sylvestre, Guy, 1918- LMS-0110 – List of Fonds and Collections – Literary Archives." Last modified 12 March 2009. Accessed 20 December 2012. http://www.collectionscanada.gc.ca/archiveslitteraires/027011-200.130-e.html.

Liebaers, Haerman. "The Dutch Tea Party of IFLA in the Seventies – A Quick Flash Back of Forty-five Years before the Dutch Tea Party." 68th IFLA Council and General Conference, August 18–24, 2002, Plenary Session I, 1–22. Accessed 20 December 2012. http://archive.ifla.org/IV/ifla68/papers/104-101e.pdf.

Lor, Peter Johan. "The IFLA-UNESCO Partnership 1947–2012." *IFLA Journal* 38, no. 4 (2012): 269–282. doi: 10.1177/0340035212463138.

———. "Secretary General's Report to Council, 2008." *IFLA Journal* 34, no. 4 (2008): 363–368. doi: 10.1177/0340035208099272.

Lumley, Elizabeth. "Campbell, Henry Cummings." In *Canadian Who's Who. 2004, Volume XXXIX,* 216. Toronto: University of Toronto Press, 2004.

———. "Erik Spicer." In *Canadian Who's Who. 2007, Volume XLII*, 1241–42. Toronto: University of Toronto Press, 2007.

———. "Scott, Marianne Florence." In *Canadian Who's Who. 2007, Volume XLII*, 1177. Toronto: University of Toronto Press, 2007.

Lunn, Jean. "Canadiana 1867–1900: A Bibliography in Progress in the National Library of Canada." *Papers of the Bibliographic Society of Canada* 10 (1971): 54–66. Accessed 9 December 2012. http://www.library.utoronto.ca/bsc/papers/197110/197110.pdf.

Lux, Claudia. "The President's Page." *IFLA Journal* 34, no. 4 (2008): 325–325. doi: 10.1177/0340035208099261.

———. "World Library and Information Congress, Québec, 2008: Closing Address by the President of IFLA." *IFLA Journal* 34, no. 4 (2008): 347–348. doi: 10.1177/0340035208099269.

———. "World Library and Information Congress, Québec, 2008: Opening Address by the President of IFLA." *IFLA Journal* 34, no. 4 (2008): 333–336. doi: 10.1177/0340035208099264.

Manning, Ralph. "Cynthia Durance." In International Federation of Library Associations and Institutions, "News," *IFLA Journal* 31, no. 4 (2005): 377–389. doi: 10.1177/0340035205061401.

McCallum, Sally. "40 Years of Technology in Libraries: A Brief History of the IFLA Section on Information Technology, 1963/4–2003." July 2003. Accessed 22 March 2013. http://www.ifla.org/files/assets/information-technology/publications/40-years-of-its.pdf.

McCormick, Paul. "Dr. Guy Sylvestre—Prime Mover: Building Collections at the National Library of Canada." In "A Tribute to Guy Sylvestre and Jean-Pierre Wallot." Friends of Libraries and Archives Canada, 2–13. Accessed 20 December 2012. http://www.friendsoflibraryandarchivescanada.ca/docs/A%20Tribute%20to%20Guy%20Sylvestre%20and%20Jean-Pierre%20Wallot%20by%20Terry%20Cook.pdf.

———. "National Librarian Guy Sylvestre, 1918–2010." *Feliciter* 56, no.6 (2010): 237–38.

McGarry, Dorothy. "IFLA 1995: Libraries of the Future. International Federation of Library Associations and Institutions." *Special Libraries* (January 1996). Accessed 23 April 2013. *AccessMyLibrary*. http://www.accessmylibrary.com/article-1G1-18545116/ifla-1995-libraries-future.html.

McGill Association of University Teachers. "Featured Retiree: Miriam Tees." January 2010. Accessed 22 March 2013. http://retirees-maut.mcgill.ca/feature/Miriam-Tees.pdf.

Moore, Kelly. "Au Revoir from Kelly Moore." *IFLA Journal* 33, no. 1 (2007): 64.

———. "Become a Librarian – See the World!" *Feliciter* 56, no. 6 (2010): 230.

———. "Director's Chair: For the Times They Are A-changin'." *Feliciter* 58, no. 4 (2012): 8.

Morrisset, Auguste-M. Letter to A.C. Breycha-Vauthier, 16 August 1961. Archives, IFLA Headquarters, The Hague, Netherlands.

Morton, Elizabeth. Letter to T. P. Sevensma, 21 April 1947. Archives, IFLA Headquarters, The Hague, Netherlands.

———. Letter to T. P. Sevensma, 29 April 1952. Archives, IFLA Headquarters, The Hague, Netherlands.

———. Letter to T. P. Sevensma, 21 August 1950. Archives, IFLA Headquarters, The Hague, Netherlands.

———. Letter to T. P. Sevensma, 12 December 1950. Archives, IFLA Headquarters, The Hague, Netherlands.

———. Letter to T. P. Sevensma, 27 June 1950. Archives, IFLA Headquarters, The Hague, Netherlands.

———. Letter to T. P. Sevensma, 7 October 1958. Archives, IFLA Headquarters, The Hague, Netherlands.

———. Letter to Anthony Thompson, 17 March 1963. Archives, IFLA Headquarters, The Hague, Netherlands.

———. Letter to T. P. Sevensma, n.d. Archives, IFLA Headquarters, The Hague, Netherlands.

National Library of Canada. "Obituary." *National Library News* 32, no. 1–2 (2000): 6. Accessed 26 April 2013. http://epe.lac-bac.gc.ca/100/202/301/nlnews/ nlnews-pdf/2000/3201-e.pdf.

National Taiwan University Library. "Keynote 1: Libraries as a Force for Change in the Digital Age." ICADL 2012. Last modified 2012. Accessed 1 May 2013. http://www.icadl2012.org/KeynoteSpeakers.html.

Nauta, Paul. "From the IFLA Secretariat." *IFLA Journal* 17, no. 4 (1991): 401–23.

Nauta, Paul, ed. *IFLA Directory 1988–1989*. The Hague, Netherlands: K.G. Saur, 1989.

Nauta, Paul, ed. *IFLA Directory 1990–1991*. The Hague, Netherlands: K.G. Saur, 1990.

Nauta, Paul, ed. *IFLA Directory 1992–1993*. The Hague, Netherlands: K.G. Saur, 1992.

New Westminster Public Library. "Library History: Librarians: 1865 to the Present." Accessed 15 December 2012. http://www.nwpl.ca/local_history_site/ heritage_site/library_history.php#librarians.

New York Public Library. "John Mackenzie Cory Records, 1949–1963." Accessed 15 December 2012. http://www.nypl.org/archives/2194.

"News Notes." *Feliciter* 21, no. 7–8 (1975): 32.

"News Notes and Miscellany." *Feliciter* 19, no. 5 (1973): 10.

Nicholson, Jennefer. "Results of the Election of President-Elect 2009." International Federation of Library Associations and Institutions. Last modified June 2009. Accessed 22 December 2012. http://www.ifla.org/news/results-of- the-election-of-president-elect-2009.

OCLC Research. "OCLC Research Activities and IFLA's *Functional Requirements for Bibliographic Records*." Accessed 19 April 2013. http://www.oclc.org/ research/activities/frbr.html.

Oliver, Chris. *FRBR and RDA: Advances in Resource Description for Multiple Format Resources*. March 2009. Accessed 19 April 2013. http://www.collections canada.gc.ca/obj/005002/f2/005002-2200-e.pdf.

Parent, Ingrid. "Introduction." In *IFLA Annual Report 2011*, edited by IFLA Headquarters. The Hague: IFLA Headquarters, 2012. Accessed 14 February 2013. http://www.ifla.org/files/assets/hq/annual-reports/2011.pdf.

———. "Libraries – A Force for Change: Inspiring...Surprising...Empowering." *IFLA Journal* 38, no. 4 (2012): 322–328. doi: 10.1177/0340035212465068.

———. "Remarks, Speeches and Presentations, Ingrid Parent Nov 2011 - April 2012. World Intellectual Property Organization (WIPO) Standing Committee of Copyright and Related Rights, 23rd Meeting, Geneva, Switzerland, November 21–23, 2011," Office of Ingrid Parent, University of British Columbia Library. Vancouver, BC. Accessed 14 February 2013.

———. "Speaking Notes. Super Conference 2012 Ontario Library Association - February 1, 2012 - Toronto, Ontario. Remarks, Speeches and Presentations, Ingrid Parent Nov 2011 - April 2012," Office of Ingrid Parent, University of British Columbia Library. Vancouver, BC. Accessed 14 February 2013.

Parker, J. Stephen. "The Developing Countries and IFLA." In *IFLA's First Fifty Years: Achievement and Challenge in International Librarianship*, edited by Willem Roelf Henderikus Koops and Joachim Wieder, 145–149. Munich: Verlag Dokumentation, 1977. Accessed 8 February 2013. http://www.degruyter.com/view/books/9783111356655/9783111356655. 145/9783111356655.145.xml?format=EBOK.

Parliament of Canada. "Bill C-8: The Library and Archives of Canada Act." Accessed 13 April 2013. http://www.parl.gc.ca/About/Parliament/Legislative Summaries/bills_ls.asp?ls=C8&Parl=37&Ses=3.

———. "The Library of Parliament." Last modified December 2006. Accessed 6 June 2013. http://www.parl.gc.ca/About/Parliament/Publications/LOP/lop-e.asp.

———. "Officers and Officials of Parliament." Last modified 6 June 2008. Accessed 13 April 2013. http://www.parl.gc.ca/parlinfo/compilations/OfficersAnd Officials/OfficersAndOfficialsOfParliament_MoreInfo.aspx?Language=E.

Peel, Bruce. Letter to Hilda Gifford, 19 September 1978. Canadian Library Association fonds, Library and Archives Canada, Ottawa, ON.

Plötz, Klaus. "The History of IFLA as a Research Theme: Challenge and Commitment." *IFLA Journal* 13, no. 4 (1987): 349–354. doi: 10.1177/034003528701300407.

Randall, S. and A. Thomson, eds. *Proceedings of the General Council, 34th Session, Frankfurt, 1968, August 18–24*. The Hague, Martinus Nijhoff, 1969.

Ranganathan, S. R. *The Five Laws of Library Science.* Madras: Madras Library Association, 1931. PDF e-book. Accessed 3 January 2013. http://babel.hathitrust.org/cgi/pt?id=uc1.b99721;seq=13;view=1up.

———. "IFLA – What It Should Be and Do." *Libri* 5, no. 2 (1954): 182–89. Accessed 31 March 2013. http://www.ifla.org/files/assets/hq/history/ranganathan_1954_libri.pdf.

Riva, Pat. "Introducing the Functional Requirements for Bibliographic Records and Related IFLA Developments." *Bulletin of the American Society for Information Science & Technology* 33, no. 6 (2007): 7–11. Accessed 19 April 2013. http://www.asis.org/Bulletin/Aug-07/Riva.pdf.

Rugaas, Bendik. "Past, Present and Future Relations between the IFLA Section of National Libraries and the Conference of Directors of National Libraries," *IFLA Journal* 20, no. 2 (1994): 141–144. doi: 10.1177/034003529402000209.

Sauvé, Pauline. Letter to Margreet Wijnstroom, 9 July 1974. Canadian Library
    Association fonds, Library and Archives Canada, Ottawa, ON.

Scarry, Patricia. Letter to Beth Miller, 30 July 1985. Archives, Canadian Library
    Association Headquarters, Ottawa, ON.

Schaepman, Susan, ed. *IFLA Annual Report 2010*. The Hague: IFLA Headquarters,
    2011.

Schobert, Tim. "IFLA Focuses on Future." *Feliciter* 28, no. 10 (1982): 1–2.

Scott, Marianne. "Conference of Directors of National Libraries: Forum for
    Discussion and Action." *Alexandria* 7, no. 1 (1995): 37–46.

Sevensma, T. P. "Twenty-Fourth Session of the I.F.L.A. Council: Madrid 12–16
    October 1958." *Feliciter* 4, no. 5 (1959): 25–30.

Shimmon, Ross. "Report of the Secretary General." *IFLA Journal* 28, no. 5–6 (2002):
    337–338. doi: 10.1177/034003520202800523.

Shimmon, Ross, ed. *IFLA Directory 2000–2001*. The Hague, Netherlands: K.G Saur,
    2000.

Shimmon, Ross, ed. *IFLA Directory 2002–2003*. The Hague, Netherlands: K.G Saur,
    2002.

Spicer, Erik. "The International Federation of Library Associations." *Feliciter* 20, no. 7
    (1974): 16–18.

Spicer, Erik J. Letter to Guy Cloutier, 5 December 1979. Canadian Library Association
    fonds, Library and Archives Canada, Ottawa, ON.

———. Letter to Guy Sylvestre, 20 September 1979. Canadian Library Association
    fonds, Library and Archives Canada, Ottawa, ON.

———. "Update, Rehabilitate, Conserve: The Library of Parliament 1995–2006."
    ELAN no. 41 (Spring 2007): 1–3. Accessed 13 April 2013.
    http://exlibris.ischool.utoronto.ca/PDF/elan_Issue_41_spring_2007.pdf.

Stibbe, Hugo L.P. "Archival Descriptive Standards and the Archival Community: A
    Retrospective, 1996." *Archivaria* 41 (Spring 1996): 259–274. Accessed 14
    February 2013. http://journals.sfu.ca/archivar/index.php/archivaria/
    article/view/12143/13145.

———. "Cataloguing Cartographic Materials in Archives." *Cataloging & Classification
    Quarterly* 27, no. 3–4 (1999): 443–463. Accessed 8 February 2013. Taylor &
    Francis Online. http://dx.doi.org/10.1300/J104v27n03_13.

Stuart-Stubbs, Basil. "1900: As We Were." *Feliciter* 46, no. 3 (2000): 130–131.

———. "1927–30: The Muddle Years." *Feliciter* 46, no. 3 (2000): 148–149.

———. "1934–46: The Long Last Lap." *Feliciter* 50, no. 3 (2004): 112–115.

"Summary of Board and Council Action." *Feliciter* 19, no. 8 (1973): 7.

Swain, Leigh. "Annual Report 1991 of the UDT Core Programme by the Programme
    Director, Leigh Swain." *IFLA Journal* 18, no. 2 (1992): 165–168. doi:
    10.1177/034003529201800217.

———. "Annual Report 1992 of the UDT Core Programme by the Programme
    Director, Leigh Swain." *IFLA Journal* 19, no. 2 (1993): 235–238. doi:
    10.1177/034003529301900225.

———. "Annual Report 1996 of the IFLA UDT Programme by Leigh Swain,
    Programme Director." *IFLA Journal* 23, no. 3 (1997): 226–229. doi:
    10.1177/034003529702300310.

Swain, Leigh, and Gary Cleveland. "Overview of the Internet: Origin, Future, and Issues." *IFLA Journal* 20, no. 1 (1994): 16–28. doi: 10.1177/034003529402000107.

Swain, Leigh, Gary Cleveland, and Louise Lantaigne. "Annual Report 1999 of the IFLA UDT Core Programme by Leigh Swain, Director; Gary Cleveland, Programme Officer; and Louise Lantaigne, Administrative Officer." *IFLA Journal* 26, no. 3 (2000): 228–229. doi: 10.1177/034003520002600310.

Sylvestre, Guy. "Foreword." In *The National Library of Canada: A Historical Analysis of the Forces which Contributed to Its Establishment and to the Identification of Its Role and Responsibilities,* by Francis Dolores Donnelly. Ottawa: Canadian Library Association, 1973.

Tees, Miriam. "Teaching Management to Information Professionals: A Practical Approach – Guidelines for Instructors." *IFLA Journal* 19, no. 3 (1993): 292–300. doi: 10.1177/034003529301900309.

Thompson, Anthony. Letter to H.C. Campbell, 27 October 1964. Archives, IFLA Headquarters, The Hague, Netherlands.

Thompson, Anthony, ed. *IFLA Directory 1971.* The Hague, Netherlands: K.G. Saur, 1970.

———. Letter to Jack Dalton, 20 February 1964. Archives, IFLA Headquarters, The Hague, Netherlands.

Tise, Ellen. "Introduction." In *IFLA Annual Report 2010*, edited by Susan Schaepman. The Hague: IFLA Headquarters, 2011. Accessed 14 February 2013. http://www.ifla.org/files/assets/hq/annual-reports/2010.pdf.

Toronto Public Library. "George H. Locke (1870–1937)." Accessed 14 December 2012. http://www.torontopubliclibrary.ca/about-the-library/library-history/locke.jsp.

———. "History of Toronto Public Library." Accessed 15 January 2013. http://www.torontopubliclibrary.ca/about-the-library/library-history.

Tunnell, A.L. "Elizabeth Morton." In *Canadian Who's Who: 1973–1975, Volume XIII,* 745. Toronto: University of Toronto Press, 1975.

"Twenty-Fifth Session of the IFLA Council: Warsaw 14–17 September 1959." *Feliciter* 5, no. 4 (1959): 9–15.

United Nations. "History of the United Nations." Accessed 17 June 2013. http://www.un.org/en/aboutun/history/.

United Nations Educational, Scientific, and Cultural Organization. "UNESCO/IFLA School Library Manifesto." Accessed 26 April 2013. http://www.unesco.org/webworld/libraries/manifestos/school_manifesto.html.

VanBuskirk, Mary. "1924 to 2009: History of the NRC Canada Institute for Scientific and Technical Information." National Research Council of Canada/Conseil national de recherches Canada. NRC Publications Archive. Accessed 20 June 2013. http://nparc.cisti-icist.nrccnrc.gc.ca/npsi/ctrl?req=%221924+To+2009+%3A+History+Of+The+Nrc+Canada+Institute+For+Scientific+And+Technical+Information%22&index=aw&pgrslts=25&action=dsere

Veaner, Allen B. "Woman at the Top: An Interview with Marianne Scott, New Director of the National Library of Canada." *American Libraries 16*, no. 1 (1985): 18–19. Accessed 12 December 2012. http://www.jstor.org/stable/25629452.

Vladimirov, Lev I. "The Socialist Countries of Europe in IFLA." In *IFLA's First Fifty Years: Achievement and Challenge in International Librarianship*, edited by Willem Roelf Henderikus Koops and Joachim Wieder, 101–107. Munich: Verlag Dokumentation, 1977. Accessed 12 May 2013. http://www.degruyter.com/view/books/9783111356655/9783111356655.101/9783111356655.101.xml?format=EBOK

Voogt, Leo, ed. *IFLA Directory 1994–1995*. The Hague, Netherlands: K.G. Saur, 1994.

Voogt, Leo, ed. *IFLA Directory 1996–1997*. The Hague, Netherlands: K.G. Saur, 1996.

Voogt, Leo, ed. *IFLA Directory 1998–1999*. The Hague, Netherlands: K.G. Saur, 1998.

Wedgeworth, Robert. "The Virtual IFLA: Moving Knowledge through Time and Space: Presidential Address." IFLA General Conference, Havana, 21–27 August, 1994. In *IFLA Annual 1994: Proceedings of the 60th General Conference, Havana, 1994. Annual Reports*. Munich: K.G. Saur, 1995, 23. Accessed 5 January 2013. http://ifla.queenslibrary.org/IV/ifla60/60-wedr.htm.

Wedgeworth, Robert, ed. *World Encyclopedia of Library and Information Services,* 3rd ed. Chicago: American Library Association, 1993.

Whiffin, Jean, ed. *International Directory of Serials Specialists*. New York: Haworth Press, 1995.

White, Janette. "Librarians in the News." *Ex Libris News* no. 16 (Autumn 1994): 4–11. Accessed 26 February 2013. http://exlibris.ischool.utoronto.ca/PDF/elan_Issue_16_fall_1994.pdf.

Whitney, Paul. "Libraries and the WTO: Why Should I Be Concerned?" *Feliciter* 46, no. 6 (2000): 302–304.

Wieder, Joachim. "IFLA's First Fifty Years: A Reprise." Edited by Harry Campbell. *IFLA Journal* 28, no. 3 (2002): 107–117. Accessed 16 January 2012. http://www.ifla.orgwww.ifla.org/files/hq/history/ifla_first_50_reprise.pdf.

———. Letter to Elizabeth H. Morton, 4 April 1959. Archives, IFLA Headquarters, The Hague, Netherlands.

———. "An Outline of IFLA's History." In *IFLA's First Fifty Years: Achievement and Challenge in International Librarianship,* edited by Willem Roelf Henderikus Koops and Joachim Wieder, 11–55. Munich: Verlag Dokumentation, 1977. Accessed 11 February 2013. http://www.degruyter.com/view/books/9783111356655/9783111356655.11/9783111356655.11.xml?format=EBOK.

Wijnstroom, Margreet. Letter to B. McNamee, 12 March 1975. Canadian Library Association fonds, Library and Archives Canada, Ottawa, ON.

———. Letter to the voting members of IFLA and the members of IFLA Consultative Committee, 8 July 1974. Canadian Library Association fonds, Library and Archives Canada, Ottawa, ON.

Wijnstroom, Margreet, ed. *IFLA Directory 1972*. The Hague, Netherlands: K.G. Saur, 1972.

Wijnstroom, Margreet, ed. *IFLA Directory 1973*. The Hague, Netherlands: K.G. Saur, 1973.

Wijnstroom, Margreet, ed. *IFLA Directory 1974*. The Hague, Netherlands: K.G. Saur, 1974.

Wijnstroom, Margreet, ed. *IFLA Directory 1975*. The Hague, Netherlands: K.G. Saur, 1975.

Wijnstroom, Margreet, ed. *IFLA Directory 1976*. The Hague, Netherlands: K.G. Saur, 1976.

Wijnstroom, Margreet, ed. *IFLA Directory 1977*. The Hague, Netherlands: K.G. Saur, 1977.

Wijnstroom, Margreet, ed. *IFLA Directory 1978*. The Hague, Netherlands: K.G. Saur, 1978.

Wijnstroom, Margreet, ed. *IFLA Directory 1979–1980*. The Hague, Netherlands: K.G. Saur, 1980.

Wijnstroom, Margreet, ed. *IFLA Directory 1981–1982*. The Hague, Netherlands: K.G. Saur, 1981.

Wijnstroom, Margreet, ed. *IFLA Directory 1982–1983*. The Hague, Netherlands: K.G. Saur, 1982.

Wijnstroom, Margreet, ed. *IFLA Directory 1984–1985.* The Hague, Netherlands: K.G. Saur, 1984.

Wijnstroom, Margreet, ed. *IFLA Directory 1986–1987*. The Hague, Netherlands: K.G. Saur, 1986.

Wikipedia contributors. "1991 Soviet Coup d'état Attempt." *Wikipedia*. Last modified 4 May 2013. Accessed 18 May 2013. http://en.wikipedia.org/wiki/1991_Soviet_coup_d%27%C3%A9tat_attempt.

———. "Canadian Library Association." *Wikipedia.* Last modified 2 July 2012. Accessed 18 August 2012. http://en.wikipedia.org/wiki/Canadian_Library_Association.

———. "CNIB". *Wikipedia.* Last modified 18 August 2012. Accessed 19 August 2012. https://en.wikipedia.org/wiki/CNIB.

———. "Expo 67." *Wikipedia.* Last modified 10 January 2013. Accessed 12 January 2013. http://en.wikipedia.org/wiki/Expo_67.

Wilhite, Jeffrey M. *85 Years IFLA: A History and Chronology of Sessions 1927–2012*. Edited by Louis Takács and Ingeborg Verheul. Berlin: De Gruyter Saur, 2012. PDF e-book. Accessed 31 January 2012. http://lib.myilibrary.com?id=394131.

———. "A Chronology of IFLA Sessions 1927–2009." The Hague: International Federation of Library Associations and Institutions, 2011. Accessed 16 January 2011. http://www.ifla.orgwww.ifla.org/files/hq/history/chronology_wilhite.pdf.

Williamson, Mary. "Harry Campbell's Association with IFLA." *ELAN: Ex Libris Association Newsletter* no. 42 (2007): 10–12.

Woolls, Blanche, ed. *Continuing Professional Education: An IFLA Guidebook.* Munich; New York: K.G. Saur, 1991.

Yarrow, Alexandra. "IFLA 2008, Days 1 and 2." *Only Connect.* Last modified 14 August 2009. Accessed 21 June 2013. http://ottawapubliclibrarian.blogspot.ca/2008/08/archived-posts-ifal-2008-days-1-and-2.html.

Wyczynski, Paul. "Joseph Jean Guy Sylvestre." *Canadian Encyclopedia.* Historica-Dominion, 2011. Accessed 22 May 2013. http://www.thecanadianencyclopedia.com/articles/joseph-jean-guy-sylvestre.

Zielinksa, Marie. "IFLA's Section on Library Services to Multicultural Populations Celebrates its 20th Anniversary." *IFLA Journal* 25, no. 4 (1999): 303–307. doi: 10.1177/034003520002600412.

———. "Report of the First Open Meeting of the Working Group on Library Service to Ethnic and Linguistic Minorities." *IFLA Journal* 8, no. 1 (1982): 68–70. doi: 10.1177/034003528200800114.

Zielinska, Marie F. *Celebrating 20 Years: A Concise History of the IFLA Section on Library Services to Multicultural Populations.* International Federation of Library Associations and Institutions, Section on Library Services to Multicultural Populations, 2001. Accessed 28 February 2013. http://www.ifla.org/files/assets/library-services-to-multicultural-populations/publications/20-years-mcult-history.pdf.

Zielinska, Marie F., and Francis T. Kirkwood, eds. *Multicultural Librarianship: An International Handbook.* Munich: K.G. Saur, 1992.

Appendix

Canadian IFLA Members and Institutional Members

Introduction

This Appendix lists over 500 Canadians and over 99 Canadian institutions that we have been able to document as IFLA members between 1931 and 2012. Compiling this Appendix of Canadian members and institutions was useful to our research, and we hope it will also be of value for future studies of Canadian participation in international librarianship. The Appendix is also an acknowledgement that many Canadians, beyond those mentioned in the text, have dedicated their time and energy to a diverse range of IFLA committees, round tables, and activities.

Although we have tried to make this Appendix as accurate as possible, we experienced certain limitations. It was not possible to compile a truly comprehensive list of Canadian IFLA members. Information in the Appendix may, at times, conflict with that in the text as they are drawn from different sources. Dates of membership provided in this Appendix should be considered estimates.

The names listed in this Appendix were taken from all available copies of the *IFLA Répertoire* (1931, 1938, 1948, 1955, 1961, 1963, and 1968) and the *IFLA Directory* (1971–1995, 1996–1997, 1998–2003, and 2005–2011). Lacunae result from the facts that the *IFLA Répertoire* does not identify all members and that the *IFLA Directory* was not published between 1995 and 1996, 2003 and 2005, and following 2012. Some names may not have been published due to privacy concerns. Whenever possible, we have corrected errors in dates and fact contained in the *IFLA Directories* through examination of the *IFLA Journal*, conference records, interviews, and IFLA's website. Despite efforts to ascertain all members' first names and IFLA positions, and to record changes to institutional names, we were not always successful in confirming full and current information for each entry.

The member section includes for each entry: member's name; estimated year of joining; approximate number of active years; and IFLA participation, such as membership in round tables or committees. The title "IFLA member" is given when no information is available as to whether an individual belonged to a committee or was a personal affiliate. For National Associates, position titles are provided in French or English, as they appear in the original sources. For clarity, we removed division and code numbers from section titles as these numbers changed over time.

The institutional section includes all institutional members and their year of first membership. As many institutions had standing agreements with IFLA, changed their names, or ceased membership for short intervals, it was not possible to compile comprehensive data on institutions' leaving and renewal dates.

The following acronyms apply to national and international associations:

ABQLA – Association des bibliothécaires du Québec – Quebec Library Association

ACBLF – Association Canadienne des bibliothécaires de langue française

ACMLA – Association of Canadian Map Libraries and Archives/Association des cartothèques et archives cartographiques du Canada

APLIC – Association of Parliamentary Librarians in Canada/Association des bibliothécaires parlementaires au Canada

ASTED – Association pour l'avancement des sciences et des techniques de la documentation

CALS – Canadian Association of Library Schools/Association canadienne des écoles de bibliothécaires

CARL – Canadian Association of Research Libraries/Association des bibliothèques de recherche du Canada

CBPQ – Corporation des bibliothécaire professionnels du Québec

CCIS-CCSI – Canadian Council of Information Studies/Conseil Canadien des sciences de l'information

CCLS – Canadian Council of Library Schools/Conseil canadien des écoles bibliothécaires

CLA – Canadian Library Association/Association canadienne des bibliothèques

IAML – International Association of Music Libraries, Archives, and Documentation Centres/Association internationale des bibliothèques, archives et centres de documentation musicaux

ICAE – International Council for Adult Education/Conseil international d'éducation des adultes

OLA – Ontario Library Association

AIESI – Association internationale des écoles des sciences de l'information

Canadian IFLA Members: 1931 to 2012

Abram, Stephen. Member: 2009.
Participation: 2009: IFLA Member.

Adams, Karen. Member: 1992–1999.
Participation: 1992–1999: Management
of Library Associations Round Table,
Executive Committee; 1992–1997:
National Associate – CLA, Executive
Director.

Alain, J. Member: 1990–1991. Participation:
1990–1991: National Associate – ASTED,
Director.

Allnutt, Vanessa. Member: 2009.
Participation: 2009: IFLA Member.

Amouzgar, Mahmoud. Member: 2004.
Participation: 2004: Personal Affiliate.

Anderson, Margaret E. Member: 1981–
1997. Participation: 1981–1989: Library
Theory and Research, Standing
Committee Member; 1989–1997:
Education and Training, Standing
Committee Member; 1993–1997:
Education and Training, Standing
Committee Member.

Anthony, Peter. Member: 1978–1985.
Participation: 1978–1985: Personal
Affiliate; 1979–1981: Round Table of
Art Librarians, Financial Officer.

Archer, John H. Member: 1961–1963.
Participation: 1961–1963: National
Associate – CLA, Past-President (1961)
and Treasurer (1963).

Arora, Ved. Member: 1993–2001.
Participation: 1993–2001: Document
Delivery and Interlending, Standing
Committee Member.

Auger, Roland. Member: 1983.
Participation: 1983: IFLA Member.

Auster, Ethel. Member: 1989–1993.
Participation: 1989–1997: Information
Technology, Standing Committee
Member; 1989–1993: Round Table of
Editors of Library Journals, Executive
Committee; 1993–1997: Library Theory
and Research, Standing Committee
Member.

Bagshaw, Marguerite. Member: 1973.
Participation: 1973: Sub-Library Work
with Children, Standing Advisory
Committee Member.

Balke, Noel H. Member: 1979–1980.
Participation: 1979–1980: Round Table
of Art Librarians, Secretary.

Ball, Katherine. Member: 1961.
Participation: 1961. National Associate –
CLA, President-Elect.

Banks, Roderick. Member: 1991.
Participation: 1991: IFLA Member.

Barber, Jeff. Member: 2006. Participation:
2006: Personal Affiliate.

Barton, J.A. Member: 1994–1995.
Participation: National Associate
– APLIC, President.

Batchelder, R. Member: 1986–1987.
Participation: 1986–1987: National
Associate – ACMLA, Secretary.

Bays, Diane. Member: 1996–2007.
Participation: 1996–1999: Libraries for
the Blind, Corresponding Member
(1996–1998; 2002–2007), Observer
(1998–1999).

Beard, C. Member: 1992–1993.
Participation: 1992–1993: National
Associate – ACMLA, President.

Beaudoin, M. Member: 1986–1999.
Participation: 1986–1987: National
Associate – CBPQ, President; 1998–
1999: National Associate – ASTED,
Secretary.

Beckman, M. Member: 1987–1991.
Participation: 1987–1991: Library
Buildings and Equipment, Standing
Committee Member.

Beglo, Jo Nordley. Member: 2001–2009.
Participation: 2001–2009: Art Libraries,
Standing Committee Member.

Bélair, Jo-Anne. Member: 2003–2013.
Participation: 2003–2007: Classification
and Indexing, Co-Editor, Head of the
Répertoire de vedettes-matière,
Standing Committee Member;
2009–2013: Classification and Indexing,
Chair/Treasurer, Standing Committee
Member.

Bélisle, Germain. Member: 1963.
Participation: 1963: National Associate –
ACBLF, Président.

Benoit-Plamondon, Francine. Member:
2011. Participation: 2011: IFLA Member.

Bernhard, Paulette. Member: 1991–2001. Participation: 1991–1995: School Libraries, Chair/Treasurer, Standing Committee Member; 1991–2001: School Libraries and Resource Centres, Standing Committee Member (1991–2001), Chair/Treasurer (1995–2001); 1991–1995: Round Table on User Education, Executive Committee Member; 1995–2001: User Education Round Table, Executive Committee.

Bernier, Gaston. Member: 1984–2011. Participation: 1984–1985: National Associate – CBPQ, President; 1998–1999: Government Information and Official Publications, Corresponding Member; 1999–2003: Library and Research Services for Parliament, Standing Committee Member; 2002–2011: Government Information and Official Publications, Corresponding Member.

Bernier, S. Member: 1984–1987. Participation: 1984–1987: National Associate: ABQLA, Secretary.

Berthiaume, Guy. Member: 2009–2011. Participation: 2009–2011: IFLA Member.

Bertram, S. 1978. Member: 1978–1980. Participation: 1978–1980: National Associate – CALS.

Bertrand-Gastaldy, S. Member: 1984–1985. Participation: 1984–1985: International Associations – AIESI, Secretary.

Best, I. Member: 1973. Participation: 1973: National Associate – ABQLA, President.

Bewley, Lois M. Member: 1984–1985. Participation: 1982–1985: National Associate – CLA, President.

Bidd, Donald. Member: 1986–1993. Participation: 1986–1993: Round Table on Audiovisual Media, Secretary (1986–1987), Executive Committee (1990–1993).

Bishop, O.B. Member: 1974. Participation: 1974: National Associate: CALS.

Bishop, S.E. Member: 1992–1993. Participation: 1992–1993: National Associate – APLIC, Co-President.

Bisson, Louis. Member: 1963. Participation: 1963: National Associate – Services des bibliothèques publiques du Québec, Vice Président.

Black, J.L. Member: 1978–1980. Participation: 1978–1980: Personal Affiliate.

Blouin-Cliché, O. Member: 1974. Participation: 1974: National Associate – ACBLF, President.

Boisvert, Claire. Member: 2009–2011. Participation: 2009–2011: IFLA Member.

Bonenfant, Jean Charles. Member: 1961. Participation: 1961: National Associate – CLA, 2nd Vice President.

Bonin, C.A. Member: 1978–1980. Participation: 1978–1980: National Associate – CBPQ, President.

Bonneau, M. Member: 1975–1978. Participation: 1975–1978: National Associate – ASTED, Executive Director.

Bonnelly, Claude. Member: 1989–2001. Participation: 1983–1993: Statistics, Standing Committee Member; 1993–2001: Information Technology, Standing Committee Member.

Bosa, Real. Member: 1991. Participation: 1991: IFLA Member.

Bouche, M.R. Member: 1984–1985. Participation: 1984–1985: International Associations – AIESI, President.

Boucher, Alain. Member: 1991. Participation: 1991: IFLA Member.

Boudrias, A. Member: 1979–1981. Participation: 1979–1981: National Associate – ASTED, Secretary.

Bourgault, Thérèse. Member: 2007. Participation: 2007: Personal Affiliate.

Bowles, Vickery. Member: 2009–2013. Participation: 2009–2013: Library Services to Multicultural Populations, Information Coordinator, Standing Committee Member.

Bowron, A.W. Member: 1961. Participation: 1961: National Associate – Affiliate of ABQLA, President.

Boxall, James C. Member: 2005–2009. Participation: 2005–2009: Geography and Map Libraries, Standing Committee Member.

Bregzis, Ilze. Member: 1983–1987. Partcipation: 1983–1987: Personal Affiliate.

Bregzis, Ritvars. Member: 1982–1987. Participation: 1982–1987: Personal Affiliate.

Brian Land, R. Member: 1984–1985.
Participation: 1984–1985: National Associate – APLIC, President.

Briggs, Geoffrey Hugh. Member: 1983.
Participation: 1983: IFLA Member.

Brousseau, Lise. Member: 1982–1987.
Participation: 1982–1987: National Associate – ASTED, President.

Brown, Christine. Member: 2009–2011.
Participation: 2009–2011: IFLA Member.

Brown, J.J. Member: 1974. Participation: 1974: National Associate – OLA, President.

Brunet, Joseph A. Member: 1948.
Participation: 1948: National Associate – CLA, Vice President.

Bryant, N. Member: 1974–1977.
Participation: 1974–1977: National Associate – ABQLA, Secretary (1974), President (1977).

Buchinski, E. Member: 1978–1981.
Participation: 1978–1981: Cataloguing, Standing Committee Member.

Buller, Nell. Member: 1986–1991.
Participation: 1986–1991: Personal Affiliate.

Brunet, Joseph A. Member: 1948.
Participation: 1948: National Associate – CLA, Deuxième Vice Président.

Burrows, Sandra. Member: 2002–2007.
Participation: 2002–2007: Executive Committee Member, Round Table Newspapers, Information Coordinator (2002–2003), Information Coordinator/Editor (2005–2007).

Burton, Melody. Member: 2009–2013.
Participation: 2009–2013: Academic and Research Libraries, Standing Committee Member.

Cabral, Louis. Member: 1992–2008.
Participation: 1992–2003: National Associate – ASTED, Director.

Calderisi, Maria. Member: 1978–1993.
Participation: 1978–1981: Round Table on Music Libraries, Secretary; 1978–1993: Bibliography, Standing Committee Observer (1978), Standing Committee Member (1979–1983, 1989–1993); 1990–1991: IAML, President.

Campbell, Brenda. Member: 2009–2011.
Participation: 2009–2011: Genealogy and Local History, Corresponding Member.

Campbell, Henry "Harry" Cummings. Member: 1955–2008. Participation: 1971–1978: Executive Board Member, First Vice President (1973–1978), Finance Committee Member (1973–1977), Observer for Executive Board (1977); 1971–1974: INTAMEL, President; 1973–1974: National Associate – CLA, President; 1974–1978: Public Libraries, Standing Committee Member; 1975–1976: Coordinating Board for Regional Activities, Coordinator; 2001: Personal Affiliate; 2002–2003: Library History Round Table, Executive Committee Member.

Campbell, Sandra. Member: 2003–2011.
Participation: 2003–2011: Personal Affiliate.

Cantello, Gillian. Member: 2009.
Participation: 2009: IFLA Member.

Cantin, Sylvie. Member: 2011. Participation: 2011: IFLA Member.

Cardin, C. Member: 1975–1977.
Participation: 1975–1977: Committee on Serial Publications, Standing Committee Member.

Carr-Wiggin, Anne. Member: 2009.
Participation: 2009: IFLA Member.

Cavill, Pat. Member: 1994–1995.
Participation: 1994–1995: National Associate – CLA, Executive Director and President-Elect.

Chang, M. Member: 1980–1981.
Participation: 1980–1981: National Associate – ACMLA, Secretary.

Charbonneau, Monique. Member: 1983.
Participation: 1983: IFLA Member.

Charbonneau, Olivier. Member: 2002–201.
Participation: 2002–2010: Student Affiliate; 2010: IFLA Member.

Chartrand, G.A. Member: 1970–1980.
Participation: National Associate – ASTED, Secretary General (1970–1971), President (1979–1980).

Cholach, Pat. Member: 1984–1987.
Participation: 1984–1987: Personal Affiliate.

Chung, Talia. Member: 2012. Participation: 2012: Personal Affiliate.

Cibic, Boris. Member: 2001–2003.
Participation: 2001: Student Affiliate; 2002–2003: Personal Affiliate.

Clement, Hope E.A. Member: 1982–1993.
Participation: 1982–1989: International
Focal Point, Chair, MARC Programme
(1982–1985), Ex officio Member
(1985–1989); 1983–1985: MARC
Network Advisory Committee; 1983–
1991: Interlending and Document
Delivery, Standing Committee Member;
1985–1989: Professional Board Mem-
ber; 1985–1991: Universal Bibliographic
Control, Advisory Committee Member,
Ex officio Member (1985–1989); 1985–
1989: Collections and Services, Chair;
1990–1991: Executive Board, Ex officio
Member, 1990–1991: Chair of
Professional Board; 1990–1991:
Programme Management Committee,
Ex officio Member; 1990–1991:
Publications Committee Member;
1990–1991: Universal Bibliographic
Control and International Marc, Chair
of Advisory Committee; 1992–1993:
Professional Board/Publications
Committee, Chair.

Cleveland, Gary. Member: 1996–1997.
Participation: 1996–1997: Universal
Data Flow and Telecommunications,
Programme Officer.

Cloutier, Guy. Member: 1980–1981.
Participation: 1980–1981: National
Associate – ASTED, President.

Clubb, Barbara. Member: 1997–2011.
Participation: 1997–2005: Public
Libraries, Standing Committee Member,
Chair/Treasurer (2000–2005); 2005–
2009: Metropolitan Libraries, Standing
Committee Member.

Cole, John. Member: 2009. Participation:
2009: IFLA Member.

Compeau, Heather. Member: 2009.
Participation: 2009: IFLA Member.

Converse, William. Member: 1992–2001.
Participation: 1992–2001: Personal
Affiliate.

Cook, C. Donald. Member: 1981–1989.
Participation: 1981–1989: Cataloguing,
Standing Committee Member.

Cook, Carol Colleen. Member: 2011.
Participation: 2011: IFLA Member.

Cooney, J. Member: 1990–1991.
Participation: 1990–1991: Round
Table for the Management of Library
Associations, Executive Committee.

Copeland, Lynn. Member: 2011.
Participation: 2011: IFLA Member.

Cordonier, J. Member: 1986–1987.
Participation: 1986–1987: International
Associations – AIESI, President.

Cote, C. Member: 1974. Participation:
National Associate – ABQLA, President.

Coté, C. Member: 1974–2003: Member:
1974. Participation: National Associate –
ABQLA, President. Participation: 1992–
2003: Personal Affiliate; 1993–1997:
University Libraries and Other General
Research Libraries, Standing Committee
Member.

Côté, Jean-Pierre. Member: 1993–2001.
Participation: 1993–1997: National
Associate – CARL, Directeur Général;
1996–2001: University Libraries and
Other General Research Libraries,
Standing Committee Member.

Coulombe, V. Member: 1979–1980.
Participation: 1979–1980: Personal
Affiliate.

Couture, Raymonde. Member: 1963.
Participation: 1963: National Associate –
ACBLF, Conseil national, Secrétaire.

Crema, Leonora. Member: 2011.
Participation: 2011: IFLA Member.

Crouch, Keith. Member: 1961. Participation:
1961: National Associate – ABQLA,
Président sortant.

Currie, C. Member: 1970–1971.
Participation: 1970–1971: National
Associate – CLA, Executive Director.

Curry, Ann. Member: 2005–2009.
Participation: 2005–2009: FAIFE
Committee Member, Library Theory and
Research, Standing Committee Member.

Dakshinamurti, Ganga. Member: 2009.
Participation: 2009: IFLA Member.

Dali, Keren. Member: 2009. Participation:
Canada Student Affiliate, 2009.

Dalidowicz, Michelle. Member: 2006.
Participation: 2006: Student Affiliate.

Dashinamurti, Ganga. Member: 1998–1999.
Participation: 1998–1999: Personal
Affiliate.

David, Sulz. Member: 2011. Participation:
2011: IFLA Member.

de Caluwé, J. Member: 1986–1987.
Participation: 1986–1987: International
Associate – AIESI, Secretary.

De Sumar, Janita Jara. Member: 2004.
  Participation: 2004: Personal Affiliate.
Dean, Kathryn. Member 2001–2003.
  Participation: 2001–2003: Personal
  Affiliate.
Delorme, Silvie. Member: 2009.
  Participation: 2009: IFLA Member.
Delsey, Thomas John. Member: 1981–1993.
  Participation: 1981–1985: Cataloguing,
  Standing Committee Member (1981–
  1989), Chair (1985–1989); 1989–1993:
  Serial Publications, Standing Committee
  Member.
Demers, Henri. Member: 1963.
  Participation: 1963: National Associate –
  ACBLF, Conseil national, Vice président.
Denis, Laurent G. Member: 1970–1971.
  Participation: National Associate –
  ABQLA, President.
Deschatelets, Gilles. Member: 1995–1997.
  Participation: National Associate – CCLS,
  Directeur.
DesJardine, C. Member: 1986–1987.
  Participation: 1986–1987: National
  Associate – ACMLA, Secretary.
Desrochers, Raymond. Member: 1996–
  1997. Participation: 1996–1997:
  National Associate – ICAE, Executive
  Director.
Dickerson, Mary. Member: 1996–1997.
  Participation: 1996–1997: National
  Associate – APLIC, Secretary/Treasurer.
Dina, Yemisi. Member: 2011. Participation:
  2011: IFLA Member.
Distad, Merril. Member: 1998–2001.
  Participation: 1998–2001: Acquisition
  and Collection Development, Standing
  Committee Member.
Divay, Gaby. Member: 2009. Participation:
  2009: IFLA Member.
Doi, Carolyn. Member: 2010. Participation:
  2010: Student Affiliate.
Doiron, Ray. Member: 2009–2011.
  Participation: 2009–2011: IFLA Member.
Dolan, E. Member: 1976–1977.
  Participation: 1976–1977: National
  Associate – CALS.
Dowding, Martin. Member: 2005–2009.
  Participation: 2005–2009: Libraries
  Serving Disadvantaged Persons,
  Standing Committee Member.

Drouillard, Beverly. Member: 1970–1971.
  Participation: National Associate –
  ACMLA, Secretary.
Drouin, P. Member: 1970–1972.
  Participation: 1970–1972: National
  Associate – ACBLF, President.
Druery, Jackie. Member: 2005–2009.
  Participation: 2005–2009: Government
  Information and Official Publications,
  Secretary, Standing Committee Member.
Dubois, F. Member: 1982–1983.
  Participation: 1982–1983: National
  Associate – CBPQ, Vice President.
Dubreuil, L. Member: 1982–2001.
  Participation: 1982–1985: National
  Associate – ACMLA, President; 1985–
  2001: Geography and Map Libraries,
  Standing Committee Member (1985–
  1993), Observer (1995–2001).
Duchesne, R. Member: 1986–1987.
  Participation: 1986–1987: Transborder
  Data Flow, Staff Member.
Duery, Jackie. Member: 2005–2009.
  Participation: 2005–2009: Government
  Information and Official Publications,
  Chair, Standing Committee Member.
Duffy, Jane. Member: 2000–2001.
  Participation: 2000–2001: Personal
  Affiliate.
Dufour, A. Member: 1978. Participation:
  1978: National Associate – ABQLA,
  President.
Duncan, Donna. Member: 1986–1997.
  Participation: 1989–1993: Classification
  and Indexing, Secretary, Standing
  Committee Member; 1989–1997:
  Classification and Indexing, Secretary/
  Treasurer, Standing Committee
  Member; 1993–1997: Bibliographic
  Control, Coordinating Board, Secretary;
  1993–1997: Editor of Newsletter of
  the IFLA Classification and Indexing;
  1996–1997: Bibliographic Control,
  Coordinating Board Member, Secretary.
Dunn, Judy. Member: 2006. Participation:
  2006: Personal Affiliate.
Dupuis, Onil. Member: 1986–2003.
  Participation: 1986–1987: Round Table
  of Editors of Library Journals, Secretary;
  1996–2003: Personal Affiliate.

Durance, Cynthia. Member: 1978–1989.
Participation: 1978–1981: Serial
Publications, Standing Committee
Member; 1978–1981: Personal Affiliate;
1981–1989. Information Technology,
Standing Committee Member.

Durance, D. Member: 1980–1985.
Participation: 1980–1985: Serial
Publications, Standing Committee
Member.

Durand, Marielle. Member: 1975.
Participation: 1975: National Associate –
ASTED, President.

Durando, Paola Valeria. Member: 2012.
Participation: Personal Affiliate.

Dwyer, Melva Jean. Member: 1978–1995.
Participation: 1978–1995: Personal
Affiliate; 1984–1991: Art Libraries,
Standing Committee Member.

Dysart, Jane. Member: 2007–2011.
Participation: 2007–2011: Knowledge
and Management, Information
Coordinator, Standing Committee
Member; 2009–2011: Library Services,
Secretary.

Easton, Harry. Member: 1973. Participation:
1973: National Associate – CLA,
President.

Ebbett, Gwendolyn. Member: 2010–2011.
Participation: 2010–2011: IFLA Member.

Eddy, B. Member: 1975–1977. Participation:
1975–1977: School Libraries, Secretary.

Ellis, Georgia. Member: 1983–1985.
Participation: 1983–1985: Personal
Affiliate.

Ellis, Richard. Member: 2002–2003.
Participation: 2002–2003: IFLA Member.

Engfield, Roy H. Member: 1983.
Participation: 1983: IFLA Member.

Eshghi, Shirin. Member: 2006. Participation:
2006: Personal Affiliate.

Evans, Gwynneth. Member: 1999–2007.
Participation: 1999–2007: Reading,
Standing Committee Member, Secretary
(1999–2003), Chair/Treasurer (2003–
2007); 2002: Personal Affliate; 2005–
2007: Professional Committee,
Chair/Financial Officer.

Farley-Chevrier, Francis. Member: 2009.
Participation: 2009: IFLA Member.

Farrell, B. Member: 1976–1977.
Participation: 1976–1977: National
Associate – ACMLA, President.

Fasick, Adèle M. Member: 1978–1997.
Participation: 1978–1980: Personal
Affiliate; 1985–1993: Children's
Libraries, Standing Committee Member
(1985–1993), Chair (1989–1993); 1990–
1991: Round Table on Research and
Reading, Executive Committee; 1993–
1997: Reading, Standing Committee
Member.

Ferland, Benoit. Member: 2011.
Participation: 2011: IFLA Member.

Figueroa, P. Member: 1986–1987.
Participation: Personal Affiliate.

Filion, Louise. Member: 1983. Participation:
1983: IFLA Member.

Filion, Paul-Emile. Member: 1982–1985.
Participation: 1982–1983: National
Associate – CBPQ, President; 1984–
1985: Personal Affiliate.

Fink, M. Member: 1980–1981. Participation:
National Associate: ABQLA, Secretary
(French).

Fink, Patricia. Member: 2011. Participation:
2011: IFLA Member.

Finlay, Mary. Member: 1983. Participation:
1983: IFLA Member.

Finsten, Hugh Alan. Member: 2005–2007.
Participation: 2005–2007: Library and
Research Service for Parliaments,
Member.

Fontaine, David. Member: 2009.
Participation: 2009: IFLA Member.

Fortin, Marcel. Member: 2005–2009.
Participation: 2005–2009: Geography
and Map Libraries, Standing Committee
Member.

Fortin, Y. Member: 1984–1987.
Participation: Personal Affiliate.

Fournier, Michel. Member: 1997–2001.
Participation: 1997–2001: Classification
and Indexing, Standing Committee
Member.

Fowlie, E.L. Member: 1989–1995.
Participation: 1989–1993: Public
Libraries, Standing Committee Member;
1994–1995: Personal Affiliate.

Foy, K.M. Member: 1985–1989.
Participation: Children's Libraries,
Standing Committee Member.

Franklin, Jonathan. Member: 2009–2013.
Participation: 2009–2013: Art Libraries,
Standing Committee Member.

Fraser-Celin, Valli. Member: 2010. Participation: 2010: Student Affiliate.

Furuya, Natsuko. Member: 1990–1993. Participation: 1990–1993: Personal Affiliate.

Galler, Anne M. Member: 1982–1999. Participation: 1982: National Associate – ABQLA, President; 1983–1987: School Libraries, Standing Committee Member, Chair; 1989–1997: Libraries Serving Disadvantaged Persons, Standing Committee Member (1989–1997), Chair (1989–1993), Editor of Newsletter of the IFLA Section of Libraries Serving Disadvantaged Persons (1993–1997), Special Adviser (1998–1999); 1990–1991: Professional Board Member – Libraries Servicing the General Public, Chair/Financial Officer; 1998–1999: Personal Affiliate.

Gardner, R.K. Member: 1983–1991. Participation: 1983–1991: Library Schools and Other Training Aspects, Standing Committee Member.

Garry, L.S. Member: 1975. Participation: 1975: National Associate: CALS, Secretary.

Gaudet, Franceen. Member: 2002–2011. Participation: 2002: Personal Affiliate; 2003–2011: Reference and Informational Services, Standing Committee Member.

Gaudet, Pierre R. Member: 2002. Participation: 2002: Personal Affiliate.

Gauthier, J. Member: 1996–1997. Participation: 1996–1997: National Associate – ASTED, Secretary.

Gauvin, Jean-François. Member: 2009. Participation: 2009: IFLA Member.

Gazo, Dominique. Member: 2008. Participation: 2008: Student Affiliate.

Gendreau, Jean-Yves. Member: 1978. Participation: 1978–1985: Official Publications, Standing Committee Member; 1978–1980: National Associate – CBPQ, Vice President.

Gendron, Céline. Member: 1992–1995. Participation: 1992–1995: National Associate – ASTED, Secretary.

Georges, M. Member: 1972. Participation: 1972: –National Associate – ACBLF, Secretary.

Gifford, H. Member: 1978. Participation: 1978: Personal Affiliate.

Gil, Olga. Member: 1984–1993. Participation: 1984–1993: Personal Affiliate.

Gill, S. M. Member: 1948. Participation: 1948: Sub-Committee on Special Libraries and Documentation Centres, Member; 1948: National Associate – CLA, Président honoraire.

Girard, Louise. Member: 1990–1995. Participation: 1990–1995: Personal Affiliate.

Gnassi, Bruno. Member: 1997–2005. Participation: 1997–2005: Government Information and Official Publications, Standing Committee Member (1997–2005), Chair (2001–2005).

Godon, Daniel. Member: 2011. Participation: 2011: IFLA Member.

Gourlay, Hugh. Member: 1948. Participation: 1948: National Associate – CLA, Treasurer.

Graham, M. Member: 1980–1981. Participation: 1980–1981: National Associate – APLIC, Secretary.

Grant, Martha. Member: 2006. Participation: 2006: Personal Affiliate.

Grenier, Hélène. Member: 1963. Participation: 1963: National Associate – CLA, Vice President.

Grieshaber-Otto, Susan. Member: 2006. Participation: 2006: Personal Affiliate.

Groen, Frances. Member: 1991–2005. Participation: 1991–1999: Biological and Medical Sciences Libraries, Chair, Standing Committee Member; 2000–2001: National Associate – CARL, President; 2001–2005: University Libraries and Other General Research Libraries, Secretary, Standing Committee Member.

Guay, Gisèle. Member: 1994–1997. Participation: 1994–1997: Personal Affiliate.

Guillemette-Labory, Louise. Member: 2007–2011. Participation: 2007–2011: Metropolitan Libraries, Standing Committee Member.

Haas, Pat de. Member: 1983. Participation: 1983: IFLA Member.

Haddad, April. Member: 2010. Participation: 2010: IFLA Member.

Hafner, Joseph. Member: 2009–2011. Participation: 2009–2011: Acquisition and Collection Development, Secretary, Standing Committee Member.

Hajnal, Peter. Member: 1989–1997. Participation: 1989–1997: Government Information and Official Publications, Standing Committee Member.

Haliwell, D.W. Member: 1979–1989. Participation: 1979–1989: Statistics, Standing Committee Member.

Hall, Alison. Member: 2000–2003. Participation: National Associate – IAML, Archives and Documentation Centres, Secretary.

Hall, M. Member: 1975–1977. Participation: 1975–1977: National Associate – CALS, President.

Hamilton, E. Member: 1982–1983. Participation: 1982–1983: National Associate – ACMLA, President.

Hang Tat Leong, Jack. Member: 2009. Participation: 2009: Personal Affiliate.

Hann, B. Member: 1975. Participation: 1975: Ad hoc Planning Group for School Library Work, Secretary.

Harlow, Neal. Member: 1963: National Associate – CLA, Vice President.

Harris, Winnifred. Member: 1990–1999. Participation: 1990–1999: Personal Affiliate.

Harrison, J.C. Member: 1975. Participation: 1975: National Associate: CALS, President.

Harrison, Tanja. Member: 2009. Participation: 2009: Personal Affiliate.

Harvard-Williams, P. Member: 1970–1973: Participation: 1970–1973: Publications Committee Member; 1973: Executive Board, Vice President.

Harvey, C. Member: 1973. Participation: 1973: National Associate – ACMLA, Secretary.

Harvie, David. Member: 2010. Participation: 2010: IFLA Member.

Havard, Mahalya. Member: 2009. Participation: 2009: Personal Affiliate.

Haycock, Ken. Member: 1978–2005. Participation: 1978: National Associate – CLA, Executive Director; 1997–2005: Education and Training, Chair (1997–2001), Standing Committee Member (1997–2005).

Hébert, Françoise. Member: 1979–1995. Participation: 1979: Working Group, Member; 1980–1983: Round Table of Libraries for the Blind, Secretary; 1994–1995: National Associate – CLA, Executive Director.

Heintz, Veslemoy. Member: 1990–1999. Participation: 1990–1999: IAML, Secretary General.

Henderson, Susan. Member: 2001–2005. Participation: 2001–2005: Libraries for Children and Young Adults, Standing Committee Member.

Hickerson, Tom. Member: 2010. Participation: 2010: IFLA Member.

Hoffman, Ellen. Member: 1999–2011. Participation: 1999–2003: Statistics, Standing Committee Member (1999–2003), Corresponding Member (2005–2007); 2007–2011: Management of Library Associations, Standing Committee Member.

Horinstein, Régine. Member: 2009–2011. Participation: 2009–2011: IFLA Member.

Hourihan, Monica. Member: 2005. Participation: 2005: Personal Affiliate.

House, Sara. Member: 2010. Participation: 2010: IFLA Member.

Houyoux, P. Member: 1980–1981. Participation: 1980–1981: National Associate – CBPQ, Vice President.

Hovius, Beth. Member: 1991–1995. Participation: 1991–1995: Libraries for the Blind, Standing Committee Member, Secretary/Treasurer.

Howarth, Lynne C. Member 1995–2013. Participation: 1995–2007: Cataloguing, Standing Committee Member (1995–2003), Metadata Discussion Group, Convenor (2003–2007); 2000–2001: National Associate – CCLS, President; 2003–2013: Classification and Indexing, Standing Committee Member.

Hubbertz, Andrew. Member: 1997–2001. Participation: 1997–2001: Government Information and Official Publications, Standing Committee Member.

Hudon, M. IFLA Member: 1973. Participation: 1973: National Associate – ACBLF, Secretary.

Huffman, S. Member: 1977–1983. Participation: 1977–1983: IFLA National Associate: ABQLA, Secretary (English).

Hunt, Karen. Member: 2007–2011.
Participation: 2007–2011: Information
Technology, Standing Committee
Member.

Hutcheson, Amy. Member: 1961.
Participation: 1961: National Associate –
CLA, President.

Icenhower, Elizabeth. Member: 2008.
Participation: 2008: Personal Affiliate.

Ingles, Ernie. Member: 1990–2010.
Participation: 1990–1991: National
Associate – CLA, Executive Director;
2010: IFLA Member.

Ireland, Willard. Member: 1955.
Participation: 1955: National Associate –
CLA, President.

Irvine, J. Member: 1984–1985.
Participation: 1984–1985: National
Associate – APLIC, Secretary.

Iseli-Otto, Sabina. Member: 2006.
Participation: 2006: Student Affiliate.

Jara De Sumar, Juanita. Member: 2009–
2011. Participation: 2009–2011:
IFLA Member.

Jensen, K. Member: 1986–1987.
Participation: 1986–1987: National
Associate – CLA, President.

Joffe-Nicodeme, Arlette. Member: 1983–
1991. Participation: 1983–1991: IFLA
Member.

Johnstone, Maria A. Member: 2002–2003.
Participation: 2002: Student Affiliate;
2003: IFLA Member.

Kandiuk, Mary. Member: 2012.
Participation: 2012 Personal Affiliate.

Kavanagh, Rosemary. Member: 1995–2003.
Participation: 1995–1999: Libraries for
the Blind, Standing Committee Member
(1995–2003), Information Coordinator/
Editor of the Newsletter of the IFLA
Section for Libraries for the Blind (1998–
1999).

Keiller, Karen. Member: 2009–2013.
Participation: 2009–2013: Information
and Technology, Standing Committee
Member.

Kertland, D. Member: 1975–1976.
Participation: 1975–1976: National
Associate – ABQLA, Secretary (English).

Kidd, B. Member: 1974. Participation: 1974:
National Associate – ACMLA, President.

Kim, Mijin. Member: 2005–2013.
Participation: 2005–2013: Library
Services to Multicultural Populations,
Standing Committee Member (2005–
2013), Chair/Treasurer (2009–2013).

Kirkwood, Frances "Frank" T. Member:
1989–2013. Participation: 1995–2007:
Personal Affiliate; 1995–1999:
Collections and Services Coordinating
Board, Secretary; 1995–2003:
Government Information and Official
Publications, Chair/Treasurer (1995–
1999), Standing Committee Member
(1995–2003); 2003–2007: FAIFE
Committee Member; 2003–2007:
Reference and Information Science,
Standing Committee Member; 2007–
2011: Reference and Information
Services, Standing Committee Member;
2007–2008: Access to Information
Network - Africa Discussion Group,
Convenor.

Kitchen, Paul. Member: 1975–1987.
Participation: 1975–1987: National
Associate – CLA, Executive Director.

Kitimbo, Irene. Member: 2009.
Participation: 2009: IFLA Member.

Koskalia, S. Member: 1980–1981.
Participation: National Associate –
CALS, Secretary.

Lackner, I. Member: 1982–1995.
Participation: 1982–1995: Personal
Affiliate.

Lafortune, Françoise. Member: 1963.
Participation: 1963: National Associate –
Services des bibliothèques publiques
du Québec Ministère des affaires
culturelles, Hôtel du Gouvernment,
Commission des bibliothèques publique
du Québec, Vice Président.

Lagacé, Eve. Member: 2005. Participation:
2005: Student Affiliate.

Laidlaw, S. Member: 1989–1997.
Participation: 1989–1993: University
Libraries and Other General Research
Libraries, Standing Committee Member;
1992–1997: Continuing Professional
Education Round Table, Secretary
(1992–1993), Executive Committee
(1992–1997).

Lamb, Kaye W. Member: 1948.
Participation: 1948: National Associate
– CLA, President-elect, premier
vice-president.

Land, Bian. Member: 1975–1976.
Participation: 1975–1976: National
Associate – CLA, President.

Landon, Richard. Member: 1985–2001.
Participation: 1985–2001: Rare Books
and Manuscripts Secretary (1985–
1987), Standing Committee Member
(1985–1993), Chair (1989–1993),
Special Adviser (1996–2001).

Langevin, Karine. Member: 2010.
Participation: 2010: IFLA Member.

Lapierre, Dominique. Member: 2010.
Participation: 2010: IFLA Member.

Large, Andrew. Member: 1998–1999.
Participation: 1998–1999: National
Associate – CCLS, Chair.

Laskaris, Ricardo. Member: 2009.
Participation: 2009: IFLA Member.

Lassonde, A. Member: 1977–1983.
Participation: 1977–1983: National
Associate: ABQLA, Secretary (French).

Lavigne, L. Member: 1989–1993.
Participation: 1989–1993: Bibliography,
Standing Committee Member.

Lavote, M. Member: 1974–1976.
Participation: 1974–1976: National
Associate – ABQLA, Library, Secretary
(French).

Law, Margaret. Member: 2010–2011.
Participation: 2010–2011: IFLA Member.

Le Sieur, Berti. Member: 1983. Participation:
1983: IFLA Member.

Leafloor, L. Member: 1974. Participation:
1974: National Associate – ACMLA,
Secretary.

Lebeau, A. Member: 1990–1995.
Participation: 1990–1995: Library
History Round Table, Executive
Committee.

LeBel, J. Member: 1977–1985. Participation:
1977–1980: National Associate – CLA,
Secretary; 1984–1985: National
Associate – APLIC, Vice President.

Leblanc, Louise. Member: 2009.
Participation: 2009: IFLA Member.

Leblanc, Suzanne. Member: 2011.
Participation: 2011: IFLA Member.

Lebland, Napoléon. Member: 1963.
Participation: 1963: National Associate –
Services des bibliothèques publiques
du Québec Ministère des affaires
culturelles, Hôtel du Gouvernment,
Commission des bibliothèques publique
du Québec, Président.

Lebowitz, Ariel. Member: 2007–2011.
Participation: 2007–2011: Library
Services to Multicultural Populations,
Standing Committee Member.

Lechasseur, Antonio. Member: 2007–2011.
Participation: 2007–2011: Genealogy
and Local History, Standing Committee
Member.

Leckie, Gloria. Member: 2002–2003.
Participation: 2002–2003: National
Associate – CCIS-CCSI, President.

Lefebvre, Madeleine. Member: 2005–2009.
Participation: 2005–2009: Management
and Marketing, Standing Committee
Member.

Leide, John E. Member: 1983. Participation:
1983: IFLA Member.

LeMay, François. Member: 1991.
Participation: 1991: National Associate –
APLIC, President. 1996–2003. National
Associate – APLIC, Secretary/Treasurer.

Leong, Jack. Member: 2009–2013.
Participation: 2009–2013: Library
Services to Multicultural Populations,
Information Coordinator, Standing
Committee Member.

L'Heureux, Sonia. Member: 2009–2013.
Participation: 2009–2013: Libraries and
Research Services for Parliament,
Standing Committee Member.

Lochhead, Sara. Member: 1998–1999.
Participation: 1998–1999: Personal
Affiliate.

Locke, Joanne. Member: 2001–2011.
Participation: 2001–2009: Libraries
Serving Disadvantages Persons,
Treasurer (2001–2007), Standing
Committee Member (2001–2007), Chair
(2003–2007), Corresponding Member
(2007–2009); 2011: IFLA Member.

Lomer, G. R. Member: 1948. Participation:
1948: National Associate – ABQLA,
Président Honoraire.

Long, Céline. Member: 2009–2010.
Participation: 2009–2010: IFLA Member.

Lunn, A.J.E. Member: 1973–1977.
Participation: 1973–1976: Committee on Bibliography, Standing Advisory Committee Member; 1973–1975: Committee on Cataloguing, Standing Advisory Committee Member; 1973–1976: Committee on Serial Publications, Standing Advisory Committee Member.

MacDonald, C. Member: 1982–1983.
Participation: 1982–1983: National Associate – APLIC, President.

Mackey, Laurette. Member: 1984–1995.
Participation: 1984–1995: Personal Affiliate.

Mackinnon, Merilee. Member: 2009.
Participation: 2009: IFLA Member.

MacLaurin, C. Member: 1985–1989.
Participation: 1985–1989: University Libraries and Other General Research, Standing Committee Member.

MacLean, Elaine. Member: 2004.
Participation: 2004: Personal Affiliate.

MacPherson, Marilyn Ceridwen. Member: 2005. Participation: 2005: Student Affiliate.

Maes, William. Member: 2002–2011.
Participation: 2002–2003: National Associate – CARL, President; 2011: IFLA Member.

Majekodunmi, Norda. Member: 2011.
Participation: 2011: IFLA Member.

Maler, Robyn. Member: 2010. Participation: 2010: Student Affiliate.

Malinski, R. Member: 1972–1978.
Participation: 1972–1978: National Associate – ACMLA, Secretary (1972), President (1978).

Manning, Ralph W. Member: 1993–2001.
Participation: 1993–1997: Management and Technology, Coordinating Board, Secretary (1993–1996), Chair (1996–1999); 1993–2001: Conservation and Preservation, Secretary/Treasurer (1993–1996), Standing Committee Member (1993–2001), Editor of the Newsletter of the IFLA Preservation and Conservation (1997–2001), Chair/Treasurer (1997–2001); 2000–2001: Chair of Professional Board, Executive Member; 2000–2001: Personal Affiliate.

Marchand, M. Member: 1978–1981.
Participation: 1978–1981: Personal Affiliate.

Mark, Timothy. Member: 1998–2009.
Participation: 1998–2005: National Associate – CARL, Executive Director; 2005–2009: Academic and Research Libraries, Standing Committee Member.

Martin, Gérard. Member: 1963.
Participation: 1963: National Associate – Services des bibliothèques publiques du Québec Ministère des affaires culturelles, Hôtel du Gouvernment, Commission des Bibliothèques publique du Québec, Secrétaire; Service des Bibliothéques publique du Québec, Directeur.

Massicotte, Mia. Member: 2006.
Participation: 2006: Personal Affiliate.

Mate, A.V. Member: 1990–1991.
Participation: 1990–1991: Personal Affiliate.

Matt, Pierre. Member: 1963. Participation: 1963: National Associate – Services des bibliothèques publiques du Québec Ministère des affaires culturelles, Hôtel du Gouvernment, Service des bibliothéques publique du Québec, Directeur adjoints (relations extérieures et publicité).

May, Michael. Member: 2010. Participation: 2010: Personal Affiliate.

McAlorum, Shannon. Member: 2009.
Participation: 2009: IFLA Member.

McAnanama, Judith. Member: 1984–1985.
Participation: National Associate – CLA, President.

McCallum, David. Member: 1996–1997.
Participation: National Associate – CARL, Executive Officer.

McClary, Maryon. Member: 2004.
Participation: 2004: Personal Affiliate.

McClintock, L. Member. 1974. Participation: 1974: National Associate – OLA, Secretary.

McDougall, D.B. Member: 1982–1983.
Participation: 1982–1983: National Associate – APLIC, President.

McGrory, Margaret. Member: 2005–2013.
Participation: 2005–2009: Libraries for the Blind, Standing Committee Member; 2009–2013: Libraries Serving Persons with Print Disabilities, Standing Committee Member.

McKee, W. Member: 1975. Participation: 1975: National Associate – ACMLA, Secretary.

McKenna, Julie. Member: 2011. Participation: 2011: IFLA Member.

McKinnon, W. Member: 1984–1985. Participation: 1984–1985: National Associate – ACMLA, President.

McNamee, B. Member: 1973–1974. Participation: 1973–1974: National Associate – CLA, Executive Director.

McQueen, L. Member: 1986–1993. Participation: 1986–1993: Libraries for the Blind, Secretary, Standing Committee Member.

McRee Elrod, J. Member: 1978–1985. Participation: 1978–1985: Cataloguing, Standing Committee Member.

Melts, Rachel. Member: 2003. Participation: 2003: Personal Affiliate.

Ménard, Elaine. Member: 2009. Participation: 2009: Personal Affiliate.

Menard, J. Member: 1978. Participation: 1987: National Associate – ASTED, Secretary.

Mertlermeyer, D. Member: 1984–1985. Participation: 1984–1985: National Associate – ABQLA, President.

Meunier, Pierre. Member: 2001–2009. Participation: 2001–2009: Statistics and Evaluation, Standing Committee Member.

Miller, Beth. Member: 1985–1991. Participation: 1985–1986: National Associate – CLA, President; 1990–1991: Round Table on Continuing Professional Education, Secretary, Executive Committee.

Mitlermeyer, D. Member: 1986–1987. Participation: 1986–1987: National Associate: ABQLA, President.

Mollel, Obianuju. Member: 2003–2007. Participation: 2003–2007: Libraries Serving Disadvantaged Persons, Standing Committee Member.

Monty, V. Member: 1989–1997. Participation: 1989–1997: Government Information and Official Publications, Standing Committee Member.

Moore, Kelly. Member: 2000–2013. Participation: 2000–2007: IFLA Membership Manager; 2007–2013: IFLA Member; 2009–2012: National Libraries, Convenor, National Organizations and International Relations Special Interest Group.

Morel, Jean. Member: 1983. Participation: 1983: IFLA Member.

Morisset, P. Auguste. Member: 1963. Participation: 1963: National Associate – ACBLF, Conseil national, Président sortant.

Morton, Elizabeth H. Member: 1948–1963. Participation: 1948–1963: National Associate – CLA, Secrétaire executif.

Moulder, Cathy. Member: 1990–1991. Participation: 1990–1991: National Associate – ACMLA, Secretary.

Mrozewski, M. Andrzej. Member: 1961. Participation: 1961: National Associate – ABQLA, Président.

Murphy, Lynn F. Member: 1990–2003. Participation: 1990–1991: National Associate – APLIC, President; 2002: Personal Affiliate.

Murray, I. Member: 1990–1993. Participation: 1990–1993: Personal Affiliate.

Mutchler, Peter. Member: 1986–1991. Participation: 1986–1991: Personal Affiliate.

Naeme, Laura. Member: 2009. Participation: 2009: Personal Affiliate.

Nagy, T. Member: 1975–1981. Participation: 1975–1981: National Associate – ACMLA, Secretary (1975–1978), President (1979–1981).

Naujokaitis, Dalia M. Member: 2003–2011. Participation: 2003–2007. School Libraries and Resource Centres, Standing Committee Member; 2006: Personal Affiliate; 2007–2011: Information and Literacy, Standing Committee Member.

Nayler, Ryan. Member: 2011. Participation: 2011: IFLA Member.

Nilsen, Kirsti. Member: 2002. Participation: 2002: Personal Affiliate.

Novack, D. Member: 1992–1995. Participation: 1992–1995: National Associate – ABQLA, Director General.

O'Brien, Leacy. Member: 1998–1999.
Participation: 1998–1999: National
Associate – CLA, Associate Executive
Director.

Oberg, Dianne. Member: 1997–2011.
Participation: 1997–2011: School
Libraries and Resource Centres,
Standing Committee Member (1997–
2001, 2007–2011); 2007–2011:
Education and Training, Standing
Committee Member

Owen, Victoria. Member: 1997–2013.
Participation: 2005–2013: Copyright
and Other Legal Matters, Standing
Committee Member (2005–2013),
Chair (2011–2013).

Packer, K.H. Member: 1975–1985.
Participation: 1975–1985: Committee
on Statistics and Standards, Standing
Advisory Committee Member (1975–
1976); 1977–1978: Library Theory and
Research, Standing Committee
Observer; 1977–1985: Statistics,
Standing Committee Member
(1977–1985).

Panneton, J. Member: 1979–1981.
Participation: 1979–1981: Public
Libraries, Standing Committee Member.

Paradis, Daniel. Member: 2010.
Participation: 2010: IFLA Member.

Paré, Richard. Member: 1986–2005.
Participation: 1986–1993: National
Associate – APLIC, Secretary;
Co-President (1992–1993); 1997–2005:
Library and Research Services for
Parliament, Standing Committee
Member.

Parent, Ingrid. Member: 1993–2013.
Participation: 1993–2001: Cataloguing,
Standing Committee Member (1993–
2001), Chair/Treasurer (1997–2001),
Editor of SCATNews: Newsletter of the
IFLA Section of Cataloguing (1998–
1999); 1998–1999: Bibliographic Control
Coordinating Board, Chair/Financial
Officer; 1999–2005: Professional Board
Member (1999–2005), Governing Board
Member (1999–2005), Executive Board
Member (2003–2005), Treasurer (2003–
2005); 2001–2003: Conference Planning
Committee, Chair; 2001–2003: IFLA/IPA
Steering Group, Co-Chair; 2005–2009:
National Libraries, Chair/Treasurer,

Standing Committee Member; 2005–
2009: Professional Committee, Vice
Chair; 2005–2009: General Research
Libraries, Chair/Financial Officer; 2007–
2009: Main Steering Bodies, Governing
Board; 2009–2011: President-Elect;
2011–2013: President.

Patrick, Jill. Member: 2008. Participation:
2008: Personal Affiliate.

Payette, Suzanne. Member: 2005–2013.
Participation: 2005–2013: Public
Libraries, Standing Committee Member
(2005–2013), Chair (2009–2013).

Payeur, Jean. Member: 2002–2003.
Participation: 2002–2003: National
Associate – ASTED, President.

Peel, Bruce. Member: 1972–1985.
Participation: 1972: National Associate –
CLA, President; 1978–1981: Rare and
Precious Books and Documents,
Standing Committee Member; 1978–
1985: Personal Affiliate.

Pekilis, Deborah. Member: 1992–1995.
Participation: 1992–1995: Personal
Affiliate.

Penney, Pearce. Member: 1982–1983.
Participation: 1982–1983: National
Associate – CLA, President.

Perron, H. Member: 1973–1974.
Participation: 1973–1974: National
Associate – ACBLF, Secretary.

Perry, H. Member: 1985–1993.
Participation: 1985–1993: Libraries for
the Blind, Standing Committee Member
(1985–1989), Secretary (1989–1993).

Peter, Anthony. Member: 1991.
Participation: 1991: IFLA Member.

Pickup, Felicity Joyce. Member: 2008.
Participation: 2008: Personal Affiliate.

Piggott, Sylvia Canada. Member: 2005–
2012. Participation: 2005–2009:
Continuing Professional Development
and Workplace Learning, Information
Coordinator, Standing Committee
Member; 2007–2012: Personal Affiliate.

Pinnell, R. Member: 1992–1993.
Participation: 1992–1993: National
Associate – ACMLA, President.

Piternick, Anne. Member: 1977.
Participation: 1977: National Associate –
CLA, President.

Plate, K.H. Member: 1974. Participation: 1974: National Associate: CALS, Secretary.

Powell, M. Member: 1986–1987. Participation: 1986–1987: National Associate – APLIC, President.

Prasada-Kole, U. Member: 1986–1995. Participation: 1986–1995: Personal Affiliate.

Prémont, J. Member: 1973–1981. Participation: 1973–1975: Parliamentary and Administrative Libraries, Standing Advisory Committee Member; 1980–1981: National Associate – APLIC, President.

Prémont, Jacques. Member: 1991. Participation: 1991: IFLA Member.

Prodrick, R. Gerald. Member: 1975–1989. Participation: 1975–1989: Social Science Libraries, Standing Advisory Committee Member; 1978: Personal Affiliate; 1980–1981: National Associate – CALS, President.

Pyper, Jane. Member: 1999–2013. Participation: 1999–2005: Library Services to Multicultural Populations, Standing Committee Member (1999–2005), Editor (2005–2013), Corresponding Member (2005–2013); 2009–2013: Metropolitan Libraries, Standing Committee Member.

Quereshi, A. Member: 1978. Participation: 1978: National Associate – ACMLA, President.

Quigley, Thomas J. Member: 2002–2009. Participation: 2002–2009: IFLA Member; 2007–2009: Literacy and Reading, Corresponding Member.

Ramdas, Lalita. Member: 1996–2001. Participation: 1996–2001: ICAE, President.

Rashke, Vera. Member: 1998–1999. Participation: National Associate – APLIC, Secretary/Treasurer.

Rebout, Lise. Member: 2009–2011. Participation: 2009–2011: IFLA Member.

Reed, Sarah Rebecca. Member: 1970–1971. Participation: 1970–1971: National Associate – CALS, President.

Reicher, Daniel. Member: 1975–1977. Participation: 1975–1977: National Associate – ASTED, President.

Ribau, Melanie. Member: 2008. Participation: 2008: Student Affiliate.

Ribeiro, Kathryn. Member: 2000–2003. Participation: 2000–2003: Personal Affiliate.

Richer, S. Member: 1989–1997. Participation: 1989–1993: Administrative Libraries, Standing Committee Member; 1993–1997: Government Libraries, Standing Committee Member.

Riva, Pat. Member: 2002–2013. Participation: 2002–2003: IFLA Member; 2005–2013: Cataloguing, Standing Committee Member.

Roberts, John. Member: 2002–2003. Participation: 2002–2003: IFLA International Association Music Libraries, Archives and Documentation Centres (IAML), President.

Robin, Randi. Member: 2008. Participation: 2008: Student Affiliate.

Robinson, Doug. Member: 1996–2003. Participation: 1996–2003: IFLA Clearing House for Canada.

Roe, Brent. Member: 2010–2011. Participation: 2010–2011: IFLA Member.

Roloff, D. Member: 1986–1987. Participation: 1986–1987: Personal Affiliate.

Romaniuk, Mary-Jo. Member: 2010–2011. Participation: 2010–2011: IFLA Member.

Rooney, Sieglinde E.H. Member: 1981–1993. Participation: 1981–1985: University Libraries and Other General Research Libraries, Standing Committee Member; 1983–1993: Acquisition and Exchange, Standing Committee Member.

Rothstein, Sam. Member: 1984–1985. Participation: 1984–1985: National Associate – CALS.

Roussel, Helene. Member: 2009–2011. Participation: 2009–2011: IFLA Member.

Rovira, A. Member: 1972. Participation: 1972: National Associate – ABQLA, Secretary.

Roy, Robert. Member: 1992–1993. Participation: Personal Affiliate.

Royer, Sophie. Member: 2005. Participation: 2005: Personal Affiliate.

Rozniatowski, D.W. Member: 1984–1985. Participation: 1984–1985: Personal Affiliate.

Ryce, Andrea. Member: 2002. Participation: 2002: Student Affiliate.

Sabourin, S. Member: 1972–1973. Participation: 1972–1973: National Associate – ABQLA, Secretary.

Sacherek, L.S. Member: 1978. Participation: 1978: Personal Affiliate.

Saint-Laurent, Audrey. Member: 2005. Participation: 2005: Student Affiliate.

Saint-Marseille, Josée. Member: 2003–2011. Participation: 2003–2011: Science and Technology Libraries, Standing Committee Member.

Saltman, Judith. Member: 2012–2013. Participation: 2012–2013: Personal Affiliate.

Sanderson, Charles R. Member: 1938. Participation: 1938: Sub-Committee on Popular Libraries, Member.

Sandiford, Susan. Member: 2002–2011. Participation: 2002–2003: IFLA Member; 2011: Student Affiliate.

Sansfaçon, Jacques. Member: 1963. Participation: 1963: National Associate – ACBLF, Trésorier.

Sauvageau, Philippe. Member: 2009. Participation: 2009: IFLA Member.

Savard, Réjean. Member: 1997–2013. Participation: 1997–2005: Management and Marketing, Chair (1997–2005), Standing Committee Member (1997–2011); 2005–2009: Main Steering Bodies, Governing Board Member; 2007–2011: Executive Committee Member; 2009–2011: PAC International Focal Point and Regional Centre for Western Europe, Africa and the Middle East, Advisory Board, Chair.

Schmidt, Janine. Member: 2003–2009. Participation: 2003–2007: Library Buildings and Equipment, Standing Committee Member; 2009: IFLA Member.

Schrader, Alvin M. Member: 2000–2003. Participation: 2000–2003: Free Access to Information and Freedom of Expression, Committee Member.

Schult-Albert, H.G. Member: 1981–1995. Participation: 1981–1989: Library Theory and Research, Standing Committee Member; 1991–1995: Library Services to Multicultural Populations, Standing Committee Member.

Schwenger, F. Member: 1993–1999. Participation: 1993–1997: Public Libraries, Standing Committee Member; 1993–1999: International Association of Metropolitan City Libraries Round Table, Secretary/Treasurer.

Scott, Marianne. Member: 1975–2003. Participation: 1975–1976: Ad hoc Planning Group for School Library Work, Standing Advisory Committee Member; 1982–1983: National Associate – CLA, President; 1985–1993: Conservation, Standing Committee Member; 1990–1991: Programme Management Committee, Ex officio Member; 1992–1993: Chair, Conference of Directors of National Libraries; 1993–1997: National Libraries, Standing Committee Member; 1993–2001: National Libraries, Standing Committee Member; 1997–2003: Committee on Copyright and Other Legal Matters, Chair (1997–2002), Staff Expert (2002–2003).

Scotti, Lucien. Member: 2005–2007. Participation: 2005–2007: PAC Advisory Board.

Sessions, V.S. Member: 1980–1981. Participation: 1980–1981: National Associate – CBPQ, Vice President.

Sharrow, Marilyn J. Member: 1985–1989. Participation: 1985–1989: University Libraries and Other General Research, Standing Committee Member.

Siglinde Ortiz Diaz, Tania. Member: 2010. Participation: 2010: Student Affiliate.

Skrzeszewski, Stan. Member: 1991–2003. Participation: 1991–1999: Library Services to Multicultural Populations, Chair (1991–1995), Standing Committee Member (1991–1999); 2002–2003: IFLA Member.

Slater, John. Member: 2008. Participation: 2008: Personal Affiliate.

Smale, Carol. Member: 2000–2009. Participation: 2001–2009: Document Deliver and Interlending, Information Coordinator, Standing Committee Member.

Smith, Christine. Member: 2012. Participation: Student Affiliate.

Smith, E.V. Member: 1989–1993. Participation: 1989–1993: Science and Technology Libraries, Standing Committee Member.

Smith, Hugh L. Member: 1961. Participation: 1961: National Associate – CLA, Treasurer.

Smith, Phil. Member: 2003: Personal Affiliate.

Sonne De Torrens, Harriet. Member: 2003–2011. Participation: 2003–2011: Personal Affiliate.

Sonnemann, Sabine. Member: 1983. Participation: 1983: IFLA Member.

Spencer, Whitney. Member: 2012. Participation: 2012: Student Affiliate.

Spicer, Erik J. Member: 1966–2001. Participation: 1966–1976: Special Libraries, Director (1967–1973), Standing Advisory Committee Member (1973–1976); 1972–1978: Committee on Official Publications, Member; 1972–1997: Parliamentary Libraries, Chair (1972–1980), Standing Advisory Committee Member (1972–1975), Standing Committee Member (1981–1989; 1993–1997), 1973–1977: Administrative Libraries, Standing Advisory Committee Member; 1975–1977: IFLA 50 Year Anniversary Program Planning Committee, Vice-Chair; 1978–1980: National Associate – CLA, President; 1978–1980: General Research Libraries, Member; 1978–2001: Personal Affiliate.

Sprovieri, C.L. Member: 1972–1973. Participation: 1972–1973: National Associate – CALS, Secretary.

St. Onge, J. Member: 1986–1987. Participation: 1986–1987: Personal Affiliate.

Stanbridge, Joanne. Member: 2010. Participation: 2010: Personal Affiliate.

Standen, Allison. Member: 2003. Participation: 2003: Personal Affiliate.

Starr, Lea. Member: 2011. Participation: 2011: IFLA Member.

Starr, Mary Jane. Member: 1998–2001. Participation: 1998–2001: Newspapers Round Table, Information Coordinator, Executive Committee.

Stayer, Marcia S. Member: 1984–1985. Participation: 1984–1985: Personal Affiliate.

Stephens, Tara. Member: 2011. Participation: 2011: IFLA Member.

Stewart, Margaret. Member: 2007–2013. Participation: 2007–2013: Cataloguing, Standing Committee Member.

Stibbe, Huggo L.P. Member: 1972–1985. Participation: 1972: National Associate – ACMLA, Secretary; 1975–1985: Geography and Map Libraries, Standing Advisory Committee Member (1975–1981; 1985–1989), Chair (1981–1985).

Stimpson, Sue. Member: 2009–2013. Participation: 2009–2013: Information and Technology, Standing Committee Member.

Stone, M.F.B. Member: 1983–1987. Participation: 1983–1987: Biological and Medical Sciences Libraries, Standing Committee Member, Secretary.

Strathern, G. Member: 1978. Participation: 1978: National Associate – CALS, Secretary.

Stuart-Stubbs, Basil. Member: 1978–1987. Participation: 1978–1987: University Libraries and Other General Research Libraries, Standing Committee Member (1978–1983), Advisory Committee (1983–1987).

Sue, Corey. Member: 2010–2011. Participation: 2010–2011: IFLA Member.

Svenonius, E. Member: 1978–1981. Participation: 1978–1981: Library Theory and Research, Standing Committee Member.

Swain, Leigh. Member: 1989–1997. Participation: 1989–1997: Information Technology, Standing Committee Member Programme Director (1989–1997), Chair (1993–1997), Editor of IT Review: Newsletter of the IFLA Section on Information Technology (1993–1997); 1990–1997: Universal Data Flow and Telecommunications, Programme Director.

Swanepoel, Marinus. Member: 2009. Participation: 2009: IFLA Member.

Swannick, Erik L. Member: 2000–2001. Participation: 2000–2001: National Associate – APLIC, President.

Swanson, Marnie. Member: 1998–1999. Participation: 1998–1999: National Associate – CARL, Executive Director.

Sylvestre, Guy. Member 1967–1987. Participation: 1977–1981: General Research Libraries, Chair; 1977–1981: National Libraries, Chair; 1982–1983: Conference of National Libraries, Steering Committee Member, Advisory Committee Member; 1986–1987: Personal Affiliate.

Tallim, P. Member: 1990–1993. Participation: 1990–1993: Universal Data Flow and Telecommunications, Programme Officer.

Teasdale, Sylvia. Member: 2007–2013. Participation: 2007–2013: Government Information and Official Public Selection, Standing Committee Member.

Tees, Miriam H. Member: 1981–1993. Participation: 1981–1989: Library Schools and Other Training Aspects, Standing Committee Member (1981–1989), Secretary (1985–1989); 1986–1987: Education and Research, Secretary/Financial Officer; 1990–1993: Personal Affiliate.

Teskey, John. Member: 2009–2011. Participation: 2009–2011: IFLA Member.

Tetreault, Ruth. Member: 1983. Participation: 1983: IFLA Member.

Thiele, Judith C. Member: 1983–1985. Participation: 1983–1985: Libraries for the Blind, Secretary, Standing Committee Member.

Thiele, Paul E. Member: 1983–1985. Participation: 1983–1985: Libraries for the Blind, Standing Committee Member.

Thompson, Pamela. Member: 2000–2001. Participation: 2000–2001: IAML, Secretary.

Tomkins, Janet. Member: 2007–2011. Participation: 2007–2011: Genealogy and Local History, Information Coordinator, Standing Committee Member.

Tremblay, A. Member: 1975–1976. Participation: 1975–1976: National Associate – ABQLA, Secretary.

Turcot, Marietta. Member: 1998–1999. Participation: 1998–1999: Personal Affiliate.

Turner, G.O. Member: 1948. Participation: 1948: Sub-Committee on Hospital Libraries, Member.

Turner, James. Member: 2003–2013. Participation: 2003–2013: Audiovisual and Multimedia, Standing Committee Member.

Urbain, Carole. Member: 2000–2001. Participation: 2000–2001: National Associate – ASTED, President.

Van der Berg, Robert. Member: 1961: Participation: National Associate – ABQLA, Trésorier.

Ven der Bellen, Liana. Member: 1970–1971. Participation: 1970–1971: National Associate – ABQLA, Secretary.

Vinet, France. Member: 1998–1999. Participation: 1998–1999: National Associate – ASTED, President.

Visscher, Ulla. Member: 2007. Participation: 2007: Student Affiliate.

Waddington, Murray. Member: 1990–1997. Participation: 1990–1993: Personal Affiliate; 1993–1997: Art Libraries, Standing Committee Member.

Waldon, Freda. Member: 1948. Participation: 1948: National Associate – CLA, Président.

Walker, Keith. Member: 2010. Participation: 2010: IFLA Member.

Wallace, Ruby. Member: 1963. Participation: 1963: National Associate – CLA, President.

Wallenius, Leila. Member: 2011. Participation: 2011: IFLA Member.

Walsh, M. Member: 1993–1997. Participation: 1993–1997: Children's Libraries, Standing Committee Member.

Walton, B. Member: 1996–1997. Participation: 1996–1997: Conservation, Corresponding Member.

Warner, Jody Nyasha. Member: 2000–2001. Participation: 2000–2001: Personal Affiliate.

Warren, Stephen R. Member: 2007. Participation: 2007: Student Affiliate.

Wellheiser, Johanna. Member: 2005–2009. Participation: 2005–2009: Preservation and Conservation, Information Coordinator/Editor, Standing Committee Member, Secretary.

Wertheimer, Leonard. Member: 1983. Participation: 1983: IFLA Member.

Whiffin, Jean I. Member: 1978–2007. Participation: 1978–2007: Personal Affiliate; 1981–1985: Serial Publications, Standing Committee; 1981–1989: Serial Publications, Standing Committee; 1989–1993: Interlending and Document Delivery, Standing Committee Member; 1993–2007: Preservation and Conservation, Standing Committee Member (1993–2001), Corresponding Member (2002–2007).

White, J.H. Member: 1972. Participation: 1972–1973: National Associate – CALS, President.

Whiteman, B. Member: 1993–1997. Participation: 1996–1997: Rare Books and Manuscripts, Standing Committee Member.

Whitmell, Vicki. Member: 1998–2003. Participation: 2000–2001: Management of Library Associations Round Table, Executive Committee Member; 2000–2003: National Associate – CLA, Executive Director.

Whitney, Paul. Member: 2000–2013. Participation: 2000–2007: Committee on Copyright and Other Legal Matters, Committee Member, (2000–2003), Committee on Copyright and Other Legal Matters Expert Resource Person (2005–2007); 2009–2013: Main Steering Body Member, Governing Board.

Wilheiser, Johanna. Member: 2001–2005. Participation: 2001–2005: Preservation and Conservation, Information Coordinator and Editor, Standing Committee Member.

Williamson, Mary F. Member: 1981–1993. Participation: 1981–1985: Classification and Indexing, Standing Committee Member; 1983–1987; 1981–1993: Personal Affiliate; Art Libraries, Standing Committee Member (1983–1987), Secretary (1986–1987).

Williamson, Nancy. Member: 1989–1993: 1989–1993: Cataloguing, Standing Committee Member (1989–1993); 1989–1993: FID, Liaison (1989–1991), Observer (1991–1993).

Wilson, M. Member: 1979–1980. Participation: 1979–1980: National Associate – ACMLA, Secretary.

Wilson, Melba. Member: 1970–1971. Participation: 1970–1971: National Associate – ABQLA, Secretary

Winearls, J. Member: 1973. Participation: 1973: National Associate – ACMLA, President.

Woods, Cheryl. Member: 1990–1991. Participation: 1990–1991: National Associate – ACMLA, President.

Woodward, F. Member: 1975. Participation: 1975: National Associate – ACMLA, President.

Wright, John. Member: 1970–1971. Participation: National Associate – CALS, Secretary.

Wu, Jane. Member: 2009. Participation: 2009: IFLA Member.

Wu, M. Member: 2007–2011. Participation: 2007–2011: Government Libraries, Standing Committee Member.

Yeo, Ron. Member: 1979–1980. Participation: 1979–1980: National Associate – CLA, President.

Young, K. Member: 1984–1985. Participation: National Associate – ACMLA, Secretary.

Young, William. Member: 2009–2011. Participation: 2009–2011: IFLA Member.

Zhao, Dangzhi. Member: 2009–2011. Participation: 2009–2011: IFLA Member.

Zielinska, Marie F. Member: 1961–2001. Participation: 1961: National Associate – ABQLA, Vice-Président; 1987–1991: Library Services to Multicultural Populations, Chair (1987–1991), Standing Committee Member (1987–1991, 1995–1999), Special Advisor (2000–2001); 2000–2001: Personal Affiliate.

Zilm, Gwen. Member: 2005–2009. Participation: 2005–2009: Information Technology, Standing Committee Member.

Canadian Institutional Members: 1931 to 2012

Association canadienne des Bibliothécaires de langue française, Université de Montréal, joined 1953.

Banque international d'information sur les Etats francophones, joined 1992.

Bell Canada, Information Resource Centre, joined 1980.

Bibliothèque administrative (Québec), joined 1975; Ministère des Communications, joined 1979; Conseil du Trésor/Service Gouvernementale, joined 1990.

Bibliothèque C. É.G.E.P. de Jonquière, joined 1970.

Bibliothèque de la Legislature: Hôtel du Gouvernement, joined 1973; Assemblée National, joined 1982.

Bibliothèque de l'Assemblée du Québec, IFLA 1986.

Bibliothèque municipal (Montréal), joined 1979; Bibliothèque de la Ville Montréal, joined 1984, Bibliothèque de Montréal, joined 1996.

Bibliothèque municipal de Montréal, joined 1975.

Bibliothèque national du Québec, joined 1961.

Bibliothèque publique, Institut Nazareth et Louis Braille (Québec), joined 1979.

Bibliothèque publique de Pointe Claire, joined 1986.

Canada Institute for Scientific and Technical Information, joined 1980.

Canadian Centre for Architecture Library, joined 1992.

Canadian International Development Agency, International Development Information Centre, joined 1979.

Canadian Library Association, joined 1946.

Canadian Museum of Civilization Library, joined 1992.

Canadian National Institute for the Blind, joined 1978 (became CNIB 2006).

Canadian National Library, joined 1970 (became National Library of Canada 1972).

Canadian Space Agency, Larkin-Kerwin Library, joined 2003.

Carleton University: Library, joined 1961.

Concordia University: Libraries, joined 1978.

Conference of Rectors and Principals of Quebec Universities, joined 1975.

Corporation des bibliothècaires professionnels du Québec, joined 1975.

Dalhousie University: School of Library Service, joined 1974; Library, joined 1979.

Dominion Bridge Company Ltd. joined 1973.

Eastern Ontario Regional Library System, joined 1970.

Faculty of Communications and Open Learning Graduate Programs in Library and Information Science, joined 1998.

Hamilton Public Library, joined 1972.

HEC Montréal, Bibliothèque Myriam et J. Robert Ouimet, joined 2008.

Institute Nazareth et Louis-Braille, joined 2002.

International Council for Adult Education, joined 1978.

International Development Research Centre, Library, joined 1975.

International Development Research Centre, Library, joined 1986.

La Centrales Bibliothèque de la Ville Montréal, joined 1982.

La Centrales des Bibliothèques (Québec), joined 1974.

La Grande bibliothèque du Québec, joined 1980.

Laurentian University: Library, joined 1975.

Legislature Library (Alberta), joined 1979.

Library Labour Canada, joined 1986.

Library of Parliament, joined 1961.

Library of the National Assembly/ Bibliothèque de l'Assemblée Nationale, joined 1990.

Library Services, Department of External Affairs, joined 1973.

Magnétothèque, joined 1982.

Manitoba Legislative Library, joined 2008.

McGill University: Library & School of Library Science joined 1961; Graduate School of Library Science joined 1970; Library Science Library joined 1974; Library and Information Studies Library, joined 1982; Libraries, joined 1996.

McMaster University: University Library, joined 2007.

Memorial University of Newfoundland: The Library, joined 1972.

Metropolitan Toronto Library Board, joined 1972.

Min. Rel. Citoyens & Immigration, Bibliothèque administrative, joined 1998.

Ministère de l'Education, Centre de Documentation, joined 1978.

National Archives of Canada, Library and Documentation Services, joined 1988.

National Gallery of Canada/Musée des Beaux-Arts du Canada, joined 1978.

National Library of Canada: Library Documentation Centre, Reference Branch, Clearing House, joined 1973; National Library/Bibliothèque nationale du Canada, joined 1978.

Okanagan University College, joined 2002.

Ontario Department of Education, Provincial Library Service (Ontario), joined 1961.

Ontario Legislative Library, joined 2002.

Ontario Library Association, joined 1967.

Ottawa Public Library/Bibliothèque publique d'Ottawa, joined 1998.

Public Archives of Canada, Library, joined 1978.

Quebec Library Association/Association des bibliothécaires du Québec, joined 1967.

Red Deer Public Library, joined 2003.

Ryerson University, joined 2009.

Saskatchewan Province: Provincial Library, joined 1978; Saskatchewan Education, joined 1988; Saskatchewan Community Services, joined 1992; Saskatchewan Municipal Government, Culture and Recreation Division, Saskatchewan Provincial Library, joined 1996; Saskatchewan Legislative Library, joined 2002.

Scarborough Public Library, joined 1961; Public Library Board, joined 1970; City of Scarborough Public Library Board, joined 1990.

Services de la Bibliothèque de ville de Laval, joined 1982.

Services des bibliothèques d'enseignement, Ministère de l'Education, Centre Administratif, joined 1973.

Services des bibliothèques publiques du Québec Ministère des affaires culturelles, joined 1961; Services des bibliothèques publiques du Québec, joined 1970.

Simon Fraser University: Library, joined 2006.

Sir George Williams University: Library, joined 1961.

Special Libraries Cataloguing, Inc. (British Columbia), joined 1980.

St. Mary's University: Patrick Lower Library, joined 2002.

Statistics Canada Library, joined 1984.

The Toronto Public Library, joined 1970 & Toronto 2B, joined 1972.

Toronto Public Library Board, joined 1982.

Université d'Ottawa: École de bibliothécaires, joined 1970.

Université de Moncton: Bibliothèque Champlain, joined 1973.

Université de Montréal: École de bibliothéconomie, bibliothéque, joined 1972; Direction des bibliothèques, joined 1973; Direction général des bibliothéques, joined 1979; La Bibliothéque de bibliothéconomie, joined 1979; Ecole de bibliothéconomie et des sciences de l'information, joined 1990; Services des bibliothèques, joined 1996.

Université de Sherbrooke: La Bibliothèque, joined 1973; La bibliothèque général, joined 1979; Services des bibliothèques, joined 1982.

Université du Québec à Montréal: direction des bibliothéques, joined 1978.

Université du Québec: coordination des bibliothèques, joined 1973.

Université Laval: joined 1961; Bibliothèque Général, Cité Universitaire, joined 1974.

University of Alberta: Library, joined in 1961; University Library, joined 1970; Faculty of Library Science, joined 1978; Augustana Faculty, joined 2007.

University of British Columbia: The Library, joined 1970; Library Processing Centre, joined 1982; School of Library, Archival and Information Studies, joined 1998; Library, First Nations House of Learning, joined 2007.

University of Calgary: Library, joined 1978; Faculty of Library Science, joined 1979.
University of Guelph: McLaughlin Library, joined 1978; Libraries, joined 2012.
University of Manitoba: Elizabeth Dafoe Library, joined 1978; Libraries, joined 1990.
University of New Brunswick: Harriet Irking Library, joined 1988; Libraries, joined 2009.
University of Ottawa: Library School joined 1961, Libraries, joined 1978; Morisset Library, joined 1982; Library Network, joined 1992.
University of Toronto: Library, joined 1961; School of Library Science, joined 1970; Faculty Library, joined 1973; Faculty of Information Studies, joined 1979; Faculty of Information Science, joined 1998; Architecture, Landscape and Design Library (Shore + Moffat Library), joined 2007.

University of Victoria: McPherson Library, joined 1978.
University of Waterloo: Library, joined 1973.
University of Western Ontario: School of Library and Information Science, joined 1972; Elborn Library, joined 1984, Graduate School of Library and Information Science, joined 1996; Graduate Library, joined 2002.
University of Windsor: Library, joined 1973; Leddy Library, joined 1984.
UTLAS International Canada, joined 1984.
Vancouver Island Regional Library, joined 2008.
Vancouver Public Library, joined 1979.
Vancouver School of Theology, Library, joined 1979.